Transition from Socialist to Market Economies

Also by Shinichi Ichimura

DECENTRALIZATION POLICIES IN ASIAN DEVELOPMENT
Roy Bahl (co-editor)

ECONOMETRIC MODELS OF ASIAN LINK
M. Ezaki (co-editor)

ECONOMETRIC MODELS OF ASIAN-PACIFIC COUNTRIES
S. Matsumoto (co-editor)

ECONOMETRIC MODELING OF CHINA
L. R. Klein (co-editor)

INTERREGIONAL INPUT-OUTPUT ANALYSIS OF THE CHINESE ECONOMY
Wang Hui-jeong (co-editor)

POLITICAL ECONOMY OF JAPANESE AND ASIAN DEVELOPMENT

Transition from Socialist to Market Economies

Comparison of European and Asian Experiences

Edited By

Shinichi Ichimura

Tsuneaki Sato

and

William James

First published 2009 by
PALGRAVE MACMILLAN

Palgrave Macmillan in the UK is an imprint of Macmillan Publishers Limited,
registered in England, company number 785998, of Houndmills, Basingstoke,
Hampshire RG21 6XS.

Palgrave Macmillan in the US is a division of St Martin's Press LLC,
175 Fifth Avenue, New York, NY 10010.

Palgrave Macmillan is the global academic imprint of the above companies
and has companies and representatives throughout the world.

Palgrave® and Macmillan® are registered trademarks in the United States,
the United Kingdom, Europe and other countries.

ISBN: 978-0-230-22803-0 hardback

This book is printed on paper suitable for recycling and made from fully
managed and sustained forest sources. Logging, pulping and manufacturing
processes are expected to conform to the environmental regulations of the
country of origin.

A catalogue record for this book is available from the British Library.

A catalog record for this book is available from the Library of Congress.

10 9 8 7 6 5 4 3 2 1
18 17 16 15 14 13 12 11 10 09

Printed and bound in Great Britain by
CPI Antony Rowe, Chippenham and Eastbourne

Contents

**Part IV   Lessons Beyond
the First Decade of Transformation**

Illustrations

Tables

Figures

Preface

This book is a comparative study of national transition experiences from socialist centrally planned to capitalist market economies in Central and Eastern Europe and East Asia. After World War II, the Soviet Union imposed rigid central planning on the Central and Eastern European countries (CEECs) under its control. Strong resistance to Soviet power broke out, for instance, in Hungary as early as 1956, but such efforts did not bear any fruit at that time. About a decade later, however, efforts at economic reform began to gain new momentum and by the late 1960s, even political efforts to move away from the Soviet-type socialism had become more pronounced in the CEECs. Their struggles began to be rewarded only with the downfall of the Soviet Union after 1989. Eventually they would achieve a higher standard of living through reform programs that allowed private enterprise and markets to develop alongside democratic political systems.

In East Asia, the foundation of the People's Republic of China (PRC) in 1949 marked the advent of Soviet-style planning. In the PRC, two distinct episodes of domestic political turmoil dominated its political and economic scenes: the *Great Leap Forward* (1958–60) and the *Great Proletarian Cultural Revolution* (1966–76) under the leadership of Mao Zedong. Both were blunders and sacrificed the lives of at least 20 million people through starvation and political repression. In late 1978, however, the new leader of the Communist Party of China (CPC), Deng Xiaoping proclaimed new guidelines that set the PRC on the path of economic reform. Deng called for *Reforms and Openness* in order to achieve the *Four Modernizations* in Agriculture, Industry, Science and Technology, and National Defense. Since then, the Chinese authorities have taken bold steps to transform the socialist planned economy steadily to a competitive market economy. The reforms succeeded in achieving historically unprecedented economic growth averaging more than 10 percent annually from the 1980s up to the present. Now the majority of Chinese people are able to enjoy a higher standard of living than they could have dreamed of prior to the reforms. There are even some signs of political reform as there is a degree of freedom of speech and limited experimentation with democratic institutions at the local level.

The objectives of this book are to examine comparatively the problems confronted and the policies adopted by the CEECs, China, and Vietnam during the transition of their economic systems and to draw some lessons for the further development of these and other economies that may be in transition in the future. This will serve not only politicians and policymakers but also academics and private businesses of our times.

Politically and intellectually Soviet-style socialism presented a great challenge to Western democracies and the capitalist free market system after the Russian Revolution of 1917. A number of leading economists in the twentieth century devoted their efforts to dealing with the challenges posed: for instance among others, L. von Mises, *Socialism*, 1922; A. C. Pigou, *Socialism versus Capitalism*, 1937; and J. A. Schumpeter, *Capitalism, Socialism and Democracy*, 1942. These books were at the center of intellectual discussions of the merits of the two systems, particularly during the world depression and upheaval that took place in the 1930s–1940s and in the immediate postwar decades. These academics showed some sympathy with the desire of socialists to overcome some of the obvious weaknesses of capitalism but the overall thrust was that they had faith in entrepreneurs' abilities to innovate and make adjustments, and so concluded that democratic capitalism was the superior system.

Earlier, in the 1920s–1930s, there had been a well-known controversy over the theoretical possibility of *collectivist planning* mimicking the market allocation of resources within the socialist system, involving such famous economists as Enrico Barone, Oscar Lange, Fred M. Taylor, Robert Mosse, Ludwig von Mises, and Friedrich von Hayek. Their conclusion was that in theory efficient collectivist planning of economic activities along lines of outcome similar to that of a free market is possible but in practice extremely difficult to achieve. Even earlier, in 1918, Max Weber in a famous speech to Austrian officers had pointed out that a socialist economy would be run not by labor representatives or labor unions but by bureaucrats and therefore could not be efficiently managed. What the CEECs and East Asian experiences have revealed bears witness to the controversy over the efficiency of planning vs. the market in determining not only the optimal allocation of resources but also the objective of an equitable distribution of wealth and income. That too is explored in this book.

Capitalism has survived not as *laissez-faire* but with markets as the dominant adjustment mechanism, supplemented by government intervention to sustain employment and output and to influence the terms of competition through regulations like antitrust laws and competition policies. Keynes' *General Theory of Employment, Interest, and Money*, 1936, provided the intellectual foundation for what has been termed the mixed economy in the West with an analytical framework for government countercyclical policymaking. Most Keynesian economists expected the degree of government intervention to increase gradually within a mixed economy under the prevailing welfare state concept. In the 1980s, however, the tide began to turn with the success of *Reaganomics* in the United States and the *Thatcher revolution* in the United Kingdom. At the turn of the century, the majority of economists accepted a diminished role for government in regulating the activities of private business, although this did not necessarily mean smaller government. This has reduced the support for socialist ways of thinking in

Western Europe and affected intellectual thought in the CEECs and even the former Soviet Union (FSU).

Accordingly, various reforms were attempted in the CEECs but did not succeed until the Soviet Union's rule of its satellite countries began to falter. The historic figures who drew the curtain on the Soviet Socialist era were the two presidents; Mikhail Gorbachev and Boris Yeltsin. Gorbachev initiated the reform of the FSU with two slogans: *Glasnost* and *Perestroika*, and broke down the iron rule of the Communist Party not only inside but also outside the FSU by indicating that it no longer intended to crush revolts in its satellite states. This immediately ignited the transformation of socialist economies in the CEECs, culminating in the fall of the Berlin Wall in 1989. In 1991 Yeltsin moved a step further forward and left the Communist Party himself before being elected President of the Russian Republic and literally gave the last rites to the *communist party-state* in Russia. His government liberalized almost all of the regulations governing the privileges of state-owned enterprises (SOEs) and collective ownership. It was he who continued the negotiations with the US started by Gorbachev, and finally ended the cold war. This marked a dramatic closing of all intellectual and political discourses on the subject of socialism vs. capitalism. The meanings of these events for the CEECs are also covered in this book.

This drama in Europe parallels the reforms initiated under Deng Xiaoping in China. Both dramas indicate how crucially important the personal roles of political leaders were in the historic transformation. Without them, what we would have observed toward the end of the twentieth century might have turned out to be a failure and have been followed by a prolonged period of stagnation and possibly of civil collapse. In the study of historic transitions, the roles of political leaders should never be missed or underestimated. A famous Japanese sociologist, Yasuma Takata once said: "Polity subjugates Economy." This was typically the case.

This historic parallel between the transitions in Europe and East Asia has attracted academic attention in East Asia, Europe, and international organizations alike. As Director of the International Center for the Study of East Asian Development (ICSEAD) in Kitakyushu City, Japan, I organized two consecutive international symposiums in Kitakyushu (March 30–31, 2000) and Budapest (November 24–25, 2000) to analyze the European and Asian experiences comparatively. This book is an updated and reedited version of the papers submitted there. The symposiums had two objectives: first, to disentangle the political economy of transformation and assess comparatively the achievements and failures of the countries in both regions; second, to evaluate the cost or sacrifices involved in transformation like unemployment, etc. Ten years of experience in the CEECs and 20 years of successful experience in East Asia were just enough to make the timing of the symposiums adequate. It was really in the 1990s that all the CEECs and Vietnam began to emerge from rigid planning to a flexible market system, and that

China moved quickly to the economic forefront with a goal of attaining a *socialist market economy*, and overtook the level attained by *creeping market socialism* in most reform-oriented CEECs.

As regards estimating the cost involved, however, the timing was hardly ideal, because until the mid-1990s a serious decline in production in the CEECs was comparable to the Great Depression in the 1930s. Even by 2000 only four countries—Poland, Hungary, Slovenia, and the Czech Republic—had barely managed to regain their pretransition (1989) per capita GDP levels. Clearly the marked progress on the political front in the CEECs during the last decade of the twentieth century accompanied an enormous economic cost. In contrast, China kept growing at 7–8 percent annually in 1997–2001, after 10 percent annually in 1986–96. As a result, its GDP more than doubled during the 1990s. Any comparison at an earlier date than the symposiums would have given the impression weighted toward the Chinese process of transition, which may not be right in the longer term.

Delegates at the first convention were László Szamuely, Eva Ehrlich, (Hungary), Tadeusz Kowalik (Poland), Le Bo Linh (Vietnam), Branislav Soskic (Serbia), Miyamoto Katsuhiro, and Sato Tsuneaki (Japan), in addition to members of ICSEAD. Participants in the second convention included such noted scholars as Wu Jinglian, Zhang Chunlin, Zuo Xuejin (China), Vladimir Benacek, Frantisek Turnovec (Czech Republic), Tran Van Tho (Japan/Vietnam), Paul Marer (USA/Hungary), Bruno Dallago (Italy), Witold Morawski (Poland), Vojmir Franicevic (Croatia), Negoslav Ostojic, Branislav Soskic, Jelena Vilus (Serbia), Olexandr Movshuk (Ukraine/Japan), Morita Tsuneo (Hungary/Japan), Ito Shoichi, Nakagane Katsuji, Okita Yoichi, Sato Tsuneaki, and Ichimura Shinichi (Japan), and several others. I wish to express my deep gratitude to all for their earnest participation, particularly those from China who came under difficult circumstances and presented frank opinions on delicate and politically sensitive topics. I wish to thank Professors Morita Tsuneo, and Eva Ehrlich who organized the Budapest conference and the memorable visits to a restaurant on the Buda Hills, Herend Factory, and a vineyard. Only I owe deep apologies for the delay of this publication to all the authors and other participants. I must express my great indebtedness to Professor T. Sato for his help in organizing two conferences and editing this volume with his expertise, and Dr. William James who kindly improved the clarity of the contents and polished up the English in the final stage of our editorial work. Lastly I wish to thank my friends Emeritus Prof. Hiroshi Kimura (Hokkaido University) and Prof. Shoichi Ito, (Kansei Gakuin University) for their advices and young colleagues at ICSEAD: Dr. Sadayuki Takii, Dr. Erbiao Dai and Dr. Hiroshi Sakamoto for their help in my editorial work and translating Den Xiaoping's speeches. Deep thanks are also due to Ms. Saori Koishi and Ms. Megumi Fukagawa, program officer at ICSEAD then.

Before closing this preface, I would like to add two remarks. One is that this book by no means covers exhaustively all of the important considerations needed to guide the future of the CEECs and East Asia. I learned about the complex nature of the issues of ethnological, religious, and historic factors in the Balkan nations when I attended the conference in Macedonia sponsored by the UN European Center for Peace and Development in 1999. A paradigm of socialist planning vs. capitalist market is only one of many wider issues for consideration. Another is that the march from socialist to market economies is now spreading to South and Central Asian countries. Studies like ours must be extended to those areas soon. I sincerely hope that many readers of this book will be motivated to tackle those issues before it is too late.

December 22, 2008
SHINICHI ICHIMURA
Emeritus Professor, Kyoto University
Honorary Counselor, ICSEAD

Contributors

Ichimura, Shinichi, Professor emeritus, Kyoto University, Honorary Counselor, ICSEAD.

Sato, Tsuneaki, Professor emeritus, Yokohama City University.

James, William E., Principal Economist, Economics and Research Department, Asian Development Bank, Manila, Philippines.

Wu, Jinglian, Professor, Chinese Academy of Social Sciences, Adviser, Economic Development Center, the State Council, China.

Szamuely, László, Professor, Hungarian Academy of Sciences, Formerly Scientific Adviser, Kopint-Datorg, Budapest.

Nakagane, Katsuji, Professor, Faculty of International Politics and Economics, Aoyama-Gakuin University, Professor emeritus, The University of Tokyo.

Tran, Van Tho, Professor, School of Social Sciences, Waseda University, Tokyo.

Zhang, Chunlin, Senior Specialist, The World Bank Office Beijing, Professor, Beijing University, China.

Ito, Shoichi, Professor, Kwansei Gakuin University, Japan.

Dallago, Bruno, Professor, Department of Economics, University of Trento, Italy.

Okita, Yoichi, Professor, Graduate School of Policy Studies, Japan.

Morawski, Witold, Professor, Institute of Sociology, University of Waszawa, Poland.

Morita, Tsuneo, Research Managing Director, Tateyama Laboratory Hungary Ltd., former Research Adviser, Nomura Research Inst., Budapest.

Turnovec, František, Professor, Faculty of Social Sciences, Charles University, the Czech Republic.

Introduction

Shinichi Ichimura, Tsuneaki Sato

This introduction offers the reader a brief summary of the main arguments in the following chapters and gives in advance a bird's-eye view of the comparative studies of two historic experiences of transition from socialist planned economies to capitalist market economies in the Central and Eastern European countries (CEECs) and East Asia.

Part I offers a *general framework for comparison of the two types of transition experiences* with three papers written by authors who are familiar with studies by both European and Asian scholars. Chapter 1: Convergence and Divergence in Transformation by T. Sato starts with a reconsideration of the conventional wisdom among European American economists that serious reform of the socialist economic system is impossible without *radical* changes in the political system: abolishing one-party rule. This became possible in the Soviet Union and Russia only after the breakdown of the party-state there in 1991. He contrasts this with the successful Chinese *gradualist* way of reforming the socialist economy under the rule of the CPC. It is a contrast between "polity first, economy next" vs. "economy first, polity next." He points out that the transformation in the CEECs is in some ways a *resumption of interrupted capitalist development*, as well as a catch-up with the developed West. China's initial conditions were different from those of the CEECs—in that it had little historic experience of capitalist development and was predominantly an agrarian economy. Thus, the two groups of countries were very divergent in their initial conditions and choice of transition strategies. Both have aimed, however, at realizing the same type of industrialized economy with efficient market systems, and are converging through different paths on similar goals.

Chapter 2: China's Transition to a Market Economy: How Far Across the River? by J. Wu gives an excellent survey of the two stages of economic reform in China and the related problems. The first stage began with Deng Xiaoping's influential words: *reforms and openness* in late 1978. The aims were four modernizations: namely, those of agriculture, industry, science and technology, and the military. The first reform was undertaken in

1

agriculture by giving farming households land use rights and then allowing the free establishment of collectively owned township and village enterprises (TVEs). With the notable success of these policies, the Chinese authorities decided to move on to industry by permitting both the establishment of private enterprises and foreign direct investment (FDI). This historic decision was made in November 1993 in the "Decision on Issues Concerning the Establishment of a *Socialist Market Economic Structure*," which was adopted by the Third Plenum of the Fourteenth Congress of the CPC. This was the clear watershed that marked the shift of the Chinese economic system from the old socialist form to a modern market economy. The *socialist market economy* became an officially affirmed goal of reforms in China. The Chinese economic development of the 1990s was unprecedented and surprised people worldwide. The paper traces the strong performance of non-state enterprises resulting from the *incremental reforms* that contributed most to this miraculous growth. Nevertheless, the road to reform was not smooth everywhere. In particular, the financial condition of state-owned enterprises (SOEs) worsened and still poses very serious problems. Unless the Chinese government overcomes them, the author cautions, it will not cross the *Rubicon*.

Chapter 3: Two Reforms under Mono-Party Political System by L. Szamuely compares the Hungarian *new economic mechanism* (NEM) of the 1960s–70s with the Chinese reforms of the 1980s–90s. It is a valuable experiment of a kind hard to find in the body of transition literature. Both countries attempted market-oriented reforms, but while the former failed, the latter succeeded. The author points out that the most serious source of failure in Hungary was the limited nature of its state sovereignty, a problem that China did not face.

Part II takes up the central problems of transformation; namely, *ownership reform* and *privatization* with two substantial papers on China and one unique paper on Vietnam.

Chapter 4: SOE Reform And Privatization in Transition: China in Comparative Perspective by K. Nakagane gives a balanced and informative assessment of the performance of SOEs and efforts at reform as regards changing the ownership structure—or privatization—in China in comparison with those in the CEECs. The paper also offers a useful survey of some theoretical discussions among transition experts in America/Europe and Asia and takes up some important issues for policy choices, such as *shock therapies* vs. *gradualism,* and three different schools of thought on transition strategies: the *market school, property rights school, and gradualist market school.* Nakagane basically endorses the ways in which China chose gradualism and shifted step by step from the market school to the property rights school, but argues that this might not have been the case with the CEECs.

Chapter 5: Vietnamese Gradualism in the Reform of State-Owned Enterprises: The First Phase of Doi Moi by Tran Van Tho gives an appraisal of SOE reform in Vietnam from a somewhat different perspectives from that of

Nakagane. In both China and Vietnam the term *privatization* is not officially used, but China's reform is getting increasingly closer to de facto *privatization*, whereas Vietnam's is not quite yet. *Socialism-oriented market economy* in Vietnam and *socialist market economy* in China must be pronounced differently, as a Chinese academician joked, with accent on market in China but on socialism in Vietnam. The author points out that the SOEs retain much more power in Vietnam and the impressive growth in Vietnam might even be termed SOE-led, at least until 2000.

Chapter 6: From Public to Private Savings: Decline of State Ownership in the Chinese Corporate Sector by C. Zhang takes up the problem of the transfer of ownership in the SOEs mainly from its financial aspects, from the points where Wu and Nakagane leave off, namely, how the SOEs could overcome the serious debts that they owe to the state banks. It delves into the sensitive area of SOE management and is really a unique piece of work which shows some ways out for the difficulties that the Chinese SOEs face in the near future.

Part III deals with *the role of the state and market in transition*. In the early phase of transformation an obsession with *market fundamentalism* tends to prevail, but the correct role of the state itself receives little attention. This explains many serious mistakes committed by some transition countries. The immediate negative impact of transformation is severe unemployment. Urgent policy priorities should be concerned with the social safety net. Available resources often become more limited after transition and naturally this is one of the most important issues in both the CEECs and China.

Chapter 7: The Social Safety Net in China by S. Ito goes knowledgably into details of various kinds of social security and their financial status. He points out the current and future difficulties of maintaining even funds at the present level or more in order to be able to collect the necessary benefits from them.

Chapter 8: The State and the Transformation of Economic Systems by B. Dallago offers one of the best expositions of the varied but appropriate roles of government in the course of transformation of CEECs with different historic heritages. He points out the varied environments of different countries that determine the appropriate functions of the state at different stages of transformation such as the level of economic development, position vis-à-vis the developed economies, resource endowments, the size of the domestic market, etc. Depending on these factors, he conjectures which type of state might be appropriate for a specific nation; the minimal state, competitive state, Keynesian state, corporative state, authoritarian state, or development state.

Chapter 9: Can the Japan Inc. Model Be a Middle Course for Transition?: Industrial Policy and Postwar Economic Development of Japan by Y. Okita offers his own answer to the question raised by Russian officials when a team of Japanese experts was invited to Moscow and asked to give their opinions independent of the International Monetary Fund (IMF) or American economists. Wartime Japan was almost as tightly controlled by the government as a socialist economy, so its postwar reconstruction experience might be thought to provide a good model for the Russians to adopt. However, after giving an incisive description of the Japanese government's role in guiding manufacturing industries through its industrial policy, and the views of many foreign and Japanese experts on the subject, the author ascribes the success of Japanese recovery and development to the particular conditions prevailing in postwar Japan and is cautious of recommending its industrial policy to transitional economies. His argument may be controversial, because some argue in favor of that as a means of dealing with *deindustrialization* phenomena.

Chapter 10: Market and Political Justice in Postsocialist Poland by W. Morawski discusses the social justice in distribution after transformation on the basis of empirical opinion polls in Poland and other countries. The author distinguishes two kinds of justice: one to be called *microjustice* and another to be called *macrojustice*. The former is related to the reward in proportion to the input of actors, while the latter is related to what the market delivers to the participants according to the rules of fairness. He carefully traces the alterations in Poles' responses to the changing social conditions in Poland that caused the change of governments as a result of the national election of October 2001. This is one important problem for any post-socialist society to face and solve. It is evident in China and many other countries.

Part IV summarizes *lessons beyond the first decade of transformation*. The two papers attempt to shed light on major aspects of transformation and derive some *lessons*, both positive and, mostly, negative. Chapter 11: Facts and Lessons of Ten Years of Transformation in Central Europe by T. Morita carefully reviews the experiences of transformation in three major Central European countries: Hungary, Poland, and the Czech Republic and concludes that the various failures in these countries are a result of the principle of *allocation* inherent in socialist economics, which is fundamentally different from the principle of exchange in the market system. But since transformation, they have already achieved through taxation the same level of income redistribution as most Western European countries. This paper also offers also a comparative picture of the performances of many CEECs in about 2000.

Chapter 12: Czech Republic 1990–2000: Lessons from the Economic and Political Transformation by F. Turnovec is brief in length, but is an incisive, critical, albeit restrained, account of the Czech transformation and derives some valuable lessons from it. He is quite critical of *voucher privatization* and seems to favor a *state capitalism* model for the first stage of transformation. It is an interesting topic, but one which he is yet to explore fully.

Thus, the book covers a variety of issues of transformation in the CEECs and East Asia and compares the two types of processes. By no means can we pretend to have exhausted the important problems of transformation or to have offered enough suggestions for policies for the years to come. Since, however, all of the papers give references to the relevant articles, books, and data sources, readers will find many materials for further study. We have laid only a foundation for comparative studies of the European and Asian experiences of transition.

Part I

General Framework of Comparison

What is written on the Banner is *Communism*,
On the signboard *Socialism*,
While the road is towards *Capitalism*
And deep in the root is *Feudalism*.
—A Chinese Joke
(Satoshi Nagumo: *Watching Chinese Jokes*,
Ronso-sha, Tokyo 2000)

1
Convergence and Divergence in Transformation: Comparison of Experiences of CEECs and China[*]

Tsuneaki Sato

1.1 Introduction

Up until the end of the 1980s, the prevailing view in Central and Eastern Europe was that no serious reform of the socialist economic system was possible without radical changes in the political system, that is, without abolishing the dominant one-party rule. This was true even in Hungary in the 1980s, when the so-called third wave of economic reform was developing. Reform-minded economists, while acknowledging willingly the need for pluralization of the political system, remained pessimistic about the feasibility of this: their discussions always noted the barriers posed by the existing political system.

In East Asia, however, China succeeded in achieving economic reform and development under Communist Party of China (CPC) rule in the 1980s. This led intellectuals in Europe to question their conventional wisdom. Contrary to their expectations, including those of this author,[1] economic reforms in China gained even stronger momentum in the mid-1990s, with only a short pause following the Tian'anmen Square incident of 1989. The success story of China, combined with the political changes in the Central and Eastern European countries (CEECs) in 1989 and Russia in 1991, prompted the most eloquent exponent of the pessimistic view in Europe,[2] W. Brus (Brus 1975),[3] to reconsider the thesis that he had been advocating for so long (Brus 1993). He acknowledged that the full-fledged marketization was possible even under a communist regime and went so far as to note the positive role that *one-party rule* might play *up to a certain point* in market development.

Now, after nearly two decades, the CEECs, particularly the frontrunners, have clearly managed almost to complete the *transition* to a capitalist market economy and accomplished the political transformation resulting from the collapse of the party-state. On the other hand, the East Asian countries—China and Vietnam, which may be classified as transition economies[4]—have pushed forward the marketization of the economy before political transformation and simultaneously achieved rapid economic growth. This is different from the European experience of the transformational depression that occurred in most CEECs in the first half of the 1990s and in Commonwealth of Independent States (CIS) countries until the end of the 1990s. However, after nearly three and two decades, respectively, China and Vietnam seem to be showing some very slight signs of democratizing their political systems at least in the long-term perspective. They may be approaching the end of developmental dictatorship *in their own way*—a trend that we have witnessed in the other East Asian countries.

This paper begins with an examination of the political transformation in the CEECs with a view to highlighting the relationships between politics and economics, and then compares the revolutionary changes in the CEECs with the evolutionary reform in China. A central focus for study is the issue of the privatization of the giant state-owned enterprises (SOEs) in these socialist countries. Ever since the CEECs embarked on their capitalist makeover, such privatization has been regarded by the so-called Washington consensus[5] as one of three pillars of systemic transformation, along with liberalization and macroeconomic stabilization.

Although the same term *privatization* is used, its background in the socialist world is utterly different from the privatization pattern in Japan or other advanced capitalist country. In the latter, a handful of inefficient public corporations had to be integrated into existing market economies dominated by dynamic private enterprises. In contrast, the former socialist states have to rein in sprawling SOEs without any existing market infrastructure. They have been all in the grip of what may be termed *obsession with ownership*. Their initial approach was, while giving a short shrift to the most crucial aspect of privatization—the establishment of management frameworks to assume risk and responsibility, simply to take legal steps to transfer corporations to private ownership as a panacea. Coupon or voucher privatization, with its inevitable failure, offers a typical example. This paper's examination bears these points in mind and looks in detail at the reform of SOEs in the East Asian countries which thus far have avoided even the term *privatization*.

At the end, a potential model of emerging capitalism in the CEECs is detailed in connection with the above discussions as well as the more general discussions of "models" of contemporary varieties of capitalism: namely, *Variety of Capitalism* (VoC) studies.

1.2 Revolutions and resumption of capitalist development in the CEECs

Two decades later, with a bit of hindsight, the 1989 *revolution* in Eastern Europe can be seen as extraordinary and unique in character. It was a great event of world historic significance, upsetting the world order of the postwar era, but admittedly it was not akin to the French Revolution of 200 years earlier which upset the social order in the pursuit of new ideals and values. The events of around 1989 may be called a *revolution* in the sense that they destroyed a sociopolitical system (one-party rule coupled with a planned economy) and paved the way for a different socioeconomic framework, that of a capitalist market economy. However, it was not a revolution in pursuit of new values but rather a consequence of having wearied of ideals or idealistic illusions. What these economies tried to adapt themselves to were the values and model economies that already existed and had been proved in the West as a result of the long historic development of capitalism and civil society.[6]

From a historical perspective, I consider this process to be the resumption of interrupted capitalist development. The CEECs belong more or less to a group of latecomers and have been pursuing modernization and industrialization following the capitalist model, floating between the West and the East.[7] This process of development was simply interrupted in 1917 in the case of Russia and in around 1948, after World War II, in the case of the CEECs.

However, what these countries subsequently sought within a socialist framework was not very different from the modernization-cum-industrialization drive in a different framework; that is, catching up with the developed capitalist countries. Since the heavily politicized postwar framework collapsed, not surprisingly, the interrupted historical development has been resumed. In no sense is this a reversal of historical development. It should be noted, however, that resumption was not as easy as was expected at the outset of transformation, because the existing system was very unusual.[8]

In this context, it must be stressed that these transition countries face the dual tasks of systemic transformation and catch-up in economic development. The latter task became harder than before, since transformation caused depression and widened the economic gap between the CEECs and EU member countries. In Russia, for example, the economy shrank to nearly half of its size in 1990. Thus, Russia at the beginning of the twenty-first century had the same economic task or need to catch up with the advanced countries as the Russia of Peter the Great or Sergei Witte, or the USSR of Stalin (Ellman 2000a).

In this respect, the difference between the CEECs and the East Asian countries, particularly China which started its transition as an underdeveloped economy, is the matter of degree rather than of qualitative nature. The argument raised by some experts[9] that the aim of reform in China (rapid economic growth) differed from that of the CEECs (systemic transformation per se) is quite misleading. It is a sheer simplification. Both require faster growth, and the difference is only a matter of degree, depending on initial conditions and historic heritage. In China, for instance, huge population pressure is particularly important for economic growth. This does not necessarily address, however, the qualitative aspect of the problem. This growth factor alone suggests that a more active role for the state is needed in the CEECs than in Western developed countries with a mature market infrastructure. This point is relevant to the discussion below on whether *transition* has already been completed in the case of the CEECs.[10]

1.3   The first stage of Deng Xiaoping's reform— the aborted NEP in China

Chinese communists prior to World War II were well aware of the backwardness of China's socioeconomic conditions and often referred to its society as semicolonial and semifeudal. Awareness of this backwardness led them to adopt the *two stages strategy* of revolution. Its clear expression can be found in Mao Zedong's *On New Democracy* (1940). According to the design, the first stage of development after the foundation of the People's Republic of China (PRC) implied that a new political power called *coalition dictatorship*, which corresponds to the *economy of new democracy* as economic base, would be a transitional stage as (new economic policy) NEP was in the Soviet economy in the 1920s. However, this coalition dictatorship was very short-lived. In 1953, the "General Line for the Transition Period" was adopted, and with the ensuing collectivization drive, the socialist character of the 1949 revolution was emphasized. The premature drive toward socialism meant that the *two stages strategy* was turned into a *one-stage strategy* that, however, did not change the core of historically inherited legacies. It was no wonder then that the first stage of Deng Xiaoping's reforms of the late 1970s and early 1980s was characterized by some features also seen in the period of the aborted NEP in China.

However, in 1984 when the official doctrine of defining the developmental stage of the country as *the initial stage* of socialism that would supposedly to last over a century was adopted, some academics advocated a theory implying almost a return to the old two stages strategy. The best version was the so-called *theory of extra lessons* from capitalism. It maintained that, in taking a shortcut to socialism, the country had to leap over the capitalist stage of development and so the newly defined *initial stage* of socialism was nothing more a period during which the country had to restore the missing link by learning an extra lesson from capitalism. In contrast to the CEECs, Chinese attempts to restore this missing link (the aborted NEP), while keeping political power intact, continued for far longer than onlookers' initial expectations and probably well beyond the intentions of the designers themselves. The economic system changed drastically, especially after the Tian'anmen Square incident of 1989.

Two contrasting developments between China and the CEECs from then to the mid-1990s are noticeable. While China achieved rapid growth and far-reaching marketization, the CEECs suffered from a deep transformational depression. They are often contrasted as being rapid (CEECs) versus gradual (China) and comprehensive (CEECs) versus partial (China) in systemic transformation; this is a gross simplification, as later developments have clearly shown.

The two are also contrasted, however, from the perspectives of freedom, human rights, and other values cherished in the West. China's approaches have been subject to a great deal of criticism from a Western perspective.[11] At the same time, there is a deep conviction among many students of comparative economics that the limitations to *partial and gradual reforms* have already been demonstrated by the Hungarian reforms of the 1970s and 1980s. These reforms were then considered as the most advanced and successful among European socialist countries. Yet, real reform in Hungary had to wait until 1989 when it got back on the track toward transition to capitalist market economy.[12]

1.4   Is the Chinese road a challenge to transition orthodoxy?

China's reform experiences have been always viewed as an anomaly in terms of its transition to a market economy and not properly accounted for by most adherents of mainstream economics. For example, the *World Development Report 1996: from Plan to Market* on transition economies (World Bank 1996) devoted little discussion to China.[13] But China has been one of the most successful transition economies by any standard. In terms of GDP it produced more than all other transition economies combined in 1998, and its per capita GDP is likely to surpass that of the 15 former Soviet Union (FSU) countries in the next decade, which was unthinkable a decade ago.[14]

Economists tend still to underestimate the significance of China's reform experiences. The most popular argument is that China was a poor agricultural country, so reform was very easy. It is true that at the outset of reform China was much less developed than the CEECs and FSU, and the latter had several challenges to face that China did not. These are, for example, the disintegration of the federal state, disruption in production linkages, problems of excess industrial capacity, and proportionally high welfare coverage relative to the country's economic potentias. This argument does not explain, however, how and why China's reform was successful. As a socialist and bureaucratically administered economy, China faced many problems similar, although not identical, to those of the CEECs and the FSU, such as the lack of property rights or a modern market system. In addition, China, as an underdeveloped country, faced many problems such as enormous population pressure, shortages of human capital, poor industrial and infrastructure bases, and lack of a modern democracy.

The reasons why China's reforms are not properly understood and appreciated by mainstream economists are deep rooted. There are strong *a priori* beliefs, based on existing knowledge of economics, about the process through which transition should take place. Such beliefs appear to have been supported by strong evidence from the unsuccessful economic reforms in the CEECs and the FSU prior to 1989–91. The theory and evidence together formed a powerful conventional wisdom about a set of *necessary and sufficient conditions for successful transition*, that is, macroeconomic stabilization, liberalization, privatization, and democratization. China's reform with its eclectic measures and rapid growth, however, seems to contradict conventional wisdom. It is true that China has also adopted many of the standard policies advocated by economists, such as open-door policies toward trade and foreign investment and enforcing macroeconomic stability, but violations of the standard policy prescriptions are also very striking. For example, for the past decades, China's reform has succeeded without *complete* market liberalization, privatization *per se*, secure private property rights, or democracy. One might think that in the absence of the aforementioned essential four factors, reform would fail. No doubt that the fact that this did no happen represented an important challenge to the *transition orthodoxy*.

As stated earlier, the most fundamental pillar and starting point of transition orthodoxy is the thesis that no major breakthrough is possible without radical change in the political system. In the CEECs and Russia, where political power and the economic system were so deeply interwoven, the collapse of the party-state immediately led to the destruction of the economic system. Even the most market-oriented reforms in Hungary in the late 1980s had not abolished this amalgamation of the political and economic spheres.

Despite high approval in the West of the collapse of the party-state, however, it had a negative aspect. That is the *desertion* of the state of its control or coordination functions. This is crucially important in the transformation process, because the formation of a modern market economy requires a long period of institution-building and cannot be left to spontaneous forces alone. As a consequence, a kind of vacuum or *Niemandsland* (no-man's-land) emerged, and this was one cause of the transformational depression that lasted for a longer time and was more severe than anticipated.[15]

In the case of the CEECs, perhaps their passage could not have been otherwise. After two decades,[16] the question could and should have been raised: "is this high-cost[17] path of shifting away from socialism[18] the only one that can be justified in historical development?" This author believes that the answer is "No," because transition in many countries has proved to have almost failed,[19] although some frontrunners have achieved relative success.

We could perhaps distinguish two possible paths for moving away from socialism: a radical but high-cost path and a gradual, evolutionary, but less costly one. The choice made depends on which pillar of the existing system is destroyed or eroded first. In terms of Marxian *political superstructure and economic base*, the first case radically destroys the political superstructure framework and this is then followed by an economic transformation that extends over quite a long period. In the second case, the economic base gradually erodes through incremental changes, taking a long time, and then this will then hopefully lead to a change in the political regime. There is no easy answer to the question of when these changes will come about. This seems to be the case in China. So long as the current leadership succeeds in making adjustments according to the economic needs of the country and while it is capable of maintaining high economic growth, albeit not as high as 10 percent annually, to improve the living conditions of the population, the current political regime could remain in power for longer than anticipated.[20]

Among the CEECs, a limited number of countries, Hungary and Poland in particular, experienced an erosion of the most important of the economic base, state ownership, through the extension of non-state ownership and the introduction of management reform in SOEs during the 1980s. However, the collapse of the political framework in a kind of chain reaction in the context of the geopolitical changes resulting from Gorbachev's perestroika was the unequivocal cause behind the dismantling of the institutional economic base. That is, it is this collapse that is identified as the precise starting point of the process of the postsocialist systemic transformation, even though many trends in this direction had already emerged prior to the political breakup.

In China features common to reform paths in all socialist countries as well as specific and unique characteristics are observable. The latter are partially related to peculiarities in the institutional, organizational, and developmental features of the Chinese system that existed even before the start of Deng Xiaoping's reform. Special mention should be made of the relatively *limited* role of central planning with little *tautness* in planning and control by regional or local authorities over a significant fraction of state or *collective* industry. Katsuji Nakagane (1981) compares Soviet planning with that of China in terms of *taut* and *slack* planning.[21] It is worth mentioning that the well-known *dual-track system* had existed even under Mao Zedong, well before Deng Xiaoping's reforms. In this writer's opinion, this Chinese *slack* planning was brought about by three factors: the vastness of the country, the limited scope of the planners' capability, and last but not least, the traditional pragmatism of Chinese culture.

1.4.1 From reform to shifting away from socialism: 1978–93

As was rightly noted by Wu Jinglian (Wu 2000), China's two-decade-long reform process (1978–98, and at the time of working on this revised version—three decades) consists of two stages: the first stage covers the period 1978–93, and the second covers the period beginning in 1994, the watershed being the November 1993 "Decision on Issues concerning the Establishment of a Socialist Market Economy Structure" that was adopted by the Third Plenum of the Fourteenth Congress of the CPC.

The first-stage reforms may be characterized as predominantly *incremental* and *evolutionary*, while the second stage, albeit preserving something of the same character, contains many elements of *shifting away* from the socialist economy and comes close to *replacing* the system as a whole. In this sense, it is a hybrid mixture of pre- and posttransformation reforms in the CEECs and FSU. This problem will be examined again at the end of this chapter.

The main objective of the early institutional changes, starting in 1979 and extending to 1993, was an ambitious *modernization* strategy coupled with a cautious approach to institutional reform. As reforms were approached in an incremental, instrumental, and pragmatic way there was no initial clear blueprint as to what the new system would be like (in fact, such a clear vision seems for all practical purposes to be absent even today). Nevertheless, a few major first-stage institutional changes can be identified:

1. the process of agricultural decollectivization;
2. entry and expansion of non-state (mostly local government) firms, that is, town and village enterprises (TVEs); and
3. market liberalization through the dual-track approach.

The most important result was the combined effect—or more precisely, the *mutually potentiating effect* to borrow a medical term—of these changes. This result, coupled with regional decentralization of administration in this huge country, contributed to creating competing, sometimes even chaotic, markets for various economic agents. Agricultural expansion and the resultant boom of local industries under the dual-track system stimulated the state industry to *grow out of the plan*[22] within a few years. Thus, China shared a common feature with the post-1990 CEECs and Russia in that the driving force for growth was new-entry firms rather than old state firms or even privatized firms.

Prices of most products were almost completely liberalized in the PRC by the mid-1990s. China achieved this result in a different way from the CEECs. In Hungary, for example, all mandatory planning was abolished after the 1968 reform, but prices were still indirectly controlled by organizations subject to bargaining for *economic parameters*. Hence, there was only *a simulated market* (Kornai 1986). After 1990, however, prices were swiftly liberalized at one stroke. In contrast, what China adopted in its *dual-track* approach was first to liberalize some prices at the margins while maintaining most basic planned prices and quotas, and then to phase these out step by step. Under the *plan track*, economic agents were assigned rights to, and obligations for, fixed quantities of goods at fixed prices as specified in the preexisting plan, whereas under the *market track* they participated in the market at free-market prices, provided that they fulfilled their obligations under the preexisting plan. Thus, markets were instigated as an institution of resource allocation in the early stage of Chinese reform.

Undoubtedly China's first stage of reform was a remarkable success. The high growth in GDP, elimination of shortages, and considerable improvement in the living standards of ordinary people would prove it. By the end of 1993, it became clear to everyone that the reform was supported by people in all walks of life. This was in sharp contrast to the frustration of Eastern European reformers in the late 1980s, who saw only a dead end to their reform efforts (Kornai 1986). Of course, Chinese reforms also contained many serious pitfalls such as excessive decentralization in favor of local governments and delay in tackling difficult measures like the bankruptcy of loss-making SOEs. Importantly, however, these achievements were basically made through institutional innovations either as ad hoc responses to a particular situation or by taking advantage of loopholes in the old system. In other words, major breakthroughs were accomplished by modifying the traditional socialist system not according to any design but through *learning by doing or walking*. The outcome of this Chinese pragmatism or eclecticism admittedly created quite a hybrid mixture of different institutions. It must be admitted that rather than the *puristic solution* of the abovementioned conventional wisdom, this *eclectic solution* gave tremendous impetus to the dynamism of China's success and opened the next road to further reforms.

1.4.2   The second stage: 1994 and thereafter

Since 1994, China's transition has moved into the second stage, aiming in practice at a shift away from the socialist system toward a capitalist market economy. First and most importantly, China has set a *goal to strive for*—which has become clearer over time—of establishing a *rule-based* market economy that incorporates internationally acceptable market institutions and practices. China has become the first and only country in which the ruling Communist Party has actively, as opposed to passively as was the case in CEECs in the 1970s and 1980s, shifted its official ideology to embrace the market system and private ownership.

Second, the advances made in several major areas toward this goal in the first five years (between 1994 and 1998) are noteworthy. Evidence shows that significant progress has been made, although in some ways contradictory, and this evidence should clarify many doubts over whether China's reform is on the right track.

1.4.2.1   *Strategic move: setting the goal for a market system*

At the outset of reform, China desired reform in order to increase productivity and improve living standards, but at no time did the leadership believe that it was going for a "full-fledged" (although this adjective has to be taken in "relative" terms) market system. This began to change in the early 1990s. However, establishing this goal was an evolutionary process, and in that respect, China is unlike most CEECs where the goal was very specific at the beginning of the transition, that is, to restore the "interrupted" capitalist development and "return" to Europe, namely to join the EU. Four consecutive milestone events should be mentioned to show how this strategic move has evolved progressively over time.

1. *The Fourteenth Party Congress of September 1992.* During much of the first stage of reform, the official ideology was one of "combining plan and market together." A more conservative version of this concept was "planning supplemented by market" and a more liberal version was "planned commodity economy." Clearly, the goal of reform was not a market system. In the spring of 1992, Deng Xiaoping made his famous southern tour to mobilize local support for further and more radical reform. The big ideological breakthrough occurred afterwards at the Fourteenth Party Congress in September 1992 when the party, for the first time, endorsed the *socialist market economy* as the goal of reform. This must be distinguished from the *market socialism* that many Eastern European reformers advocated in the 1970s and 1980s. In market socialism, the market is a simulated one that serves the purpose of socialism based on predominantly public ownership (Kornai 1992). In contrast, in a socialist market economy, development of a market economy is the goal and *socialist* is just an adjective.

2. *The Decision of November 1993.* The details of the transition to the *socialist market economy* became clearer one year later. The final output was the "Decision on Issues Concerning the Establishment of a Socialist Market Economic Structure" adopted by the Third Plenum of the Fourteenth Party Congress in November 1993. With the objectives of establishing a market system in mind, this landmark document made four major advances in reform strategy.

First, unlike the previous strategy of "groping for stones to cross the river," the decision emphasized the importance of coordination among various aspects of reforms. It advocated a coherent package and an appropriate sequencing of reforms, known as *combining package reform with breakthrough in key areas.*

Second, in abolishing in the first stage of reform aspects of the peculiar contracting system such as fiscal contracting, managerial contracting, and household contracting, the decision called for a rule-based market system to create an *equal-footing* basis for various economic agents. It included the decision to unify the foreign exchange rate and tax rates among all enterprises, regardless of ownership.

Third, the decision focused on the building of market-supporting institutions, such as formal fiscal federalism, a centralized monetary system, and a social safety net. Separation of central and local taxation and their administration was a critical step toward fiscal federalism. Revenue transfers between the central and provincial governments were to be based on a fixed formula rather than achieved though bargaining. Another example was the strengthening of the central operation of the People's Bank in order to minimize the local governments' influence on monetary policies.

Finally, the decision addressed the enterprise reform issue in terms of property rights and ownership. It was different from the former *expanding enterprise autonomy* in that it intended to transform the SOEs into *modern enterprises with clear property rights, well-defined responsibility and authority, separation of enterprises from the government, and scientific internal management.* For the first time, it also left the door open regarding the *privatization* of SOEs: As for small state-owned enterprises (SOEs), the management of some could be contracted out or leased; others could be shifted to the partnership system in the form of stock sharing or sold to collectives and individuals. But the major breakthrough on ownership issues still had to wait for longer.

3. *The Fifteenth Party Congress of September 1997.* In the decision of November 1993 state ownership had been regarded as a *principal component* of the economy, while private ownership was a *supplementary component.* This congress made a major breakthrough on this issue: State ownership was downgraded to *a pillar of the economy* and private ownership was elevated to *an important component of the economy.* In Chinese politics, these subtle changes of rhetoric imply an important change in ideology. The document recognized that *varieties of ownership should develop together.* Although private ownership had been discriminated against for decades, this statement meant that it gained *legitimacy.* Furthermore, the meaning of public ownership was redefined; it could have *many different forms* such as joint-stock corporations with shares divided among many owners. Finally the official ideology became *friendly* toward private ownership.

The second major breakthrough taken by the same congress was its emphasis on *the rule of law.* This is not the same as *democracy* in Western terminology. For example, the two typical market economies of Hong Kong and Singapore have established the rule of law but are not full democracy by Western standards. China considered this rule of law as crucial to a modern market economy and gave priority to it over democracy in its sequencing of political reforms.

4. *The Constitutional Amendments of March 1999.* Private ownership and the rule of law were incorporated into the Constitution in March 1999. An amendment to Article 11 of the Constitution places private businesses on an equal footing with the public sector by changing the original clause "the private economy is a supplement to public ownership" to "the non-public sector, including individual and private businesses, is an important component of the socialist market economy." Furthermore, Article 5 of the Constitution was amended to include the principle of "governing the country according

to law." These constitutional amendments indicate China's official commitment to a full (again not to be taken in absolute sense) market system based on the rule of law.

1.4.2.2   Major accomplishments in the first five years (1994–98)

The failure of Eastern European reforms prior to 1990 seemed to make the argument for the necessity of democratic political reform before economic transformation (Kornai 1992) persuasive, but China provided a case not possible in the CEECs. China is the first and only country under a Communist Party to embrace private ownership and a market system based on rule of law in its Constitution.[23] Among the new major measures introduced during the first five years, five are commonly cited:

1. unification of foreign exchange rates and current account convertibility;
2. overhaul of the tax and fiscal systems;
3. monetary centralization and financial reform;
4. reduction in the size of government bureaucracy; and
5. *privatization*[24] of SOEs and layoff of SOE workers.

Privatization of SOEs was started by local governments in a few provinces as experiments. Later, the central government promoted the trend with the slogan "grasping the large and letting go the small." *Grasping the large* was interpreted to mean keeping about 1,000 large firms in state ownership. But small SOEs were viewed differently. China's industrial SOEs were dominated by small and medium-sized enterprises mostly under the supervision of county or town governments. Most of them were converted to TVEs. The process had slowed down somewhat by 1998 because of the Asian financial crisis, but the trend had already become irreversible.

1.5   Reflections on the political economy of transition

Three decades ago few economists, myself included, predicted that China would go so far and accomplish such a great deal. Past performance is no guarantee of future success, but there are good reasons for reduced pessimism. Today, the ideology against markets and private ownership has subsided in China. Goals for reform have been clearly set to build up many market-supporting institutions, and the Chinese leadership is more determined than ever to integrate their economy with the global one.

1.5.1   Lessons from China

The Chinese transition path has been unusual enough to cast doubt on much of the conventional thinking on transformation strategies (Chow 1997). Economists should learn as much from lessons as they would teach

(Walder 1995). China's success was not an achievement of any grand program of transition to the market economy but a cumulative process of various reforms in agriculture and the rural economy, manufacturing industries at various levels, trade and services (an extension of various hybrid *non-state* enterprises, the enhanced dual-track regime in state industry, the introduction of temporary employment for industrial workers, and an extension of early experiences with the open-door policy, relations with foreign partners), and so on. All of these appear to be mutually reinforcing. Such Chinese experiences seem broadly to show some similarities to the reform processes in European socialist economies in the 1980s.

As stated earlier, in China, beginning in the early 1990s, some institutional reforms were introduced that went above and beyond previous attempts. This is also similar to the experiences of the CEECs in the 1980s, where radical reform measures were introduced only after the political changes of 1989. These reforms included the opening of stock exchanges (1990), the externalization of social protection from state enterprises (e.g., the privatization of housing and formation of social welfare funds), and movement toward external current account convertibility. The phases of the reform measures were not strictly sequential but overlapped one another and the edges were sometimes blurred by the contradictory political cycles that marked the whole process.

In China, a chain of sequences of reform was accompanied by a corresponding relaxation in socialist ideology. This also occurred in other countries, although the changes were scattered over time and over different CEECs. The most salient feature in the Chinese case is that the ideological accommodation always provided an ex-post facto justification of actual changes already made. Yet, the ideological evolution of the communist regime has been remarkable. Similarly to the history of official doctrines in other socialist countries, the general trend has been a gradual relaxation of socialist ideology that has evolved into a process of increasing blurring of the postulated contrasts between socialism and capitalism. The process of *hollowing out* of the official ideology has in some respects gone further in China than it did in Poland or Hungary in the late 1980s.

At the current stage of development it is very important to acknowledge the *mixed* character of Chinese reforms. They contain elements or components of reforms from such reform-oriented countries as Hungary and Poland in the 1980s along with those reform measures which were implemented *only after* the collapse of the party-states in the CEECs in 1989 and in Russia in 1991. On top of that, nowhere in the CEECs was there a decline in the SOE sector—about 25 percent of industrial production at the end of 1989—before political changes took place, as was the case in China. Lack of understanding of this seems to have given rise to a great deal of confusion in the discussion on China's transition. Emerging institutional and organizational forms, which often had to be adjusted to the socialist legacies in

China, have a hybrid character or are disturbingly nonconformist in the eyes of the *transition orthodoxy* (Rawski 1994).

This is an important point in the debate between the standard and opposing views. The former emphasizes the irrelevance of the Chinese experiences to the transition debate, while the latter maintains the uniqueness of the Chinese reforms in the broad context of systemic transformation. It challenges the conventional views about the nonreformability of the socialist system under one-party rule and the standard preemptive prescriptions about transition policies, even though the Chinese lessons may have little relevance to current policies in the CEECs.

For example, the *nonconformist* way of transformation is seen even in agriculture, which is commonly regarded as having succeeded most easily among Chinese reforms. Land ownership has remained formally *collective*, while use of it is granted to peasant households for a period of up to 30–50 years. Leases can be sublet or passed on to children, but the land itself cannot be bought or sold. The system is a kind of family farming with the state as *landowner*. But at the recent Central Committee Plenum (October 2008) the important decision was taken to promote the creation of "transfer markets" of subcontracting rights of farmers to land utilization, which seems to open the door to the de facto *privatization* of land ownership.

In other areas, the most remarkable feature is the expansion of the so-called non-state sector. This broad and indistinct category includes collective enterprises, both urban and rural—the latter mainly consisting of the famous TVEs, *individual* enterprises in cities or the countryside, and *other* (*private* and mixed Sino-foreign) *forms* of firms. The broad category, *collective*, is hard to define as these enterprises can be public, semipublic, quasi-private, mixed, hybrid, or vaguely defined cooperatives.[25] In any case, they are not highly dependent on a hierarchical management structure. Despite widespread interference by local authorities, TVEs have been the most dynamic sector. No doubt China's success has been primarily brought about by hybrid non-state enterprises and foreign capital enterprises including joint ventures.

While the notion of *privatization* has remained taboo or been evaded, *restructuring of state assets* has accelerated since 1993. Policies in favor of incorporation promoted the initiatives of enterprises in developed urban areas like Shanghai to take over. Many changes took place in ownership, the distribution of property rights, and the forms of organizations. The analysis of these changes was difficult because of the indistinctness of the semiformal or informal categories of new organizations. Chinese academics had no clear conceptual framework for interpreting the changes, and this was linked to the ambiguity of official ideological schemes. In fact, state ownership was transferred to collective, private, or foreign ownership through a number of ways: leases, spin-offs, and joint ventures. Various models of *shareholding system* were discussed in diverse circles and localities, and cross-ownerships of different kinds were extended, reminiscent of the *recombinant property*[26] or *interwoven ownership* (Sato 1997) that was typical of the postsocialist East European economies in the first decade of transformation. In China this occurred, in most cases, without bank involvement—unlike the East European experience. Thus, Chinese reforms in the 1980s led to the emergence of a socialist mixed economy with growing institutional and organizational varieties that evolved in the 1990s into a kind of *postsocialist mixed economy*. In this later version, original Chinese innovations are combined with similar features found in the CEECs in the 1990s.

Another major aspect of transformation is the changes in the coordination mechanism during the transition process, which cannot be simply reduced to the simple notion of switch *from plan to market*. Both capitalist and socialist economies have had complex coordination mechanisms combining various modes of *coordination mix* (Sato 1997), such as government control, markets, networks, and microhierarchies. Radical reform of socialist systems, or postsocialist transformation, is typically marked by significant changes in the coordination mix with the configuration evolving closer to the *genetic* mix consistent with capitalist systems. Some modes of coordination can quickly go through qualitative transformation—for example, state coordination through the abolition of megahierarchy or the switch from sellers' markets to buyers' markets (Kornai 1995). In general, however, such a transformation is a complex process, and it is not easy to draw a line between the two systems. The Chinese path was relatively more complicated, since it had to mix the elements of "socialist" reforms and postsocialist transformation. Microregulation by the state has shrunk and now covers only a small portion of industrial production. The megahierarchy has been fragmented in the process of devolution of control to lower levels of state administration, and its significance has been reduced by the gradual extension and generalization of horizontal links for state enterprises. Central government regulation has shifted from microregulation to *indirect bureaucratic coordination*,[27] and rather polycentric state administration has partially replaced the megahierarchy. The decrease in the degree of redistribution has implied a hardening of budget constraints even for the SOEs, although the constraint is generally harder in the non-state sector. Traditional social and industrial networks, with stabilized individual or organizational relations based on traditional mutual trust and reciprocity, have played an important role under Chinese socialism and they have been transformed, restructured, and sometimes extended in the process of changing the coordination setup.

The character of the emerging Chinese *capitalism* mixes elements of the Chinese tradition of *bureaucratic capitalism* from the 1920s and 1930s, postsocialist features of intricacies between the state and non-state sectors, cross-ownership ties of various kinds (Stark and Bruszt 1994), and characteristics typical of Asian capitalism, in which business networks and family groups play a very important role (crony capitalism).

1.5.2   Alternative paths toward postsocialist transformation

The distinguishing feature of the socialist system is the combination of a one-party regime and the dominant role of state ownership. The system is compatible with a variety of other institutions. As a consequence, the dislocation of the institutional economic base, which signifies a shift away from the socialist system to the capitalist system can take place in two ways: by the political superstructure being dismantled or state ownership in the economic system being eroded.

The first has been illustrated by the CEEC and FSU countries, and the second by China—and by Vietnam to far lesser extent. Gradual erosion of state ownership in China has progressively dismantled the institutional base and its relative coherence and produced a significant qualitative transformation of the economic system. But the piecemeal hollowing out of communist ideology regarding the contrast between socialism and capitalism was also instrumental in this dismantling. The crumbling away of the institution's structure affected its stability and coherence, even before its second pillar—that is, the dominance of state ownership—had begun to crack. The Chinese experience, as noted by W. Brus (1993), suggests that the domination of communist ideology should be distinguished from one-party rule.

There is an asymmetry between the formation of a socialist system from capitalism or proto-capitalism and postsocialist transformation. In the first case, the imposition of a one-party regime leads in all cases to the building of the second pillar of the institutional base, state ownership. This, in turn, has consequent effects in terms of regularity and coordination of doing business and mode of life. The role of ideology is fundamental in this process of transferring ownership. J. Kornai writes about a *genetic program*[28] based on the political block (one-party regime plus ideology) that transmits through a quasispontaneous process the characteristics of the system to every cell or single social relationship. The Kornaian *main line of causality* explains principally the process of the formation of the socialist system, its extension from one national economy to others, and its reproduction during periods of relative institutional stability.

But in the process of systemic sliding that results from continuous economic reforms, the main line is modified, reversed, or broken. Gradual *deprogramming* becomes irreversible. Changes in subsystems interact with the institutional base. Evolution in coordination mix and organizational diversification influence the ownership sphere as well. The political system is gradually modified by institutional and societal changes. When the Communist Party abandons the fundamental theses of its old ideology, is converted to the *market economy*, and accepts the limitations of state ownership to restricted spheres of the economy, it comes close to the category of authoritarian regimes compatible with a capitalist economic system. Such a *quiet revolution from within* was maturing in Poland, and especially in

Hungary, in the late 1980s before the communist regimes' demise, and the same process went much further in China during the 1990s.

1.5.3 Reflections on the principles of systemic change

China differs from the CEECs and Russia in many important ways, including in its initial conditions. China had a large agricultural sector which was the springboard for its reform. The greater amount of *slack* in China's planning system made it natural to pursue reform in a more decentralized way based on regional experiments. The ten-year turmoil of the Cultural Revolution discredited central planning and substantially weakened the government and the party bureaucracy and its vested interests. Thus, China is unlikely to provide a straightforward model for CEECs or Russia to follow. However, since the conventional wisdom on transition was based almost exclusively on the experiences of Eastern Europe, it is useful to incorporate into this analysis lessons based on careful observations of the case of China—the largest member of all transition economies. It is common to compare China's experiences since 1978 and often up to 1994 with those of the CEECs and Russia after 1990 and to contrast the difference between the two as *gradualism* vs. *Big Bang*. However, this is an inappropriate comparison. In the CEECs, reforms began as early as 1968 in Hungary, 1980 in Poland, and 1985 in the FSU. China, Hungary, Poland, and the FSU all went through a two-stage process: first the reform of the planned system and then the building of the market system. When setting China against the CEECs at a comparable stage, three conclusions can be drawn.

The first conclusion, based on China's achievements during the first 15 years of reform, is that transforming a planned economy, both as a single event and as a step along the longer path, can be successful. The reforms in the CEECs prior to 1990 were not as successful, and in fact, nearly failed. In analyzing the CEECs' experiences, Kornai (1992) reached the following conclusion: "In spite of generating a whole series of favorable changes, reform is doomed to fail: the socialist system is unable to renew itself internally so as to prove viable in the long run." In retrospect, the reforms undertaken in China between 1978 and 1993 were much more comprehensive and radical than those in the CEECs prior to 1990. For example, the latter had no serious dynamic development of non-state enterprises, and this is one reason why China's early reform was more successful. Thus, the evidence from China is compelling and demonstrates that the Eastern European experience is not universal.

The second conclusion, based on China's experience of the 1990s, is that changing from a planned system to a market one can occur without a *political revolution*. The East European reforms of the 1970s and 1980s led to a dead end because "the system is incapable of stepping away from its own shadow" (Kornai 1992). It eventually resulted in a political revolution that jump-started the transition of the 1990s. Although it is still too early to predict that China can complete its transition to a capitalist market system successfully, there is enough evidence to believe that the goal is set, the journey is now underway, and the chances of attaining the goal are, to say the least, not bad. If China attains its goal, it will disprove the Kornai thesis.

The third conclusion is that there are diverse paths for a successful transition. Institutional changes, in particular, require consideration of country-specific conditions. China has provided a feasible alternative form of transition with no prior political revolution, unlike the Eastern European cases. Some argued that China was a special case because it was a poor agrarian country, but others argued that Hungary and Poland were also special because their early reforms were constrained by their not being truly independent from the FSU (Szamuely 2000) and that their later transformation was facilitated by their aspirations to join the EU. The principles of system change are more complicated than most specialists originally believed.

1.5.4   Reflections on the theory and practice of transition

Transition was the most significant economic event during the twentieth century. During the last decades of the century, there were two major surprises. One was the sharp initial decline in output followed by recovery in most CEECs and the FSU, known as the *U-shaped output response* (Blanchard 1997). Another was China's remarkable success in taking a different path of transition. Both surprises force us to admit that there are limits to our economic knowledge on transition and there seem to be two related components to this. First, our knowledge about the working of market economies is not sufficient. Present-day economics offers an excellent explanation of the price mechanism, but it does not provide satisfactory expositions of the role of various institutions and the political economy in markets. Ronald Coase (1992) said, with reference to transition economies: "Without the appropriate institutions no market economy of any significance is possible. If we knew more about our own economy, we would be in a better position to advise them." Douglass North (1997) agreed: "While neoclassical theory is focused on the operation of efficient factor and product markets, few Western economists understand the institutional requirements essential to the creation of such markets since they simply take them for granted. A set of political and economic institutions that provides low-cost transacting and credible commitment makes possible the efficient factor and product markets underlying economic growth." Obviously, to build a market system from scratch, nothing can be taken for granted.

Second, our knowledge about the transition process is even more limited. Even if we have perfect knowledge about the destination, how to get there is a separate issue. Since transition from plan to market is unprecedented, the practice of transition is brand new and the theory of transition is in its infancy. Even Anatoly Chubais (1998), one of the so-called leading architects of the Russian reform, acknowledged after the Russian financial crisis in 1998: "We must recognize that we did not fully understand the scale of the process which we had undertaken. We thought there would be very difficult three years, five years, and eight years. Now, unfortunately, it is clear that reform will take decades."

Deng Xiaoping and other Chinese reformers were pragmatic, rather than naïve or cynical, recognizing from the very beginning that they did not know what would make the reforms succeed. Studying China's experiences should add a great deal to economics as a social science. After all, this is a country that may become, as Maddison (1998) exaggeratedly mentioned, the largest economy—once again the largest in the world—in less than two decades.

1.6 Tentative conclusions

What this chapter has tried to say in comparing the experiences of the CEECs and China may be summarized as follows.

1. In the first stage of reform in China (1978–93), incremental and evolutionary changes prevailed. This period could be compared to most radical reforms in some CEECs, Hungary in particular, in the 1980s, to which this author once applied the term "creeping market socialism" (Sato 1996)[29] although in some respects China's reforms went further. With Kornai (1986), we could speak of a *mixed economy of a socialist type*.

2. Although the picture is still blurred, the second stage (1994 and after) of China's evolutionary approach away from the socialist system, seems to show both a progressive move from radical reforms of the 1980s type toward postsocialist transformation and a hybrid mixture of the two. Here we may well speak of the gradual formation of an economy, which could not be understood without a hypothetical term that we coined: *postsocialist mixed economy*.

3. The hybrid and mixed character of today's Chinese economy leaves the door open to different interpretations and views. One could draw different conclusions from observing the same ongoing facts or processes. Yet, one cannot close one's eyes to the fact that some *dialectical* development from quantitative into qualitative change has taken place, approaching the crossing of the systemic *Rubicon*. It must be ensured, however, that the hybrid mixture of different institutions is gradually *put in order* to approach a more *orderly*, normal market structure.

4. Setting the exact *dateline* of this qualitative change is, however, difficult and open to controversy. Actually no clear-cut line divides systemic orders in the sphere of coordination setup or ownership, as shifts of dominance gradually take place. The case of postsocialist transformation in the CEECs is no exception. As for the case of China, however, this writer may offer a

tentative conjecture as hindsight: the *Rubicon* might have been crossed in the late 1990s, when the institutional bases were dismantled through ownership transfer and ideological conversion. Quite interesting in this regard is that Kornai in his latest paper (Kornai 2007) takes practically the same view as us. Judging from three yardsticks of systemic transformation (the *Rubicon*)—a dominant role for the private sector, the predominance of market coordination, and the evolution of the Communist Party to a ruling party not *antagonistic* to capitalism—he considers that the major characteristics of capitalism either apply or are near to applying in China.

5. Chinese development accompanied gradual systemic changes with a growing heterogeneity, or even contradictoriness, and a lack of affinity among various components of the system. How to theorize the development pattern in such *fuzzy*, nonconformist and unconventional forms may be a challenge to economists.

6. Most CEECs and the FSU took a long detour called *state socialism* and then resumed their interrupted capitalist development paths after 1989. China skipped the capitalist development stage and tried to modernize itself within the framework of socialism with Chinese characteristics. The two paths trodden were divergent in the past but might become more *convergent*[30] in the future. Authoritarian one-party rule may fulfill the same role as the market-friendly *developmental dictatorship* of some East Asian countries, the role of which has been to promote capitalist development. With the end of the ability to play that role, however, they came to an end in most countries in the region. No doubt, authoritarian one-party rule is not a good thing as such, but under Chinese conditions in the transition process it might have performed the necessary *role of the state*, the *desertion* of which caused the confusion in the CEECs in the first phase of transformation. Perhaps otherwise transition could not have happened in China.

The problem remains naturally regarding to what extent the current political system can accommodate the next stage of transformation toward a capitalist makeover. At least one thing seems clear: the political system should be modified according to the pressing needs of the economy, together with further modification of its ideology. If—this is a big *if*—the present political system can accommodate these needs with its high rate of growth, a unique case in history may be seen in that an authoritarian regime succeeds not only in maintaining itself for a long time but also in promoting capitalist society in a large country with socialist legacies.

1.7   Comparative economic systems and variety of capitalism studies

This writer believes that now the door may be open to pondering the following question. What types of capitalistic market economies are emerging in the former socialist countries in the current transformation process? This is an extension of the study on postsocialist transformation of the VoC Studies and enriches Comparative Economic Systems Studies which has once again been acknowledged as an important field of economics. It is an intellectual counterpart paralleling the integration of postsocialist countries into the world capitalist order.

Comparative Economic Systems Studies as an academic discipline was first included in the lecture programs of many American universities in the early 1950s at the time of the Cold War, and appeared to aim to demonstrate the superiority of capitalist over socialist systems. The discipline then tried, however, to be more *neutral* by incorporating cybernetics and information theory in the 1970s (e.g., Montias 1971). But the attempt was not as successful as was hoped for, since such theories as cybernetics or systems theory were not capable of analyzing the heavily politicized actual socialist systems.

In the late 1980s the name changed to *Refornomics* (Reform Economics). Once transformation was under way, this was proclaimed the *Economics of Transition* (Lavigne 1995, 1999). Having come a long way, Comparative Economic Systems Studies a comparison of *grand systems*—appears to have withered away as the postsocialist economies became integrated into the capitalist world, including emerging capitalism with socialist legacies. There still remains much scope for Comparative Economic Systems Studies to study this type of emerging capitalist economy within the framework of VoC studies. Hanson (2006) was quite right in raising the question of *the long-term viability or lack of it of non-Anglo-Saxon versions of capitalism*, but not correct when he tended to put weight on *lack of it*. As this writer argued earlier, although the boundaries of the models of capitalism sometimes seem blurred amidst fierce market competition under globalization, there is no noticeable trend toward one-way convergence to the Anglo-Saxon type of capitalism. It goes without saying that capitalism in general should be upheld against *really existing socialism*, but it does not necessarily mean that *really-existed capitalism* should be defended in its every form and model. Here is a large untapped field for VoC Studies.

As Kornai (2005) rightly put it, this does not mean that the tasks of *transitology*—as applied to the incompletely transformed countries of China, Vietnam, Cuba, or even Iraq— are over. The big remaining question is whether the Chinese type of *capitalism of developmental dictatorship* might be analyzed within the framework of *VoC studies*. We have seen many less-developed countries that achieved capitalist development under an authoritarian regime, but China is the first case of that kind under the Communist Party rule.

From the viewpoint of VoC Studies, there seem to be very mixed and contradictory processes being pursued in the world. On the one hand, as noted by Giannetti and Nuti (2007), claims of the *death* of the European social model are a gross exaggeration, but undoubtedly it has been *wavering* in the midst of globalization and somewhat diluted by EU enlargement to postsocialist CEECs, as some of them adopted a seemingly *hyper-liberal socio-economic model*. On the other hand, Russia under former President Putin and the Medvedev-Putin *tandem* leadership is increasing the tendency toward capitalism with an authoritarian dictatorship, although formally communist one-party rule has been abolished. The similarity of, and differences between, the two big transforming countries, China and Russia, could be an important subject for VoC Studies. Certainly VoC Studies must cover not only advanced capitalist countries like America, *old* Europe, and Japan but also most of the transforming economies in the postsocialist CEECs, Russia, China, Vietnam, and others. Everything is in progress and awaiting economists' careful observations and analyses rather than premature judgments.

Notes

This paper was first presented at the Second ICSEAD Workshop on Transitional Economies in Central Eastern Europe and East Asia, held in Budapest at the Hungarian Academy of Sciences on November 24–25, 2000 and revised and updated December 1, 2008. The author wishes to thank László Szamuely for his helpful comments in the revision.

1. Sato wrote just after the Tian'anmen Square incident in June 1989: "Henceforth, although the economic reforms in China would remain in name, the substance would be lost." This was quite in line with the conventional wisdom at that time. In hindsight, undoubtedly Sato was wrong.
2. Here László Szamuely's cautious reservation is quite interesting (Szamuely 2000). Referring to János Kornai's (Kornai 1992) concept of "genetic program," he writes: "So, when we accept the Kornaian concept of the anti-reformist 'genetic program' inherent in every CPE under a mono-party regime it should be always in our mind that the actual realization of the program takes place neither in a vacuum nor on an isolated island. The international economic and political environment or context always play a significant, often decisive, role in it, both in negative and positive sense, i.e., hindering or furthering market-oriented reforms. In the case of Hungary, a small country with a highly trade-dependent economy, the promising process of economic reform was kept back perhaps not so much by any foreign political and/or ideological constraints as by the very simple fact of the extensive and tight cooperation with the economies of the other countries of the Soviet bloc, in the first place with the Soviet Union."
3. Brus (1993), pp. 437–439. Here "marketization" refers to the change in coordination mechanisms as propounded by J. Kornai (1984); this involves, namely, a shift from "bureaucratic" to "market" coordination, the former including two forms: direct (administrative) and indirect (parametric).
4. Ellman (1999) raises a strong objection to applying the term "transition economy" to China. He writes in a book review: "This, however, is a very doubtful classification, since China's economic policy goals are in fact very different [as Pomfret (1997) has pointed out] and it has not experienced a political revolution." Despite my deep admiration for my old friend M. Ellman, I cannot agree with his

argument, since it is hard to refuse the use of the term to those countries where "marketization" has gone far beyond the scope and degree of the most market-oriented reforms in CEECs in the 1980s by any standard.

5. Washington Consensus is what is regarded as some basic ways of thinking behind the policy advices of the World Bank or IMF to developing countries' governments.

6. This was extensively discussed by T. Sato, Takayuki Ito, Nobuo Shimotomai, and Susumu Takahashi in a Round-Table Discussion (1999).

7. Ivan Berend (Berend 2000b), citing the early 20th century Hungarian poet-prophet, Endre Ady, writes, "The region is, in the middle of Europe...like a ferry-boat...sails from the East to the West, but more likely back to the East."

8. This point is extensively discussed in Sato (1995). As to Sato's "non-reversal-resumption" arguments, he agrees with Szamuely (2001) who cautioned, while naturally regarding "socialism" as a "failed experiment," that "it would be a grave mistake to neglect all kinds of real progress made in general education, social and health services. Even if some may deride these achievements as manifestations of a premature welfare state, this inheritance of the socialist era, if properly administered, could be a great advantage for the former socialist countries."

9. See, for example, Pomfret (1997).

10. See, for instance, Berend (2000a). Berend argues, citing Tsuneo Morita (1999), that "if they [i.e., the transition countries] achieve a growth rate in the range of 4.5 to 6.0 percent annually against an assumed 3 percent growth in the low-income countries of the EU, it may take, in the best possible scenario, about 30 years. The Czech Republic may reach that level in 10–15 years, Hungary, Poland and Slovenia in 20–25 years." In the same context, G. Kolodko (1999) rightly refers to the "necessity of equitable growth" as the missing link in "transition orthodoxy." (See also Kolodko (2000) for more on this). In addition, according to László Csaba (2001), it will take more than 25 years for Hungarian wages to reach 60 percent of the European Union average. "Hungary could shorten the time period, but that would just increase unemployment and result in about 80 percent of medium-sized enterprises closing down," as was the case in East Germany.

11. Jeffrey Sachs, Wing Thye Woo and Xiaokai Yang (2000) argue, "There are two patterns of transition. One is adopted by Eastern Europe and Russia, in which market-oriented reforms are just a small part of the transition of constitutional rules. The other is adopted by China and Vietnam, in which market-oriented reforms are implemented under communist game rules (i.e., a communist monopoly of political power)." Although, of course, this writer is not against constitutional development, he is against such a shift in argumentation which does not seem to justify the failure in the "small part of transition" in Russia. It is less convincing, as the "constitutional development" itself in Russia under an authoritarian president is open to question, to put it most mildly. See Sato (2000).

12. Here, too, Sato appreciates the comments of László Szamuely (2001), who reminded him of the importance, when discussing the "limitations" of reforms of Hungarian type in the 1980s, of taking into account the issues of "national sovereignty" which the CEECs did not possess, while China did.

13. This was because the World Bank could not determine at that time where to place China according to the various measurement parameters, and instead illustrated the Chinese experience mainly in boxes rather than in the text.

14. According to Maddison's (1998) calculation based on purchasing power parity, without taking into account the 1998 Russian economic crisis, China's per capita GDP will surpass that of the 15 former Soviet Union countries by 2010. As of writing this revised version (2009), China has become the third economic power in the world after the USA and Japan, surpassing Germany in terms of GDP.

15. Grzegorz Kolodko (1993) rightly refers to the "policy failure which almost negated the intermediate control mechanism which was to be applied to the enormous state sector, in turn increasing the uncertainty at the enterprise level, leading to further decline in production." As to the institutional vacuum, see Sato (1995). Note should be taken here of Szamuely's (2001) comments that what matters here "is not so much the lack of regulation as the quality or nature of this regulation," which in turn does not justify a *dictatorship of law* of the type advocated by the former Russian President Putin.

16. There were many papers published in 2002 which, either in the titles or subtitles, included this phrase. Most are apologetic in character with only a few exceptions. Among papers on this subject, János Kornai's (2000a and 2000b) is one of the relatively few that are objective. Kornai gave this paper again at a lecture given at the 6th EACES Conference in Barcelona, September 7–9, 2000. He added orally, "I think ownership reforms in China are following the Strategy A [where Strategy A refers to a *strategy of organic development* in privatizing SOEs]." Kornai also refers to the *success* and *disappointment* in transition in a more recent paper (Kornai 2005).

17. The most comprehensive analysis of the costs of transformation is given in a remarkable paper by Ellman (2000b). See also Szamuely (1997).

18. This subtitle is from Kornai's book published in 1990, as quoted above.

19. Stiglitz (1999) refers particularly to Russia's case, but it is also true of most southeastern European countries where, to quote the statement by Daniel Daianu (2000), former Minister of Finance of Romania, "People no longer understand the transition as a regime change to a miraculous state of market economy. Mistakes had been made, and...what is now evident is the need to catch up and to grow."

20. A few years ago, some Japanese experts on Chinese economy were arguing that the socialist market economy in China is a form in which *euthanasia* of socialism is to be implemented. In the unforeseeable long term, this might be the case, but it is probably not true in the foreseeable medium- or fairly long term.

21. See Nakagane (1981) and Granick (1987).

22. See Naughton (1995) and Fan (1997).

23. Quite interestingly, Kornai (1998), in stark contrast to his former views, emphasized that what constituted a necessary basis for a market system was not *democracy* but a political power *friendly* to private property and the market.

24. Officially China does not use the term *privatization*, substituting it with other terms such as *transformation of ownership* or *restructuring of ownership*, quite similar to the use of *nonpublic ownership* as a proxy of *private ownership*.

25. See Perotti, Sun, and Zou (1998). The idea has been further developed in a generalized form in Sun (2000).

26. Stark first raised this notion in 1992, but developed it more extensively in Stark (1993), to which this writer also contributed. See also Stark (1994).

27. Kornai (1992, chap. 6) distinguishes between two types of *bureaucratic coordination*: direct and indirect. An earlier version of this notion is found in Kornai (1984).

28. See Kornai (1992) and Szamuely's cautious reservation (Szamuely 2000).
29. This notion is quite close to Nuti (1990). Kornai's notion of *market socialism* (i.e., state ownership plus market economy) is too narrow to reflect the reality in some most advanced reform-oriented countries even in the 1980s, since the share of non-state ownership was increasing there and the economy was becoming more *mixed*. It was a *creeping* approach to market socialism, which, however, was overtaken by the drastic political turnaround of 1989 and thus remained unfinished.
30. *Convergence* does not necessarily mean that two systems become the same, but rather that the *distance* between the two becomes closer. See Tinbergen Jan (1980).

References

Berend, Ivan. 2000a. "From Plan to Market, From Regime Change to Sustainable Growth in Central and Eastern Europe." UN/ECE Spring Seminar, Geneva, May 2.

Berend, Ivan. 2000b. "The Future Enlargement of the European Union in a Historical Perspective." Paper presented at the International Symposium in commemoration of the 120th anniversary of the Hosei University, Tokyo, Oct. 3.

Blanchard, Olivier. 1997. *Economics of Post-Communist Transition*. Oxford: Clarendon Press.

Brus, Wlodzimiez. 1975. *Socialist Ownership and Political Systems*. London: Routledge and Kegan Paul.

Brus, Wlodzimiez. 1993. "Marketization and Democratization: The Sino-Soviet Divergence." *Cambridge Journal of Economics* 17: 437–439.

Chow, Gregory. 1997. "Challenges of China's Economic System for Economic Theory." *American Economic Review* (May) 87: 321–327.

Chubais, Anatoly. 1998. *Russia Today Online*, September 24, Reuters.

Coase, Ronald. 1992. "The Institutional Structure of Production." *American Economic Review* (Sept.) 82: 713–719.

Csaba, László. 2001. *Budapest Sun*, April 6.

Daianu, Daniel. 2000. UN/ECE informal seminar on The Economic Regeneration of South-East Europe, Geneva, May 3.

Ellman, Michael. 1999. "Book Review" in *Economic Systems* 23(4): 381–383.

Ellman, Michael. 2000a. "The Russian Economy under El'tsin." Paper delivered at the International Symposium on The End of the Yeltsin Era, organized by the International Center of Hosei University, Tokyo, Feb. 21. Also in *EUROPE-ASIA Studies* 52(8).

Ellman, Michael. 2000b. "The Social Costs and Consequences of Transformation Process." Paper presented at the UN/ECE Spring Seminar From Plan to Market: The Transition Process after Ten Years, Geneva, May 2.

Fan, Gang. 1997. "Growing into the Market: China's Economic Transition," UNU/WIDER Project Meeting, Transition Strategies, Alternatives and Outcomes, Helsinki, May 15–17.

Giannetti, Marilena, and Mario D. Nuti. 2007. "The European Social Model and its Dilution as a Result of EU Enlargement." *TIGER Working Paper Series*, No. 105 (July).

Granick, David. 1987. "The Industrial Environment in China and the CMEA Countries." In *China's Industrial Reform*, Gene Tidrick and Chen Jiyuan (eds.). New York: Oxford University Press.

Hanson, Philip. 2006. "The Tasks Ahead in Comparative Economics—What Should We Be Comparing?" (mimeo), Paper delivered at the Annual Conference of JACES (Japan Association for Comparative Economic Studies), Hitotsubashi University, Tokyo, June 10.

Kolodko, Grzegorz. 1993. "From Output Collapse to Sustainable Growth in Transition Economies." *Institute of Finance Working Papers*, No. 35.

Kolodko, Grzegorz. 1999. "Ten Years of Post-socialist Transition: The Lessons for Policy Reforms." *World Bank Development Research Group Working Papers*, No. 2095 (Apr.).

Kolodko, Grzegorz. 2000. "Globalization and Catching-Up: From Recession to Growth in Transition Economies." *IMF Working Paper*, No. 100 (June).

Kornai, János. 1984. "Bureaucratic and Market Coordination." *Osteuropa Wirtschaft* 29(4), 306–319.

Kornai, János. 1986. "The Hungarian Reform Process: Visions, Hopes, and Reality." *Journal of Economic Literature* (Dec.), 24(4): 1687–1737.

Kornai, János. 1990. *The Road to a Free Economy—Shifting from a Socialist System: The Example of Hungary.* New York: W.W.Norton.

Kornai, János. 1992. *The Socialist System: The Political Economy of Communism.* Oxford: Clarendon Press.

Kornai, János. 1995. "Eliminating the Shortage Economy: A General Analysis and Examination of the Developments in Hungary." *Economics of Transition* 3(1/2).

Kornai, János. 1998. "From Socialism to Capitalism." *Center for Post-Collectivist Studies*, Paper No. 4, London.

Kornai, János. 2000a. "Ten Years After 'The Road to a Free Economy': The Author's Self-Evaluation." Paper presented at the World Bank ABCDE/Annual Bank Conference on Development Economics, Washington, Apr. 18–20.

Kornai, János. 2000b. "What Does the Change of the System from Socialism to Capitalism Does and Does Not Mean." In *Annual Bank Conference on Development Economics 2000,* Boris Pleskovich and Nicholas Stteern (eds.). Washington DC: The World Bank: 49–66.

Kornai, János. 2005. "The Great Transformation of Central Eastern Europe: Success and Disappointment." Presidential Address, delivered at the 14th World Congress of the International Economic Association (IEA) in Marrakech, Morocco, Aug. 29.

Kornai, János. 2007. "What does 'Change of System' Mean ?" In *From Socialism to Capitalism* (forthcoming) J. Kornai. Budapest: Central European University Press.

Lavigne, Marie. (1995, 1999). *The Economics of Transition.* 1st and 2nd Edns., London: McMillan.

Maddison, Angus. 1998. *Chinese Economic Performance in the Long Run.* Paris: OECD Development Centre.

Maddison, Angus. 2007. *The World Economy: A Millennial Perspective/Historical Statistics.* Paris: OECD (Development Centre Studies).

Mao Zedong. 1940. *On New Democracy—Selected Works of Mao Zedong* [Japanese Translation], Vol. 4. Tokyo: San-ichi Publishers, 1952.

Montias, John M. 1971. *Comparison of Economic Systems.* New Haven: Yale University Press.

Morita, Tsuneo. 1999. "The Hidden Growth Potential of EU Candidates." *World Bank Newsletter, Transition* 10(5).

Nakagane, Katsuji. 1981. "China: The Structure of Socialist Economic System and Development." In *Contemporary Socialism, Economic Systems Series*, Vol. 4, Masayuki Iwata (ed.). [In Japanese.] Tokyo: Toyokeizai-Shimposha.

Naughton, Barry. 1995. *Growing out of the Plan: China's Reform 1978–1993*. New York: Cambridge University Press.

North, Douglass. 1997. "The Contribution of the New Institutional Economics to an Understanding of the Transition Problem." *UNU/WIDER Annual Lectures*, Assembly House of the Estates (Säätytalo), Snellmaninkatu 9–11 Hall 15, Stockholm, Mar, 7.

Nuti, Domenico Mario. 1990. "Market Socialism: A Model that Might Have Been but Never Was." Paper presented at the World Congress of Slavic Studies, Harrogate, England, July 22.

Perotti, Enrico C., Laixiang Sun, and Liang Zou. 1998. "Enterprises in China." *UNU/WIDER Working Papers*, No. 150 (Sept.).

Pomfret, Richard. 1997. "Growth and Transition: Why Has China's Performance Been so Different?" *Journal of Comparative Economics* 25(3).

Rawski, Thomas G. 1994. "Progress without Privatization: The Reforms of China's State Industries." In *Changing Political Economies: Privatization in Post-Communist and Reforming Communist States*, Vedat Milor (ed.). Boulder, CO: Lynne Rienner Publishers.

Round-Table Discussion. 1999. "Ten Years after the Revolution in Eastern Europe." [In Japanese.] *Sekai* [The World], Atsushi Okamoto (ed. in chief), (Dec.). Tokyo: Iwanami Shoten Publishers: 88–105.

Sachs, Jeffrey, Wing Thye Woo, and Xiaokai Yang. 2000. "Economic Reforms and Constitutional Transition." *Center for International Development Working Paper*, No. 43 (Apr.).

Sato, Tsuneaki. 1989. "Comparative Study of Economic Reforms." In *Economic Transformation in Contemporary China*, Vol. II. [In Japanese.], Kazuo Yamanouchi (ed.). Tokyo: Iwanami Shoten.

Sato, Tsuneaki. 1995. "How Extensive Has the Transition to a Market Economy Been?" *Moct=Most*, 5(1, 2): 1–12.

Sato, Tsuneaki. 1996. "Adjusted Concept of Transformation Policies: Some Cordial Suggestions." In *Reevaluating Economic Reforms in Central and Eastern Europe since 1989*, NIRA (Japan) and KOPINT-DATORG (Hungary), Proceedings of the International Workshop, Budapest, Sept. 1995, Budapest, 1996.

Sato, Tsuneaki. 1997. "Possibilities for and Limitations to a 'Mixed Economy' in the Systemic Transformation." In *Economic System of Post-Socialism*. [In Japanese.], Tsuneaki Sato (ed.). Tokyo: Iwanami Shoten Publishers.

Sato, Tsuneaki. 2000. "Russia's 'Market Economy' in the Putin Era." *Russian Studies*, JIIA (The Japan Institute of International Affairs), No. 31 (Oct.). [In Japanese.]: 55–87.

Stark, David. 1992. "Path-Dependence and Privatization Strategies in Eastern Europe." In *Transition to Capitalism? The Communist Legacy in Eastern Europe*, Janos Matyas Kovacs (ed.), (1994). New Brunswick and London: Transaction Publishers.

Stark, David. 1993. "Recombinant Property in East European Capitalism." Paper presented at the Annual Conference of the Society for the Advancement of Socio-Economics (SASE), New School for Social Research, New York, Mar. 27–28.

Stark, David. 1994. "Not by Design: Recombinant Property in East European Capitalism." *Document du Travail*, IRSES, MSH, Paris.

Stark, David, and L. Bruszt. 1994. "Restructuring Networks in the Post-socialist Economic Transformation." *Cornell Working Papers on Transition from State Socialism* 94(9).

Stiglitz, Joseph. 1999. "Whither Reform? Ten Years of the Transition." Keynote address given at the World Bank ABCDE/ Annual Bank Conference on Development Economics, Washington DC, Apr. 28–30.

Sun, Laixiang. 2000. "New Paradigms on Ownership of Firms: A Comprehensive Analysis across Development Stages and Institutional and Technological Contexts." *UNU/WIDER Working Papers*, No. 192 (Aug.).

Szamuely, László. 1997. "The Social Costs of Transformation in Central and Eastern Europe." *Department East European Studies, University of Uppsala Working Papers*, No. 31 (Jan.).

Szamuely, László. 2000. "Two Market-oriented Reforms under a Mono-party Socio-political System." Paper presented at the ICSEAD Workshop on the Comparison of Transition, Kitakyushu City, Japan, Mar. 30–31.

Szamuely, László. 2001. "Comments on the Paper by Tsuneaki Sato." Mimeo.

Tinbergen, Jan. 1980. "De Convergentietheorie: Balansa na 20 Jaar." *Civis Mund.*

Walder, Andrew. 1995. "China's Transitional Economy: Interpreting its Significance." *China Quarterly* (Dec.).

World Bank. 1996. *World Development Report 1996: From Plan to Market.* New York: Oxford University Press.

Wu, Jinglian. 2000. "China's Transition to a Market Economy." Paper presented at the Budapest Workshop, Nov. 24–25.

2
China's Transition to a Market Economy: How Far Across the River?

Jinglian Wu

2.1 Introduction

We view China's reform as an evolutionary process in two stages. The first stage spans about fifteen years from 1978 to 1993, and the second begins in 1994. There is a clear division between the two. The watershed is the historic November 1993 "Decision on Issues Concerning the Establishment of a *Socialist Market Economic Structure*" adopted by the Third Plenum of the Fourteenth Congress of the Communist Party of China (CPC). The review in Section 2.2 below of the nature of the first-stage reform will allow better understanding of the significance of the decision. First, the reform started step by step to expand the market incentives for resource allocation, while keeping the basic institutional framework of central planning almost intact. It achieved a great success outside the state sector and dramatically improved people's living standards, eliminating the shortages common to all planned economies.

This success was utterly different from the similar reforms in the Central and Eastern European countries (CEECs) prior to 1990. As early as 1968, Hungary pioneered its serious economic reform by abolishing mandatory planning targets for enterprises. For Chinese reformers in the early 1980s, it was a role model, but it failed to eliminate shortages and its economy stagnated (Kornai 1986). Poland and the Soviet Union underwent similar stories. These early failures later gave the CEECs an impetus to take more radical measures for reform but only after the fall of the communist regimes in around 1990. By contrast, China demonstrated a surprising alternative means of transition from a planned to a market economy.

Section 2.3 explains in detail the November 1993 decision as a historic and strategic shift in China's course of reform. Then, China opted to abolish the planned system altogether for the first time, and set a new goal of establishing a modern market system which would eventually incorporate internationally recognized *best practice* institutions. This second stage of reform, beginning in 1994, was comparable to the reforms in the CEECs after

1990 and the former Soviet Union (FSU) countries after 1992. Section 2.4 describes the experiences of reform during the first five years after 1994. China attempted several radical reforms in accordance with the November 1993 decision. The major reform measures included unification of exchange rates and current account convertibility, the overhaul of the tax and fiscal systems with the separation of national and local taxation administrations, and the reorganization of the central bank, including establishing cross-province (regional) branches. China also began to privatize small-scale state-owned enterprises (SOEs), lay off surplus state employees and establish a social safety net.

Despite great achievements, China still has a long way to go on its journey toward a modern market economy. Section 2.5 investigates the remaining challenges, mainly surrounding the core issue in the Chinese economy: the government-business relationship and its change to an arm's-length type with a free and competitive enterprise system. This is the foundation of any modern market system, which requires China to tackle three urgent tasks: (1) transforming SOEs, (2) promoting private enterprise, and (3) establishing the rule of law to govern government-business relations. Finally in Section 2.6, in conclusion, we recognize many opportunities for China, including those granted by its accession to the WTO. We are cautiously optimistic about China making a quantum leap in its transition to a market economy within a decade after its 2001 accession to the WTO.

2.2   The nature of the reform in the first stage: 1978–93

During this period, China's GDP grew at an average annual rate of about 9 percent, or 7.5 percent on a per capita basis. The living standard of ordinary people improved significantly. For example, an average Chinese consumer tripled his/her consumption of edible vegetable oil, pork, and eggs. Per person living space doubled in urban areas and more than doubled in rural areas, and total household bank deposits to GDP ratio increased from less than 6 percent in 1978 to more than 40 percent in 1993. The number of people living in absolute poverty substantially decreased from more than 250 million to fewer than 100 million. By the end of 1993, people in all walks of life were enthusiastic supporters of reform simply because almost everyone had benefited from it. This contrasts sharply with the frustration of CEECs' reformers in the late 1980s, because they saw only a dead end to their decades-long efforts at reform (Kornai 1986, 1992).

The reason why China could avoid the failures of the CEECs was that it made deeper institutional changes than they did (Wu 1992) by introducing dramatic changes outside, rather than inside, the existing core of central planning in the form of *incremental reform* (*zengliang gaige*), including the *non-state sector* which rose rapidly (Qian and Xu 1993; Wu 1999 and Qian 2000). By the early 1980s nearly 100 percent of agricultural activities were in the form of household farming. In the nonagricultural sectors, a variety of forms of ownership for non-state enterprises prevailed, including collectives, cooperatives, private businesses, joint ventures with foreign firms, and sole foreign-invested firms. Unlike the SOEs, non-state enterprises operated outside the scope of central planning and were subject to harder budgetary constraints, facing keener competition, and soon became the engine of growth and industrialization. In 1978, the state sector accounted for 78 percent of the nation's industrial output: by 1993 the share had declined to only 43 percent. Similarly, the state's share in commerce declined from 55 percent in 1978 to 40 percent by 1993. With no privatization of the SOEs taking place during this period, such declines were entirely as a result of the rapid growth of the non-state sector. In the CEECs, despite decades of reform, the *second economy* (the non-state sector) remained insignificant, especially in industry, even in the late 1980s (Kornai 1986). During this period foreign direct investment in China made up less than 5 percent of total investment by the early 1990s, and domestic private firms were not significant either. In fact, most non-state firms were collective enterprises like rural Township and Village Enterprises (TVEs) controlled by local government.

Accompanying the rise of the non-state sector was the development of markets. Price reform began under a *dual-track* mechanism, that is, prices were free at the margins while planned prices were maintained for planned quantities and were frozen for some time (Wu and Zhao 1987). As a result, true domestic market prices were quickly established for all goods as early as the mid-1980s. The planned track was largely phased out in the early 1990s. By 1993 more than 90 percent of prices—in terms of industrial output values—were determined by market forces. In Hungary, however, where mandatory planning targets were abolished as early as 1968, most prices continued to be *administered* even in the late 1980s by bureaucrats, not determined by the market (Kornai 1986). China's market development was also pushed by the rapid expansion of foreign trade. As a result of the open-door policy, both exports and imports increased much faster than GDP. Thus, the exports to GDP ratio increased from less than 5 percent in 1978 to more than 20 percent by the early 1990s. The interaction between foreign and domestic markets helped push convergence of the two tracks. All of these changes were also forms of *incremental reform*.

In the CEECs, reforms were often *ad hoc* responses to particular constraints of planning or took advantage of its loopholes. For example, "contracting" prevailing between different levels of government and enterprises/households was effective in eroding central planning, but these contracts were subject to frequent renegotiations and change. Thus, the core of central planning remained in the early 1990s.

Lenin's *State and Revolution* characterized a centrally planned economy as a *State Syndicate* and a *Party-State, Inc.* Lenin's original description referred to a situation where the entire society becomes one factory and all the people become employees of the party-state. In its narrow sense, his description does not apply even to prereform China or the Soviet Union, because of the complex structure of internal organizations involving both the state and collective sectors. The essential point of Lenin's party-state remained valid, however, for both pre- and postreform China. The party-state is reflected in the following three areas. First, the SOEs are still controlled by the state and the party in an old-fashioned way, if not in daily operations, certainly in the making of strategic decisions. No single SOE was privatized and almost none went bankrupt. No state employees were ever laid off for economic reasons. The CPC appoints top managers in SOEs. Although the state sector shrank significantly in relative terms, it expanded in absolute terms of employment, output, and assets. Second, truly private enterprises did not develop at a healthy pace. Truly private enterprises accounted for less than 15 percent of industrial output by the end of 1993, and almost all of the domestic private enterprises had fewer than eight employees. Most non-state enterprises, such as TVEs, were collective or joint ventures, which were essentially local government-controlled and not truly private. Local governments are, of course, parts of the state. Third, new market-supporting institutions were not put in place to replace the old planning institutions. China did not have a market-supporting fiscal system, financial system, system of corporate governance, social security system, or modern legal system, for example. Fundamentally, there was no rule of law, and the CPC and the state, not laws, governed the economy.

2.3   The essence of the November 1993 decision

To show the significance of the November 1993 decision, its main contents and several follow-up decisions are discussed first. Then follows analyses of the political and economic basis for the leadership to have made such a strategic shift as well as the intellectual inputs contributing to the decisions.

2.3.1   The November 1993 decision and subsequent ideological changes

At the outset of reform, the Chinese leadership wanted to increase productivity and improve people's living standards, but at no time did they think of introducing a full-fledged market system (Perkins 1994). During the first 15 years of reform, the official ideology was one of *combining plan and market together*. In the early 1990s, the mind-set of the leadership began to change. In the spring of 1992, Deng Xiaoping made his famous southern tour to mobilize local support for further and more radical reform. The big ideological breakthrough occurred afterwards at the Fourteenth Party Congress in September 1992 when the CPC, for the first time, endorsed the *socialist market economy* as China's goal for reform. This must be distinguished from CEECs reformers' *market socialism* of the 1970s and 1980s. In the latter, the market is a simulated one designed to serve the purpose of socialism based on public ownership (Kornai 1992), whereas in the former *socialist* is just an adjective and the goal is *market economy*. The difference is fundamental.

The makeup of the socialist market economy became clearer a year later. In 1993, the CPC's Economics and Finance Leading Group, headed by Party Secretary General Jiang Zemin, worked with economists to prepare a broad strategy of transition to a market system. Several research teams were formed to study various aspects of transition ranging from taxation to fiscal and financial systems, enterprises, and foreign trade. The final output was the "Decision on Issues Concerning the Establishment of a Socialist Market Economic Structure" adopted by the Third Plenum of the Fourteenth Party Congress in November 1993 (*China Daily*, Nov. 17, 1993).

Its essence was to replace China's centrally planned system with a modern market system and eventually to incorporate the international institutions recognized as the *best practice*. This landmark document represented a turning point on China's road toward a market economy and, together with several subsequent decisions, marked a decisive historic event.

The decision made two major breakthroughs. First, it called for the creation of market-supporting institutions, such as formal fiscal federalism, a centralized monetary system, and a social safety net. For example, separation of central and local taxation and their administration was a critical step in moving toward formal fiscal federalism. Revenue transfers between central and provincial governments were to be based on a fixed formula rather than through bargaining. This represents the beginning of a rule-based system.

Second, the decision addressed the issue of enterprise reform in a more fundamental way regarding property rights and ownership. It was decided to transform SOEs to *modern corporations* with "clarified property rights, clearly defined responsibility and authority, separated from the government, and scientific internal management." In addition, for the first time, it opened the door to privatization of SOEs: "As for the management of small SOEs, some may be contracted out or leased; others may be shifted to the partnership system in the form of stock sharing, or sold to collectives and individuals." But no further breakthrough on ownership issues came until later. In this decision, state ownership was still a *principal component of the economy*, while private ownership was a *supplementary component of the economy*.

In September 1997, the Fifteenth Party Congress made two additional major breakthroughs. The first was on ownership: state ownership was downgraded to a *pillar of the economy*, whereas private ownership was elevated to an *important component of the economy*. In Chinese politics, these subtle changes of rhetoric imply a significant change in ideology. The document recognized that "varieties of ownership should develop together." Since private ownership had been discriminated against for decades, the only new message here was that private ownership had gained legitimacy.

The rhetoric of public ownership remained, but its meaning was redefined, because it may take many *different realization forms* such as joint stock companies with investment by several owners rather than a single one.

The second major breakthrough was somewhat overshadowed by the aforementioned ownership issue but is more important. That is its explicit emphasis on the rule of law. As always in China, the content of the rule of law will evolve over time. The rule of law is not the same as democracy. For example, the two most free-market economies, Hong Kong and Singapore, have rule of law but are not democracies by Western standards. The Chinese leadership seemed to decide to give priority to the rule of law over democracy. This is not hard to understand since the former is clearly crucial for a modern market economy but does not directly or immediately threaten the governing power of the CPC as the latter might.

In March 1999, both private ownership and the rule of law were formally incorporated into the Chinese Constitution.[1] An amendment to Article 11 placed private businesses on an equal footing with the public sector by changing the original "the private economy is a supplement to public ownership" clause to "the non-public sector, including individual and private businesses, is an important component of the socialist market economy." Article 5 was also amended to include the principle of "governing the country according to law and establishing a socialist, rule of law country." These amendments were major steps for the transition toward a full market system based on the rule of law.

The failure of the CEECs' economic reforms before 1990 led to persuasive arguments on the need for democratic reform to precede economic transition (Kornai 1992). Communist parties there were unwilling to change their ideology, and the logical consequence was their collapse. In China the CPC itself made the ideological shift and China became the first former socialist country voluntarily to embrace a market economy and private ownership. What follows is an attempt from political, economic, and intellectual perspectives to answer the question what set the Chinese leaders' mind on these changes.

2.3.2   The political will

The primary objective of the CPC must be to maintain its power, and the political will of the leadership toward economic reform is shaped by both domestic political events and international geopolitics. The central proposition seems that economic reform is good for economic development, which in turn is good for maintaining the CPC's power. In this regard, the important legacy of the Cultural Revolution must be highlighted. It taught the Chinese leadership an important lesson: economic development is the key to maintaining its power. During the Cultural Revolution between 1966 and 1976, the central focus of the CPC was *political movement*, which resulted in disastrous consequences to the national economy and the people's standards of living. Economic disaster fueled mass resentment against the party, although such resentment was officially targeted toward the *Gang of Four*. This experience had an enormous impact on the mind-set of some of the top leaders and convinced them that without economic development the party could not survive; in other words, a necessary condition for maintaining the party's power and regaining popular support was economic development. Thus, to a large extent, the displacement of dogmatic ideology in favor of pragmatism was a result of the backlash of the Cultural Revolution. The argument for economic development became even more compelling after the 1989 Tian'anmen Square Incident, because it was the only source from which the government could gain its legitimacy. In Deng Xiaoping's own words, "(economic) development is the hard rule."

In the light of the lessons learned from the Cultural Revolution, reverting to Soviet-type central planning was out of the question. In fact such a system has not prevailed in China since 1958. The only debate centered on the scope of the market relative to central planning and the extent of any opening up. Information arriving from China's neighbors provided strong evidence in favor of increasing the role of market and opening up. Most Chinese were stunned by the impressive economic development of Japan and the *Four Little Tigers* of Hong Kong, Taiwan, Singapore, and South Korea. Referring to the success of Hong Kong, Deng Xiaoping reportedly said that although he did not have a good knowledge about economics, he could tell a good economy when he saw it. All these spurred the party leaders to accelerate reforms. As the so-called "emancipation of mind" in 1977 and 1978 preceded the start of economic reform in 1979, so the mentality of the CPC changed before the November 1993 decision.

The political will of the CPC was also influenced by China's geopolitics. By the early 1990s, the neighboring countries' *East Asian Miracle* and their increased overseas investment put her under increased pressure, and more importantly the collapse of the Soviet Union at the end of 1991 changed her geopolitics forever. Both the CEECs and FSU countries began their radical transition toward market systems. The CPC's leaders feared that their power would be undermined if those former socialist countries were democratized and overtook China in economic development.

2.3.3   The economic motivation

The political will of the leadership was also faced with economic reality. The dramatic change in the economic landscape in China from the late 1970s to the early 1990s began to add new pressures for more radical reforms as follows.

First, the state sector had become increasingly problematic. Although the SOEs underwent a sequence of reforms along the lines of *expanding enterprise autonomy and increasing profit incentives* for more than ten years, their performance remained disappointing despite disproportional allocation of resources in their favor. For example, their ratio of total profits and taxes to capital declined from 24.2 percent in 1978 to below 10 percent in 1993. Their losses increased dramatically, and the state banks' accumulated non-performing loans accounted for about or over 20 percent of the total outstanding loans. Moreover, the rise of the non-state sector brought increasing competitive pressure, so maintaining the SOEs became very costly. The old *expanding enterprise autonomy and increasing profit incentives* were no longer good enough. More radical reforms were required to address key issues of property rights, ownership, and corporate governance.

Second, even the TVEs needed reforms including privatization. They played an important role in the first stage of reform, but many problems arose through the lack of clear property rights and good governance. Their weaknesses became increasingly noticeable, for example, in Southern Jiangsu. As TVEs grew larger, their management became bureaucratic, resembling that of SOEs but with the disadvantage that they had to face market competition. They began to lose good managers to foreign and joint venture firms as the latter offered higher salaries and shares. The rapid entry of domestic private enterprises and foreign firms changed the product market from a seller's market to a buyer's market, eroding the profit margins that the TVEs had enjoyed as early starters in the 1980s.

Third, the old-style administrative control methods of central planning could no longer maintain macroeconomic stability in an increasingly decentralized economy. Inflation began to run away in late 1992 and early 1993, which put pressure on the exchange rate. Both the state and non-state sectors overheated the economy, but the government had little control over inflation in part because of the excessive financial decentralization of the 1980s. A more comprehensive and indirect or market-oriented approach to macroeconomic management was imperative (Lou 1997). Reforms of the taxation and fiscal system, monetary and financial system, and a flexible exchange rate policy were urgently needed in order to manage the decentralized and market-oriented economy. This was one of the immediate reasons, although by no means the only one, for the November 1993 decision.

Fourth, the combination of planned and market economy gave rise to rampant corruption and rent-seeking activities. Government officials at all levels used their power to divert income and strip assets from enterprises for personal gain. They also used their power to collect bribes through the granting of licenses and land-use rights, approving of Initial Public Offerings (IPOs), exempting taxes and many other means. The problem here is the lack of any market-supporting institutions, based on the rule of law, to constrain the government or bureaucrats. As a result, corruption and rent-seeking created a major constriction in China's sustained economic growth.

2.3.4   The intellectual inputs

Economists' ideas also contributed important intellectual inputs to the November 1993 decision. Unlike most CEECs and the FSU countries, China's reform has never relied on foreign advisers, but the influence of Chinese domestic economists and some foreign economists was considerable. Throughout the 1980s, academic exchange with the West and East European countries as well as new economic education gave enormous impacts on old, middle-aged and young economists. The so-called Western economics in education and research has gradually replaced Soviet-style economics and taken root in the economics profession. After almost thirty years of economic reform and academic exchange, the body of knowledge obtained on the market economy has no comparison with that in the late 1970s.

These ideas had important intellectual impacts on the 1993 decision, which in fact incorporated many ideas coming out of research done in the early 1990s. Some of the key research results were later collected and published in a collective volume (Wu et al. 1996). Starting in 1990 at the low point of economic reform after the Tian'anmen Square incident, a group of researchers worked on a medium-term integrated design for reform. The research focused on several key areas of reform including detailed studies on new fiscal and monetary systems, monetary policy in transition, currency convertibility, reforms of state commercial banks, financial restructuring of enterprises and banks, a social safety net, incorporation, the changing role of government in the economy, etc. These studies utilized the body of economic knowledge that had developed in the West, including both neoclassical economics and new institutional economics. In addition, they incorporated the lessons learned from the reform experiences of China and Eastern Europe in the 1980s. The fusion of economic theory with the reform experiences made these studies applicable to the actual situation in China and suitable for policy purposes.

Many important ideas can be traced to the period of intellectual debates on reform strategies in the 1980s. One of the key ingredients of the decision—building market-supporting institutions such as taxation and financial systems—has its intellectual roots in the *integrated reform* school (Wu et al. 1988). This group of economists recognized early on the shortcomings of piecemeal reforms and emphasized the importance of coordinated reform in several key areas such as liberalization of prices, building market-oriented taxation and fiscal systems, and monetary and financial reforms. They were in favor of a systematic approach and considered a *mini-bang reform* as key to the establishment of a market system. Although their proposals were initially accepted, they were rejected by the leadership later in the 1980s. However, their intellectual contribution influenced subsequent economic thinking and had specific impacts on the formulation of the 1993 decision.

Dong (1979) recognized before anyone else the importance of ownership reform, and then other Chinese economists introduced the ideas of property rights, ownership, and share-holding companies in the 1980s, and the concept of corporate governance in the early 1990s. The limits of earlier profit contracting practices and the knowledge of the functioning of Western corporations and the stock market contributed to the subsequent decisions on incorporation, diversification of ownership structure, and the development of the securities market.

2.4   Progress in the first five years in the second stage: 1994–98

From January 1994, a series of reforms was launched in accordance with the November 1993 decision in five main areas: (1) foreign exchange and external sector reform, (2) tax and fiscal reform, (3) financial reform, (4) SOE reform, and (5) the establishment of a social safety net. A review of the progress in each area is given here.

2.4.1   Foreign exchange and external sector reform

Before 1994, foreign exchange markets, like many others, had a *dual track*: an official rate and a *swap rate* (i.e., the market rate). The market track, however, had grown dramatically, and by 1993 the plan-allocated foreign exchange's share had fallen to less than 20 percent. On January 1, 1994, with the abolishing of the planned allocation, the two tracks were merged into a single market track.[2] In December 1996, China went one step further and announced the current account convertibility of the yuan but retained capital account control, which is one important reason why China weathered the Asian financial crisis, even with its weak financial system.

This reform succeeded in stabilizing the foreign exchange rate between 1994 and 1998 and even increasing it slightly from 8.7 yuan to 8.3 yuan per US dollar. Exports and FDI increased dramatically, and the country's foreign exchange reserves increased from US$ 21 billion to US$ 145 billion. Even during the crisis years, China continued to attract annually FDI of about US$ 45 billion.

2.4.2   Tax and fiscal reform

Before 1994, the fiscal contracting system had played a positive role in providing the incentives badly needed for local governments, but it was not rule-based. China had no national taxation bureau, because all taxes were collected by local governments. After the 1979 reform, local governments often used their power to reduce or exempt taxes meant to be transferred to the central government.

On January 1, 1994, China achieved major taxation and fiscal reforms that were closer to international practices by distinguishing clearly between national and local taxes, and establishing a national taxation bureau and local tax bureaus, which were each responsible for their own tax collection. This reform made it very difficult for local governments to erode national taxes as in the past (Dong 1997) and established firm rules for the transfer of taxes between the national and local governments. For example, under the new system, value-added tax (VAT) became the major indirect tax shared by the national and local governments at a fixed ratio of 75:25, although local governments were compensated for their revenue losses for three years.

In 1995, the new Budget Law took effect and prohibited the central government from borrowing from the central bank. The central government was prevented from financing its deficit from its current account but not its capital account, although it could finance the deficit by issuing government bonds. The law imposed more stringent restrictions on local governments at all levels. It required them not only as before to have their budgets balanced but strictly controlled their issuing of bonds and restricted their borrowing on the financial market.

To enforce this law, an independent auditing system was introduced. In 1996 the State Auditing Agency audited the Ministry of Finance's implementation of the state budget for the first time since the founding of the PRC (Dong 1997). Tax reform and the Budget Law made local governments' budget constraints much harder.

These fiscal reforms are the most profound and comprehensive institutional transformation made during this period. The decline in government revenue as a share of GDP halted and then reversed. Its share of GDP declined from 11.2 percent in 1994 to 10.7 percent in 1995 but increased to 10.9 percent in 1996, 11.6 percent in 1997, and 12.4 percent in 1998 (*China Statistical Yearbook* 1999). In 1999, its share of GDP passed 13 percent. Nevertheless, many thorny issues remained unresolved, such as the problem of transferring revenue between central and local governments, the troubling sub-provincial tax and fiscal system, and problems related to extra-budgetary and off-budgetary fees and funds. The tax and fiscal reforms made a reasonably good start, but much still remained to be done.

2.4.3   Monetary and financial reform

China's monetary system was in bad shape before 1994. As much as 70 percent of the central bank's loans to state commercial banks were made by its local branches, which were heavily influenced by local governments. In 1993, after Vice Premier Zhu Rongji became its governor, the central bank centralized its operations. Since then, its local branches have been supervised entirely by the headquarters of the central bank. In 1995 the new Central Bank Law was passed to give the central bank the mandate for monetary policy independent of local governments. Thus, the local governments' influence on monetary policy and credit allocation was substantially reduced (Xie 1996), and their overall budget constraints became much tighter fiscally and financially in the 1990s than they had been in the 1980s. In 1998, the central bank replaced its 30 provincial branches with nine cross-province regional branches, like the U.S. Federal Reserve system, located in Shenyang, Tianjin, Jinan, Nanjing, Shanghai, Guangzhou, Wuhan, Chengdu, and Xi'an. This reform minimized the local governments' influence on monetary policies.

The reform of the central Bank was remarkable, but reform of other financial organs was very limited and unsatisfactory. After 1994, attempts were made to commercialize four major state banks, that is, the Industrial and Commercial Bank of China, the Agricultural Bank of China, the Bank of China, and the Construction Bank of China, They account for more than 80 percent of total outstanding loans. After the passing of the Commercial Banking Law in 1995, they began to adopt the international accounting standard for bank assets and risk management and became more conscious of profitability and the quality of loans. They also began to compete with each other when their business dealings overlapped. Their operations came one step closer to conventional commercial banks in 1998, when the central bank abandoned credit allocation ceilings and replaced them with standard reserve requirements, asset-liability management, and interest rate regulations. They did not face any serious competition, however, with foreign banks, because the foreign banks were not allowed to conduct local currency business and could not operate outside special economic zones and some major cities.

In terms of regulation, China basically followed the old American model along the lines of the Glass-Steagall Act; not only is commercial banking separated from investment banking, but commercial banks also cannot hold shares in stock companies. Three different government agencies were brought in to regulate commercial banks, security firms, and insurance companies respectively. In 1998, for the first time, several high-profile banks and investment companies—such as the Hainan Development Bank and the Guangdong International Trust Investment Company (GITIC)—went bankrupt and closed down.

Despite the large amount of capital infused into the four state banks in 1997, the status of the banking and financial system was even more fragile by the end of 1998 than it had been in 1994, mainly because of the delay in reform of the SOEs and governance of state banks. The lack of SOE reform meant that the nonperforming loan problem worsened. The four state banks did not improve their governance and remained 100 percent state owned and administratively subordinate to the central bank.

2.4.4 SOE reform

China did not privatize any SOEs before 1992, and its industrial SOEs were dominated by small and medium-sized enterprises, most of which were under the supervision of county and city governments. Privatization of small SOEs began to emerge on a large scale in 1995 (Cao, Qian, and Weingast 1999).[3] This trend had begun among local governments as experiments in a few provinces such as Shandong, Guangdong, and Sichuan as early as 1992. Later, in 1995, the central government endorsed privatization with the slogan of "grasping the large and releasing the small" (*zhuada fangxiao*). This process slowed down in 1998, partly because of the Asian financial crisis, but picked up again in 1999. Privatization of small SOEs progressed unevenly, some provinces like Zhejiang, Guangdong, and Shandong moving very fast, while others like Northeast China lagged behind.

Many SOEs were either nonviable or overwhelmed with excessive numbers of employees, and their main concern was the reallocation of labor. About ten million workers were laid off by SOEs and urban collectives each year from 1996 to 1998. Ironically, these massive layoffs and the associated unemployment were often painted as serious *problems* of Chinese reform by the mass media, but they should really have been viewed as significant achievements of the second-stage reform. Never before had state employees been laid off or state enterprises closed, but layoff was an essential step in any serious SOE reform. In contrast, the lack of labor-shedding in Russian enterprises even after privatization was clearly a sign of failure rather than achievement. In the late 1990s, total employment in government agencies and enterprises began to shrink after peaking in 1995 and declined to the level of the late 1980s—below 100 million (*China Statistical Yearbook* 1999).

As far as ownership and governance issues are concerned, however, reform in large-size SOEs has had no breakthrough. The failure of several attempts in the past may be revealing. First, in 1997, there was an experiment to try to reform 100 large SOEs by incorporating them through introducing several investors in each. However, this resulted in more than 80 of them remaining solely state owned. Second, many incorporated SOEs, including those already listed on China's two stock exchanges, suffered from the conflict between the so-called three old committees (i.e., the party committee, the employee representative committee, and the workers union) and three new committees (i.e., shareholders, boards of directors, and supervisory committees). In some cases, the conflict between the party secretary and the top manager (such as the chairman of the board) was so severe that it interfered with the enterprise's normal operation. Third, in response, some enterprises opted to place the same person in the positions of both party secretary and chairman of the board. But this led to another problem: "insider control." Fourth, to address this problem, from 1998 on, hundreds of external "special inspectors" (*jicha tepaiyuan*) were sent by the central government to large SOEs to supervise their operation. However, the inspectors were mostly retired high-level bureaucrats who had no knowledge of business operation and accounting. Not surprisingly, they could not play any constructive role in addressing the corporate governance problem. Fifth, after abolishing the special inspectors, the government came up with another solution and set up within the CPC's Central Committee the Large Enterprise Working Committee (*daqiye gongwe*) with direct responsibility for appointing top managers in large SOEs in collaboration with the Ministry of Personnel. After so many years of reform of large SOEs, China went full circle and almost returned to where it began.

2.4.5   Establishment of a social safety net

Establishing a social safety net is regarded as essential for both more radical reform of SOEs and healthy development of private enterprise. In China, it mainly concerns urban residents and consists of four programs; pensions, health care, unemployment insurance, and minimum living standard support. Thus far, China has no unified national program of any kind, and only provincial and municipal governments are responsible for implementing their own local programs.

Financially, the most costly programs are pensions and health care, especially the former. According to the November 1993 decision, the goal of pension reform is to move from an enterprise-based pension system under central planning to the one combining *social responsibility* and *individual accounts*. The former follows a pay-as-you-go principle and the latter is a fully funded program. After several years of effort, the pension scheme already covered at least nominally employees in almost all SOEs and urban collective enterprises as well as those in more than half of private enterprises. However, two serious problems remain. One is the proportion of *social responsibility* and *individual accounts*. Another is the issue of compensation for old and retired employees who cannot contribute sufficiently to their individual accounts. Many old industrial cities have a high proportion of old and retired employees and face more serious challenges in pension reform. These regions are more inclined to go for smaller individual accounts in order to pay for the immediate obligations toward current retirees.

In 1997, the State Council introduced the following framework: a mandatory amount of 11 percent of payroll should go to individual accounts, of which 8 percent is contributed by employees and 3 percent by enterprises; local governments decide the amount of the social responsibility contribution, often around 17 percent of payroll. Under this framework, individuals contribute 8 percent and enterprises contribute a total of 20 percent of payroll. This system poses two problems. First, the total tax rate for pension purposes is too high, around 28 percent of payroll. This dramatically increases labor costs for enterprises. Second, the problem of compensation for old and retired employees remains unresolved. The original proposal to use a proportion of state assets or government bonds for compensation is not implemented yet. As a result, most individual accounts of old employees remain empty, and the programs continue to rely on the pay-as-you-go mechanism. This practice erodes the individual accounts of new employees, because part of their contributions is used for current retirees. This will certainly create problems for the future and defeats the purpose of creating fully funded individual accounts.

2.5   The challenges ahead

Although the state sector produces only one-third of GDP the government allocates two-thirds of the country's capital resources to it through administrative fiat. The market has not begun yet to operate as the primary allocating mechanism for economic resources. The reason lies in the core of the old state-owned economic system. The key feature of the old system is a unification of the three entities—the CPC, the government, and the economy. Some people, particularly the social and political élite, have a tremendous interest in maintaining this old system. If they did not regard the interest of the entire society as primarily important, they would use whatever excuses, including political ones, to hinder the progress of reform and restructuring. Thus, the reforms face enormous resistance.

China's accession to the WTO made the need to push for more rapid domestic reform urgent; otherwise, foreign competition could throw a devastating blow. Joining the WTO might provide the political momentum for further economic reform. The time was right to push for the next wave of reform in the direction put forward in the November 1993 and subsequent decisions.

2.5.1   What is the core issue?

The assessment of the first five years of reform since 1994 is mixed. Reform was on the right track and made several impressive strides but was disappointing in many areas. China still faces many challenges. For example, each of the five areas listed above has an unfinished agenda, and to that list, one may add needed reforms in regulation and competition policy, improvement in social equality, and a crackdown on corruption, etc. What is the core issue?

This writer's view is that it is the establishment of a free and competitive enterprise system. It requires a change in the government-business relationship into one of an arm's-length type. Specifically, China must undertake the three tasks (1) transform existing SOEs, (2) promote new private enterprises, and (3) establish the rule of law. The first two concern the governance of enterprises, whereas the last concerns the governance of the entire economy. They are interrelated. Without transformation the SOEs will continue to divert resources away from private enterprises and suppress their development. The development of private enterprise requires support from the rule of law because both the government and the markets must be constrained by the law and regulations. In the end, solving the core issue means dismantling of what Lenin called *the State Syndicate* or *the Party-State Inc.* and establishing an economy that is basically insulated from politics.

Scholars studying the institutional foundations of economic development monitor the nature of the government-business relationship. Economic historians, such as North (1981) and Rosenberg (1986) attribute the rise of the West in the eighteenth and nineteenth centuries to a fundamental change in that relationship. They cite a sequence of events like the Glorious Revolution in England in 1688 and the commercial codes and company laws developed later as the factors that insulated businesses and commerce from arbitrary intervention by government. Through these institutional evolutions, governments in the West were able to keep at an arm's length distance from economic activities. This provided room for entrepreneurial activities to be largely free from government intrusion. Scholars of contemporary economic systems drew similar lessons in a different context. For example, in his study of socialist economies, Kornai (1992) considered party-state control and the bureaucratic coordination of economic activities as the main cause of the recurrent troubles.

Addressing the core issue provides a key link to many other reform issues. Take government fiscal revenue as an example. Some economists tend to regard the lack of government revenue as the source of many problems including inflation, regional inequality, and the lack of a social safety net. However, a deeper problem behind it is that of SOEs. They are both the government's main source of revenue and its main fiscal burden. Similarly, as regards the problem in the financial sector, the SOEs accumulated massive bad loans, and the state banks which lent these loans were themselves state enterprises. As for the social safety net, the main obstacle concerns the compensation for old and retired employees. This demands that a proportion of state assets be invested in individual accounts, and this again requires enterprise reform. As far as external reform and further opening up of the economy are concerned, if domestic reforms lag behind and the government continues to stand in the way of business, domestic enterprises will lose out in competition with foreign firms, which would lead to a backlash against opening up. Finally, addressing the core issue by the rule of law is beneficial in solving certain social problems like fighting corruption.

2.5.2   Transforming SOEs

SOEs still account for about one-quarter of industrial output, and a much higher proportion in such services as wholesale commerce, transportation, communication, and banking. The state has a virtual monopoly in some sectors such as airlines, telecommunications, and banking. Large-scale SOEs continue to constitute the backbone of the economy, and the state sector continues to place a disproportionately large burden on economic resources. For instance, the SOEs' share of bank lending remained nearly at 60 percent at the end of 1998. The SOEs remained the main revenue source, accounting for more than half of the total but also represent the largest financial burden. Even after two decades of reforms, the financial performance of SOEs continued to deteriorate and to be responsible for the financial sector's problems.

The document on SOE reform adopted by the Fourth Plenum of the Fifteenth Party Central Committee in September 1999 may be said to be one of the most significant breakthroughs after the Fourteenth Party Congress. It specified three new policies.

The first and perhaps most important was a *readjustment of the layout of the state economy* which in essence dramatically narrowed the scope of the state. Specifically, the government decided to concentrate its control over enterprises in the following four main areas but to gradually withdraw from others: (1) industries related to national security, (2) natural monopoly industries, (3) industries providing important public goods and services, and (4) pillar industries and backbone enterprises in high and new technology. SOEs were operating in almost all sectors of the economy, ranging from fighter plane production to hotel operation, and from bookselling to toymaking. Thus, the government's commitment to withdraw from most industrial and service sectors was a significant and encouraging step forward. These policies, however, could have been even better. The most controversial area was the fourth, the so-called *pillar industries* and backbone enterprises in high and new technology industries. This provision appears to have been a political compromise. They were vaguely defined and could include many industries such as banking, telecommunications, or the Internet. Unsurprisingly, politicians used this loophole to slow down privatization.

The second new policy concerned the diversification of ownership for the enterprises over which the government still wished to maintain control. A few enterprises were chosen to remain under 100 percent state ownership, but all the others became joint stock companies with multiple owners. The new owners could be either domestic private investors or foreign investors. The government regulatory body, the China Securities Regulatory Commission (CSRC), had already been authorized to formulate the regulations for the sale of state shares. This policy change was quite significant, because when the government had selected 100 large SOEs for reform experiments just a couple of years earlier, as many as 80 of the 100 had still had the state as a single owner in the final analysis.

This diversification reform began in 1999. Sectors with a high concentration of SOEs, such as petroleum, telecommunications, the railways, and electric power, underwent industry-wide restructuring with the following targets: (1) the separation of administrative and corporate functions and establishment of a new framework though which the government would exercise regulatory power; (2) the removal of the sector monopoly of some SOEs to give way to competition; and (3) the fulfillment of public listing of restructured SOEs in domestic and overseas capital markets. Two examples are discussed.

1. *The revamp of the petroleum sector.* The petroleum industry was under the monopoly of state agencies at the time. The Ministry of Petroleum and Natural Gas Industry and the Ministry of Petrochemical Industry were consolidated into three vertically integrated companies: CNPC, Sinopec, and CNOOC. In November 1999, CNPC divested its core business ranging from oil recovery to the sale of processed oil products to its subsidiary PetroChina, which was listed in Hong Kong (H shares) and New York (ADS) in March 2000. With the flotation, state ownership in PetroChina was reduced to 90 percent, with further reductions intended. Apart from the state's share, the rest is owned by foreign investors. Sinopec Group grouped its core assets to form Sinopec Ltd. in February, 2000 and in October it went public in Hong Kong, New York, and London. After the flotation, China Petrochemical Corp. (Sinopec Group), Sinopec's parent company, held a 56.06 percent stake, while state asset management companies and China Development Bank held 22.73 percent and foreign shareholders—including oil giants such as Exxon Mobil, Shell, and BP Amoco—make up the rest.

2. *The revamp of the telecommunications sector.* China's telecommunications sector was completely monopolized and operated by the then Ministry of Post, representing the central government. To introduce competition to the sector, the government set up China Unicom in 1994, based on a merged wireless communications business that was originally affiliated with the then Ministry of Electronics Industry. Nevertheless, even long after that, primary telecommunications resources in China—for example, the telecommunications network infrastructure—remained under the monopoly of China Telecom, a new SOE based on the Directorate General of Telecommunications (DGT) under the Ministry of Post. China Unicom was not allocated even the necessary resources and was severely short of capital, so it could not compete with China Telecom. The government had to reshape the whole telecommunications sector in 1999.

The restructuring had three basic concepts, the first of which was separation of the administrative and corporate functions. The Ministry of Information Technology and Telecom Industries (MII), with its telecommunications functions transferred from the DGT would have all its corporate capacity revoked and become a regulatory body of the industry representing the government. Second, China Telecom would be divided into four parts based on different lines of business operation. Third mobile telecommunications, paging, and the Internet telephone business would be gradually opened to foreign investors in order to form true competition. China Unicom was listed in New York and Hong Kong in June 2000, raising US$ 6.278 billion, the largest IPO deal in non-Japan Asia. After the flotation, the state held an 80 percent stake in the company.

The third new policy concerns the establishment of *corporate governance*. The very term appeared in a CPC document for the first time here. Once a firm has several investors other than the state, the demand for this issue emerges. The structure of corporate governance concerns (1) how control rights are allocated and exercised, (2) how boards of directors and top managers are selected and monitored, and (3) how incentives are designed and enforced. In market economies, major issues of corporate governance concern the legal rules limiting agency problems, protecting shareholders and creditors, and providing room for managerial initiatives.

Corporate governance reform is expected to be the most difficult of the three policies affecting SOEs to implement. The difficulty arises in the political position of the Communist Party. In all past policies, the fundamental principle of *party controlling personnel* remained unchallenged. The party not only appoints cadres to administrative posts but also appoints the managers of enterprises that are wholly owned by the state. The combination of the expanding autonomy for enterprises and the power of the party over personnel leads to a dilemma (Qian 1996): delegating more effective control rights to managers provides them with incentives to increase current production but also enables them to plunder state assets, which results in high agency costs. On the other hand, maintaining party control over the selection and dismissal of managers serves to check managerial asset stripping somewhat but is also the ultimate means of political interference.

As for the party's role in corporate governance, the decision on SOE reform sent out mixed signals. On the one hand, the government intended to follow international common practice in hiring, empowering, and rewarding top managers for its enterprises, including the award of shares. On the other hand, the decision reiterated the fundamental principle of *party controlling personnel*, although it said that the methods of control would be improved. Party control gave the enterprise's party committee extraordinary power in making strategic decisions, and presented a fundamental problem in corporate governance. In the coming years, we would see conflicting forces on corporate governance reform. Withdrawing the party from its role in making managerial appointments would be the first test of the political limits of economic reform. Unless the state, institutional investors, and individual investors were all put on an equal footing, political intervention by the government would continue to plague the performance of firms. The issue of the party's role must be addressed before the goal of *separation of government and enterprise* can be achieved. For this reason, corporate governance for large state-controlled enterprises remains one of the thorniest issues.

Reforming of state banks was another issue. Many studies of the financial system focus on nonperforming loans. The ultimate problems are the SOEs and the state-owned banks. In 1999, the state owned 100 percent of all four state commercial banks through the legal form, *sole state ownership* (*guoyou duzi*). A useful reform might be made through diversification of the banks' ownership to make them truly commercial banks and build up their corporate governance. There were two possibilities, each of which had a precedent in China.

The first would be a partial diversification of state ownership through the issue of bank shares to the public in domestic or overseas stock markets. In 1999, Pudong Development Bank of Shanghai issued 400 million yuan (US$ 48 million) worth of shares to the public and was listed on the Shanghai Stock Exchange. Traditionally, households in developing countries favor bank stocks and regard them as *blue chip*, so an issue of bank shares might help to rejuvenate the Chinese stock market. Therefore, the experience of Pudong Development Bank provided one possible model for the four major state commercial banks. Diversification of ownership to include the public would be one way to force a bank to establish better corporate governance.

The second model was the example of the Bank of Communications. Established in 1987, it is the fifth-largest bank in China and arguably the best-run bank, being the most profitable and having the lowest proportion of nonperforming loans in its assets. It was a joint-stock bank but in 1999 was not listed on the stock market when its shareholders were other SOEs and organizations. Although all the shares of the bank were ultimately owned by the state, these investors had strong financial interests in the sound operation of the bank. Corporate governance of this bank was quite different from that of the four major state banks because it has no direct administrative link to a particular government agency, while others did. Diversification of ownership to include multiple institutional investors is another way to improve corporate governance because one state administrative organ would no longer possess monopoly control.

Either way, the state would continue to hold majority shares of the four major banks. Their performance would improve further with better corporate governance and more competition, especially with foreign banks. In many countries, privatization of banks often came later than that of industrial firms. In Taiwan most banks are state owned. In Germany more than a half of all banks are still publicly owned in terms of assets mostly by local governments. They appear to perform not too badly as compared to private banks, perhaps because banks must be regulated by the government anyway. Entrepreneurial scope for operating a bank rather than an ordinary firm may be smaller, and regulations are well enforced.

The government launched two reform programs to clean up the accumulation of nonperforming loans in state banks. The first was the creation of four Asset Management Companies (AMCs): Xinda, Dongfang, Changcheng, and Hua-rong, to take over the nonperforming loans of the Construction Bank of China, the Bank of China, the Agricultural Bank of China and the Industrial and Commercial Bank of China, respectively. The second and related program was the *debt-equity swap* to reduce the debt burden of selected SOEs. Because Chinese banking law did not allow commercial banks to hold equity, the newly established AMCs were responsible for implementing the debt-equity swaps.

While both AMCs and debt-equity swaps can be useful, they are not substitutes for banking reform as described above. Moreover, transferring bad debts from state banks to AMCs and debt-equity swaps are merely accounting exercises, because the state still owns the bad assets of SOEs through its ownership of AMCs. These exercises would not address banking reform, that is, improving the governance of state banks. Worse, large-scale transfers of bad debts and debt-equity swaps would introduce the moral hazard problem to state banks and state enterprises. It means that if done unconditionally, the state would actually be handing out cash, like an emergency blood transfusion, to save troubled banks and enterprises.

2.5.3 Promoting private enterprises

The second task for establishing arm's-length government-business relationship is to promote private enterprises, especially small and medium size enterprises (SMEs). By 1998, they accounted for 37 percent of total industrial output, as Table 2.1 shows.

As regards retail sales of consumer goods private enterprises accounted for more than 50 percent (Table 2.2) but had a much smaller share in other services. For example, in telecommunication and banking, they virtually did not exist.

At the beginning of transition in the CEECs, economists paid great attention to the mass privatization of large-scale SOEs and believed that this would soon lead to superior performance. Voicing a minority opinion, Kornai (1990) argued, however, that transition economies would be better off by promoting *de novo* private enterprises to be created by entrepreneurs. These entrepreneurial firms always start small, and since each entrepreneur has a substantial personal stake in the firm, he would be better positioned to avoid many pitfalls at the initial stage of transition in governance that beset large firms.

Table 2.1 Composition of ownership in industrial output (%)

	1978	1980	1985	1990	1995	1998
State-owned or controlled	77.6	76.0	64.9	54.6	32.6	27.0
Collectives	22.4	23.5	32.1	35.6	35.6	36.3
Private	0.0	0.5	3.1	9.7	31.8	36.8

Note: State-owned means 100 percent state ownership, and state-controlled means that the state has a 51 percent or more share in joint-venture or joint-stock companies. Collectives refer to urban collective enterprises and rural TVEs. Private enterprise refers to the rest, including foreign firms.

Source: *China Statistical Yearbook*, various years.

Table 2.2   Composition of ownership in retail sales of consumer goods (%)

	1978	1980	1985	1990	1995	1998
State-owned or controlled	54.6	51.4	40.4	39.6	39.8	20.7
Collectives	43.3	44.6	37.2	31.7	19.3	16.6
Private	2.1	4.0	22.4	28.7	40.9	62.7

Note: State-owned means 100 percent state ownership, and state-controlled means that the state has a 51 percent or more share in joint-venture or joint-stock companies. Collectives refer to urban collective enterprises and rural TVEs. Private enterprise refers to the rest, including foreign firms.

Source: China Statistical Yearbook, various years.

Evidence from the CEECs demonstrated that growth indeed came from such *de novo* private SMEs. The striking case comes from Poland, which had not implemented any mass privatization of large-scale SOEs because of workers' opposition. Despite or because of this, Poland is one of the most successful transition economies mostly through the achievements of newly created private enterprises. Chinese economists spent a great deal of time and energy debating the issue of how to reform or privatize large-scale SOEs and after all found that the growth impetus mainly came from SMEs.

Even in market economies, both developed and developing, newly created SMEs have played important roles in economic growth. The boom of the American economy in the 1990s benefited greatly from the deregulation and structural changes of the 1980s. More and more small enterprises entered previously monopolized industries, and new high-tech companies mushroomed. In Silicon Valley new start-up firms emerged at a record rate, becoming the pillars of the Internet revolution. In Taiwan, the phenomenal growth of its high-tech industries was driven largely by entrepreneurial SMEs. In recent years the electronic industry overtook that of South Korea, which relied heavily on a few conglomerates (*chaebol*), and became the third-largest producer in the world after America and Japan.

Private enterprise in China can take three forms. First, it could take the form of *de novo* private enterprise. The Chinese people do not lack entrepreneurship, rather, they are hampered by legal restrictions on entrepreneurial activities. In 1999, the People's Congress passed the Law on Individually-owned Enterprises, which provided legal protection for entrepreneurial firms for the first time. The second form may emerge from the privatization of small and medium-size SOEs. The 1995 government policy of *releasing the small* was further relaxed to *releasing the small and the medium* by the decision of September 1999 on SOE reforms (*China Daily*, Sept. 27, 1999), with a potentially significant impact on the development of private enterprises, because in China, unlike CEECs, the distribution of SOEs by size was skewed toward small ones. In 1993, small and medium-size SOEs employed about

67 percent of state workers and produced about 43 percent of state industrial output. With no privatization of large SOEs, therefore, just releasing the small and medium-size SOEs would easily reduce the share of the state in industry by almost half. The third, form is privatized collective enterprises. By 1998, collective enterprises accounted for about 36 percent of total industrial output and most were TVEs. Their competitive advantage gradually declined. From 1995, more TVEs were transformed into *stock cooperatives* or privatized outright.

In the last two years before the turn of the century, a relevant institution and policies were established in different agencies under State Council. In July 1998, for example, the State Economic and Trade Commission (SETC) set up a new division dealing with SMEs with various types of ownership in order to regulate corporate reform, support their initiatives with newly formulated policies as appropriate, and promote the buildup of a focused service system. Following that, the PRC Law for the Promotion of Medium-Size and Small Enterprises underwent its investigatory and drafting procedures. In it financial and fiscal policies and social service systems in favor of such enterprises were improved. The development of private SMEs is likely to be the growth engine and the brightest spot of the Chinese economy for many years to come (Figures 2.1 and 2.2).

Optimism is supported by the evidence from Zhejiang province that experienced rapid development in private enterprises, and this may be a future development trend for the rest of the country. Zhejiang province, just immediately south of Shanghai, is the mid-point of China's coast line. It has a population of 44 million, the same size as that of South Korea. For some time before 1978, Zhejiang was a median performer among 29 provinces in terms of economic development. Two decades later by 1998, however, Zhejiang had jumped to the fourth position behind Beijing, Shanghai, and Tianjin in terms of GDP per capita. In 1998 and 1999, while the national economy slowed down, Zhejiang kept its momentum and became the star province.

Zhejiang's outstanding performance can be attributed to the rapid development of its private enterprises. In the 1990s, they grew at an amazing speed. By 1998, the relative shares of industrial output of state, collective, domestic private and other types of enterprises (including foreign and joint venture) were 11, 32, 45, and 12 percent, respectively. In 1999, the state sector's share was 7.9 percent, and of companies with foreign investment, it was 11 percent. This means that the proportion of private industrial business was above 80 percent.

More interestingly, private enterprises in Zhejiang began to take over ailing state enterprises. For example, in 1999, Renmin Electronic Equipment Group, a private enterprise from Wenzhou, bought 230 mu (15 hectares) of land in the Pudong area of Shanghai for its electronic equipment manufacturing facility. At the same time, it acquired 34 SOEs in Shanghai. Most of these

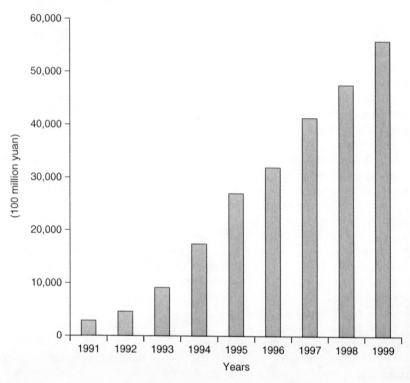

Figure 2.1 Gross industrial output value by private enterprises
Source: *China Statistical Yearbook*, various years.

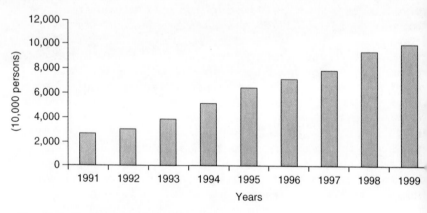

Figure 2.2 Number of staff and workers in private sector
Source: *China Statistical Yearbook*, various years.

SOEs were making losses but endowed with excellent locations and some technological and human capital advantages. The private enterprise had a complex with six subsidiaries and more than 300 sales companies all over China, with total sales of 300 million yuan ($ 36 million) in 1998 (*People's Daily*, Sept. 17, 1999).

Several other features of private enterprise development in Zhejiang are worth mentioning. First, private enterprises in rural areas are the main driving force in its industrialization. Between 1992 and 1997, three-fourths of the increase in industrial production came from rural enterprises. In 1997 private enterprises were responsible for two-thirds of rural enterprise output (*Zhejiang Online*, Sept. 1, 1999). Second, as a coastal province, Zhejiang does not boast a particularly impressive record in attracting FDI, which accounts for less than 10 percent of industry. Domestic private enterprises have been the primary force in its impressive development. Third, it mainly relies on domestic markets, not exports for its development. Its development seems to fit neither the strategy of import substitution nor that of export-orientation.

Zhejiang represents China's future. In a historical perspective, it led the country in ownership changes. In 1984, the proportion of non-state industrial output (collective and private) was already more than 50 percent, at a time when the national average was 35 percent. Eight years later, in 1992, the national average of non-state industrial output managed to rise to over 50 percent. In 1998, the proportion of private industry in Zhejiang, surpassed 50 percent while the national average stood at 37 percent. Other provinces sent *study teams* to visit Zhejiang to find out why this province grew faster than them. The lesson is clear: it was a result of faster development of private enterprises. With other provinces learning lessons from Zhejiang's experiences, it was felt that it would be no surprise to see the share of private industrial output at the national level might surpass 50 percent within the following decade.

2.5.4 Establishing the rule of law

Transforming SOEs and developing private firms would require a fundamental change in the rules of the game. Ultimately, changing the government-business relationship into an arm's-length type requires the establishment of the rule of law. Interestingly, the Chinese government has separated legal reform from other *political reforms,* and this allowed it to make considerable progress in a few years. In 1996, the Chinese parliament passed the Lawyers' Law, which is considered by many as a milestone for legal reform. Public hearings, open trials, and even live TV coverage of trials followed, although still in limited scope. The Constitutional Amendment of March 1999, which incorporates the principle of the rule of law is another major development.

The economic advantages of the rule of law over *ad hoc* arrangements are transparency, predictability, and uniformity, which help to reduce idiosyncratic risks, rent-seeking, and corruption. These features will, in turn, reduce transaction costs and increase economic efficiency. Therefore, the rule of law is more than simply putting the government's words into public codes. It concerns the rules of the game in a modern economy fundamentally governing the relationship between the state and markets in a way that is most conducive to economic development.

The rule of law has two economic roles. The first is that the law should be applied to the government; that is, the government is constrained by law vis-à-vis other economic agents in the market. The rule of law binds the government, and thus guarantees a credible commitment to the provision of private incentives, which are the ultimate force for economic development. Thus, the rule of law provides the foundation for limited government and secures private property rights against government intrusion. By reducing government discretion, the rule of law is also a powerful instrument for limiting corruption and rent-seeking.[4] Under the rule of law, individuals have the right to sue the government. Private businessmen and farmers have begun to use these legal means to protect themselves against excessive government fees. For example, *The Wall Street Journal* (1999) reported the case of Peijiawan village in Shaaxi Province, where in 1996 12,000 farmers filed a class-action lawsuit against the local government for levying excess taxes of $75,000. In the fall of 1998, the local court made an initial ruling in favor of the farmers. The local government appealed, and the case was before the Shaaxi Provincial Supreme Court at the time of the newspaper report.

The second economic role of the rule of law is that the government needs to protect private property rights, to enforce contracts, to create a level field for competition, and to regulate the market if necessary. To achieve this goal, the government needs to become a neutral third party, and this involves a fundamental shift from its role of manager or administrator of economic activities under central planning. In early 1998, a major reform to streamline the government bureaucracy took place. The number of ministries in the central government was trimmed from 45 to 29, and the number of civil servants was cut by half, from 8 million to 4 million. Most of the former industrial branch ministries were downgraded to bureau status and placed under the jurisdiction of the State Economic and Trade Commission (SETC). Their previous enterprise management functions were removed and their direct administrative links with state enterprises were severed.

One example is the Ministry of Information Industry. This ministry used to administer China Telecom, the telephone monopoly, directly. After the breakup, the ministry became the regulatory agency for the telecommunication industry, playing the same role as the U.S. Federal Communications Commission (FCC). Another example concerns government regulation of financial institutions and markets. With China's accession to the WTO and its commitment to grant market access to foreign banks and insurance companies, the need for prudential regulation became urgent.

2.5.5 Can the current political institutions accommodate the change?

Thus far the three major areas of the core issue have been addressed. An important question is whether or not these desirable reforms can be implemented within the present Chinese political system. There is no easy answer to this. The reforms may be divided into three categories according to current political feasibility. The *first* includes the reforms that can be or have been implemented by the present political institutions. Such reforms include developing private SMEs, introducing multiple investors in large-scale state-controlled enterprises, and public listing and ownership diversification of major state commercial banks.

The *second* concerns the reforms that are currently being openly debated but for which consensus has not yet been reached. For example, in connection to SOE reform, the issue on reducing the CPC's decision-making role in large state-controlled enterprises is hotly debated. Many are in favor of adopting the practice according to the Company Law in which no special role is given to the party. In fact, as early as 1980, Deng Xiaoping himself pushed the idea that the party committee (*dangwei*) in SOEs should not be involved in the day-to-day decisions of enterprises (Deng 1993). But others continue to insist otherwise.

The *third* includes the reforms that are not openly discussed now, but where promising indirect resolutions could be adopted. An example is judiciary independence, a term that has been avoided by newspapers. Interestingly, *legal reform* in China is separated from *political reform*. Just like the concept of market economy, the rule of law is also written into the Chinese Constitution. However, political reform, which is currently not on the agenda, mainly refers to free elections and freedom of political association. It is not clear how far legal reform can go without political reform. However, the possibility exists that substantial judiciary independence can be adopted through innovative legal reforms.

2.6 Concluding remarks

To assess how far China's reform has progressed, an overview and analysis of the economic reforms since 1994 was provided, then the core challenges that China must face in order to complete its transition and realize its full potential were identified and assessed. A clear trend of development such as private enterprise development in some areas can be observed. In other areas multiple possibilities can be expected to unfold, such as corporate governance of large-scale state-controlled enterprises; yet in other areas we see only a beginning of change such as the rule of law.

Realization of Chinese growth potential depends on whether reform can keep pace with economic development or not. From the analysis above, it can be seen that great difficulties lie ahead but cautious optimism about the future of China's reform is justifiable. After the successful reforms, the non-state sector already forms the bulk of the economy and popular support for further reforms remains strong. These are the domestic factors favorable for further reforms. Another external factor is China's accession to the WTO. The WTO sets the rule of law for global market competition. By joining the WTO, China was integrated into the global economy, with in order to survive globally, no choice but to accelerate the transition to a full-fledged market system incorporating international best practices, thus tilting the domestic political balance more in favor of further and faster reform. Demand within China for speeding up the transformation of SOEs, developing private enterprises, and establishing the rule of law strengthened and continues.

Therefore, the WTO factor provided an important and timely impetus for China's transition to a market economy. History is never short of surprises. Twenty years before, few would have predicted the great success of China's reforms in the next two decades. Past performance is no guarantee of future results, and there are always contingencies that are beyond anyone's predictions. Nevertheless, barring catastrophic events, China's journey toward the other side of the river, that is, a modern market economy, seems likely.

Notes

1. "Top lawmakers yesterday overwhelmingly endorsed China's landmark constitutional amendments which enshrine the 'rule of law' and bolster the status of private businesses" (*China Daily*, March 16, 1999).
2. However, for those organizations that were accustomed to receiving cheap foreign exchange, annual lump-sum subsidies in the domestic currency that were sufficient to enable the purchase of the previous allocation of foreign exchange were offered for a period of three years to compensate for losses.
3. The Chinese do not use the term *privatization* but rely on several other terms, such as *transformation of ownership* (*zhuanzhi*) or *readjustment of ownership structure* (*suoyouzhi jiegou tiaozheng*). Similarly, the Chinese often use *nonpublic ownership* as a substitute term for *private ownership*.
4. Democracy is another way to limit corruption. China has held elections only at the village level.

References

A Statistical Survey of China. Various years. *A Statistical Survey of China*, various issues. [In Chinese.] Beijing: China Statistical Publishing House.

Cao, Yuanzheng, Yingyi Qian, and Barry R. Weingast. 1999. "From Federalism, Chinese Style to Privatization, Chinese Style." *Economics of Transition* 7(1): 103–131.

China Daily. Various years. Various issues.

China Statistical Yearbook. Various years. *China Statistical Yearbook*, various issues. [In Chinese.] Beijing: China Statistical Publishing House.

Deng, Xiaoping. 1993. "Dang he guojia lindaozhidu de gaige" [Toward the Reform of the Leading System of the Party and the State]. In *Selected Works of Deng Xiaoping,* Volume 2. [In Chinese.] Beijing: The People's Press: 322–323.

Dong, Fureng. 1979. "Guanyu wo guo shehuizhuyi suoyouzhi xingshi wenti" [On the Form of Our Country's Socialist Ownership]. *Jingji yanjiu* [Economic Research Journal] 1.

Dong, Fureng. 1997. *Jingji Fazhan Yanjiu* [Studies on Economic Development]. [In Chinese.] Beijing: Jingjikexue Chubansh [Economic Science Publishing House].

Kornai, János. 1986. "The Hungarian Reform Process: Visions, Hopes, and Reality." *Journal of Economic Literature* 24(4): 1687–1737.

Kornai, János. 1990. *The Road to a Free Economy.* New York: Norton.

Kornai, János. 1992. *The Socialist System: The Political Economy of Communism.* Princeton: Princeton University Press.

Lardy, Nicholas. 1998. *China's Unfinished Economic Revolution.* Washington, DC: Brookings Institution.

Lou, Jiwei (ed.). 1997. "Macroeconomic Reform in China: Laying the Foundation for a Socialist Market Economy," World Bank Discussion Paper No. 374. Translated from *Hongguan Jingji Gaige: 1992–1994 Beijing, Shexiang, Fangan, Sanzuo.* Beijing: Enterprise Management Publishing House, 1995.

Naughton, Barry. 1995. *Growing Out of the Plan: Chinese Economic Reform, 1978–1993.* New York: Cambridge University Press.

North, Douglass C. 1981. *Structure and Change in Economic History.* New York: Norton.

People's Daily. Various years. Various issues.

Perkins, Dwight. 1994. "Completing China's Move to the Market." *Journal of Economic Perspectives* 8(2): 23–46.

Qian, Yingyi. 1996. "Enterprise Reform in China: Agency Problems and Political Control." *Economics of Transition* 4(2): 427–447.

Qian, Yingyi. 2000. "The Institutional Foundations of China's Market Transition." In *Proceedings of the World Bank's Annual Conference on Development Economics 1999,* Boris Pleskovic and Joseph Stiglitz (eds.). New York: World Bank.

Qian, Yingyi, and Cheng-Gang Xu. 1993. "Why China's Economic Reform Differ: The M-form Hierarchy and Entry/Expansion of the Non-state Sector." *Economics of Transition* 1(2): 135–170.

Rosenberg, Nathan, and L. E. Birdzell, Jr. 1986. *How the West Grew Rich: The Economic Transformation of the Industrial World.* New York: Basic Books.

Wall Street Journal. Mar. 25, 1999.

Wu, Jinglian. 1992. *Tongxiang shichang Jingji Zhi Lu* [The Road Toward a Market Economy]. [In Chinese.] Beijing: Publishing House of Beijing Industrial University.

Wu, Jinglian. 1999. *Dangdai Zhongguo Jingji Gaige: Zhanlue Yu Shishi* [The Contemporary Chinese Economic Reform: Strategy and Implementation]. [In Chinese.] Shanghai: Shanghai Far East Publishing House.

Wu, Jinglian and Renwei Zhao. 1987. "The Dual Pricing System in China's Industry." *Journal of Comparative Economics* 11: 309–318.

Wu, Jinglian, Zhou Xiaochuan, Lou Jiwei, and others. 1988. *Zhongguo Jingji Gaige de Zhengti Sheji* [The Integrated Design of China's Economic Reform]. [In Chinese.] Beijing: China Outlook Publishing House.

Wu, Jinglian, Zhou Xiaochuan, Rong Jingben, and others. 1996. *Jianshe Shichang Jingji de Zongti Gouxiang Yu Fangan Sheji* [The Road to a Market Economy: Comprehensive

Framework and Working Proposals]. [In Chinese.] Beijing: Central Compilation and Translation Press.

Xie, Ping. 1996. *Zhongguo Jinrong Tizhi de Xuanze* [The Choice of China's Financial System]. [In Chinese.] Shanghai: Far East Publishing House.

Zhejiang Online. Various years.

3
Two Reforms under Mono-Party Political System: The Hungarian NEM in the 1960s–70s and the Chinese Reform

László Szamuely

3.1 Introduction: political reform vs. economic reform

Does the transition of an economy from socialist to market require a prior or simultaneous change of political regime as happened in the Soviet Union and Eastern Europe or might it grow out of successive economic reforms with no substantial change in political institutions as was the case in China? No a priori answer can be given to this question, but some clues may be found in the recent history of reforms of Soviet-type economies.

The socialist experiment in Russia in 1917 created a well-known centrally planned economy (CPE) based on a combination of four elements: centralized mandatory planning, public ownership of the means of production, a dictatorial mono-party political system, and an inward-looking almost outright autarkic economic policy. During the history of the Stalinist and other socialist economies, four functioning alternative models appeared. Chronologically the first was a mixed economy model, introduced by the new economic policy (NEP) in Russia in 1921. Important as the NEP was for the evolution of economic thinking in socialism in that it reintroduced money, trade, and banking into the socialist economy, it lasted only five to seven years and proved to be a stage of gradual transition *from a* market *to a socialist economy.*

The second model was the system of economic self-management of the former Yugoslavia. It lasted almost four decades, but its experiences seem to have little relevance to our subject. Public and scholarly discourses during the period were concerned with the peculiar problems generated by the new Yugoslavian system. The decentralized institutional system made the national market increasingly fragmented, and brought about rising economic inequalities and sharp rivalry between regional power elites. In the end all these factors led to an explosion of nationalistic enmities and ended up with a breakup of the multiethnic state.

The third model was seen in Hungary, and the fourth in China. They presented two similar alternatives in the sense that the Soviet-type CPE was reformed and functioned without substantial changes in either political regime. In Hungary the reform started in 1968, in China ten years later. Some regarded the Hungarian reform as half-success and half-failure, while others saw it as a total failure. It is true that the new economic mechanism (NEM) in Hungary "failed to produce the breakthrough that the reformers expected" (Brus and Laski 1989, 66). It was some 20 years later that the disappearance of Soviet dominance brought about a general systemic change toward a full-fledged market economy.

In China three decades of economic reforms successfully transformed the poor and backward country into the fastest growing economy in the world, rapidly expanding its share in the international trade and attracting huge inflows of FDI. Nothing seems to block its progress yet. A comparison of the Chinese success with the case of the NEM in Hungary seems to show not only some traits common to both but also factors that hindered progress in Hungary but were absent in China. Thus, we may be able to discern possible caveats that endanger the reform process even in China.

This chapter deals primarily with Hungary because the early history of Hungarian reform should not be forgotten by researchers of transitional economies. Section 3.2 recapitulates its essential features, its achievements, and contradictions similar or parallel to those of the Chinese reform. The last section discusses the possible future for Chinese reform.

3.2   The achievements and contradictions of NEM

Analysts of the NEM argue that the abandonment of the directive planning system did not lead to any form of market economy (Kornai 1986; Kornai and Richet 1986; Brus and Laski 1989). With the operation of NEM over twenty years *a third kind of centrally planned economy* came about in Hungary besides the hitherto known Soviet- and Yugoslav-types. It was an indirectly controlled CPE that functioned primarily through financial regulation. This system resulted not only from deliberate actions but also from compromises adopted as a result of the mistaken neglect of essential factors and unforeseen international and domestic developments.

First, let us start with the factors internationally acknowledged as achievements, innovations, and positive results of the 1968 reform.

First, *a planned economy was realized without detailed prescriptions, that is, plan targets regarding the volume and mix of goods by the central bodies.* The elimination of the difficult and costly mechanism of "breaking down" the plan made it easier to realize the government's targets. This feature was the *differentia specifica* of the Hungarian reform. It is the most widely known characteristic that makes the Hungarian reform different from those in the

other Central and Eastern European countries (CEECs). Only Hungary realized, with all its *pluses* and *minuses*, what had been a theoretical assumption
or a timid proposal of reform-minded economists in socialist countries ever
since the mid-1950s, including in the proclaimed intentions of the militarily
suppressed *Prague Spring* in 1968.

Second, the other achievement of the reform that proved to be lasting was
*the shift from the earlier allocation of material inputs in physical terms to trading
in producers' goods.* This created a market of consumers' and producers' goods
and provided the foundation for the autonomy of enterprises, which was an
important objective of reform in other socialist countries as well. Without
these free and direct contracts among enterprises, the free choice of buyers
and sellers, the free spending of money by the enterprises, and entrepreneurial autonomy, profit-mindedness and initiatives could not have been
more than a pious wish.

Thus, the financial indicators replacing the plan targets given in physical
units helped enterprise managers to develop a way of thinking in terms of
money, costs, and realizable profit, although the size of the last was centrally manipulated. Managers were given limited but real autonomy and
so they became the decisionmakers, not simply the executors of central
instructions. In this way, the indirect system of control and management
proved to be a useful interim phase of learning on the road to a genuine
market economy.

Third, NEM acknowledged and partly realized, despite detours and retreats,
the multisector nature or pluralism of the economy. The equal rights of
state-owned and cooperative enterprises in agriculture, manufacturing, and
commerce as well as individual small ventures, independent merchants,
etc were not only accepted in principle but also realized in practice. In the
beginning progress was made in acknowledging the equal status of state
and cooperative ownership. However this reform concept—accepted by the
Hungarian leadership in 1966—did not remove the superiority of state ownership but made deliberate efforts to apply business organization, management, and enterprise forms to state-owned enterprises (SOEs), as tested in
the cooperatives, that is, non-state sector of agriculture. This step-by-step
approach led later, mostly in the 1980s, to the widening of the sphere of
private entrepreneurship in its open and hidden forms—the so-called second economy. The authorities waivered between harassing, tolerating, and
encouraging private enterprises. This ambivalent and stop-and-go attitude
was ingrained in the concept of the reform as a compromise between the
preservation of central planning and the development of a market-oriented
economy. As it were, the reform policy of the Kádár régime wanted to have
its cake and eat it too.

Fourth, linking external and internal markets, or pulling down the wall
between domestic production and external markets, was another important objective of the 1966 reform. However, this was carried out very incon-
sistently because of the oil-price hikes in the mid-1970s and early 1980s

and the wrong policy being used to handle them. Nevertheless, after 1968 much was attained: first, the introduction of uniform foreign exchange coefficients, then a uniform exchange rate; second, the creation—in principle only in many cases—of choice between domestic and foreign selling and buying; third, granting the right of foreign trade to Hungarian producers, commercial enterprises, and cooperatives; fourth, a gradual assimilation of world market prices into domestic price formation, etc. All of these achievements led Hungarian producers, if very slowly and unsatisfactorily, to become better oriented to foreign markets.

Next, some deficiencies or weaknesses of the 1968 reform can be traced back to its original conception.

First, the intention was to reform only the economic mechanism, as the title of the May 1966 party resolution stated. Notice that the reform in Hungary was enacted on January 1, 1968 but the decision was made in May 1966. Even within the economic sphere it did not revise the objectives of the country's economic policy or development strategies. On the contrary, the party and state leadership never doubted that their economic policy was correct, and that only the instruments and methods used to attain its aims needed improvement. In fact, economic policy aimed only at Council for Mutual Economic Assistance (CMEA) autarky: that is, the satisfaction of the demands of the CMEA/Communist Economic Community (COMECON) market in the first place. This was the strategic objective of the so-called second wave of industrialization that started in the Soviet bloc countries at the end of the 1960s. The real objective was not to manufacture up-to-date items of ever higher technological standards exposed to competition in the world market but only to increase the volume of poor-quality goods of an old pattern or construction. This was promoted by the centrally financed, large-scale development programs in the 1970s. Such economic policies were moreover carried out through the indirect economic control and management system, but it could not have been done in the case of self-regulating markets.

Second, *the Hungarian NEM lacked a capital market.* The reform left decisions on investment and its financing mainly in the hands of central government agencies. The idea requiring the centralization of investment in a socialist economy goes back to Marx and even to pre-Marxian socialists. Its theoretical basis was given in the early 1960s by the argument of Brus (1961), a distinguished Polish (later British) economist, about centralized and decentralized models of the socialist economy. His writings became known in Hungary in the 1960s and provided Hungarian reformers with theoretical ammunition in fighting antimarket dogmas and prejudices. His view was that simple reproduction might be left to enterprises, but extended reproduction had to be within the scope of authority of the state. The Hungarian reform extended the sphere of return payments for investment fund allocations. Since, however, the reform's measures still entrusted related decisions to the national economic plan, "earmarking" credits by objectives and frequently by "addressees" made the requirement of repayment merely a formality in practice. Under such conditions the "investment hunger" of enterprises was not mitigated, and the efficiency of fixed asset management did not differ much from how it had been under conventional directive planning. After all, the 1968 reform hardly affected the institutional system and its decision-making procedures.

Third, in reality, the reform was not intended to touch the system of economic and political institutions, that is, the power structure of society, but was intended to change how power was exercised. Among the questions that arose after the reform, the narrowly interpreted economic institutions received the most serious attention. Hungarian analysts widely discussed the problems of contradictions and obstructions related to SOEs. They were given decisionmaking autonomy, but they remained part—more exactly lower rungs—of the hierarchy of economic control and management. The managers of the SOEs were, for instance, selected and appointed by the competent bodies of the party-state. What was discussed in the relevant literature only later—mainly as a result of changes in the economic institutions in the early 1980s—was that the reform did not affect the division of labor between the party and the state. More exactly, the reform ignored the lack of such a division. It did not abolish the amalgamation of the political and the economic spheres, nor did it put an end to the interchange of economic and political criteria in decisionmaking. The reform also left the power structure of the party-state untouched.

The 1968 reform required only formal changes in party activity. It did not seek to change the all-embracing role of party control. The Hungarian leadership took special care to ensure that the reform process, as well as the functioning of the reformed economic mechanism, remained under the guidance and control of party organs. Thus it is unnecessary to search for the reason why there was no further impulse to transform the indirect economic management and control system established in the first stage of the reform into some variety of market economy, including a regulated one. Market control was incompatible with party control—at least in the manner conceived by the 1966 party resolution.

Fourth, the other built-in "guarantee" of restraining the reform was the *unchanged official ideology*, which preserved, even in the post-reform period, the concept of a socialist society and economy according to Stalin's canon. Quite a few theoretical changes of the Hungarian reform were not adopted in official ideology. For example, there were different models of the socialist economy, the plurality and equality of different state and non-state forms of ownership, the commodity-producing nature of a socialist economy, and the enterprise autonomy vs. control by the state. It was a strange situation, in which two aspects of the party leadership worked at cross-purposes. Economic management recognized the need for reform, while ideology tried with its huge propaganda apparatus to maintain an ideal of socialism, which was far from solving real problems.

This state of affairs did not come about spontaneously as a consequence of some failure in *agit-prop* activities or because of inertia. The Kádár regime, which lasted more than 30 years, was basically characterized by its efforts toward preserving stability. Continuity was interrupted only in exceptional cases. Even then, any such change was interpreted as a minor correction of the well-proven line. Working out the blueprint for reform was always done behind closed doors, and the intentions underlying any radical change were often hidden from the public for a long time. Needless to say, this secrecy had also an outward-looking motivation. The Hungarian leadership took great pains to prevent the risk of any Soviet accusation of *revisionism*. Ideology, agitation, and propaganda were always directed at keeping up continuity; that is, at justifying the correct and unbroken line of the party policy. This accounts for the fact that in neither the 1960s nor the 1970s was it pronounced that the 1968 reform had in fact been a realization of the concepts formulated in 1956–57, that is, before, during, and after the popular uprising of October–November 1956. It was not revealed either that after 1957, those concepts had been branded by the same party leadership as *revisionist*. For the sake of face-saving and not to irritate the Soviet such sensitive issues were always evaded.

3.3   Dissimilarities of the two cases

At first sight it may seem ridiculous to make any comparison between such different countries as China, a big Asian power with of population of 1.2 billion and Hungary, a small Central European country populated by 10 million people. The issue is, however, the old controversy about the possibility of reforming CPE, and we only wish to draw some conclusions from this comparison.

János Kornai (1992) gave a theoretical model to Soviet-type socialism and called it *classical*. He introduced an apt notion, the *genetic program* of the socialist system, borrowing the term from biology. According to him, this *genetic program* consists of two elements: the undivided political power of the Communist Party and the dominant influence of the official ideology—Marxism-Leninism. This program "transmits the main characteristics of the system to every cell within it. This is the seed of the new society from which the whole organism grows" (Kornai 1992, 368). However, even Kornai is cautious—one would say ambivalent—when discussing the possibilities of a radical reform under the conditions of a mono-party system. On the one hand, he draws a rather definite conclusion from his analysis of the attempts at reforming classical socialism (mostly in Eastern Europe): there cannot be "a comprehensive and consistently radical transformation in the other spheres, while the key feature of the old classical structure, the Communist party's power, remains. Although the monopoly of power is shaken and the official ideology begins to break down, they remain strong enough to obstruct any consistent, full change in the system's other elements" (Kornai 1992, 566). On the other hand, he doesn't exclude—implicitly—a situation "when this genetic program is modified" (Kornai 1992, 569). Later he makes this point more explicitly: "a considerable change must take place in the thinking of the Communist party leadership before it can bring itself to make appreciable departure from the classical model, or at least resign itself to such a departure taking place" (570).

History bears witness to at least two cases when Communist leaderships resigned themselves to such "appreciable departures" in Eastern Europe prior to the systemic changes of 1989–90. One was the case of Czechoslovakia in 1968 when a radical sociopolitical change initiated by the Communist Party leadership was suppressed by the Soviet military invasion.

The other was the case of the Hungarian reform, at least I presume. Of course, nobody knows how far the Hungarian leadership would have been ready to go along the road of market-oriented reform, had it been fully sovereign in its decisionmaking. But it wasn't and the Hungarian leadership was fully aware of it. The presence of Soviet troops in the country since World War II was a fair reminder of the fact, and the Czechoslovakian episode reinforced this. Despite its awareness of the situation the Hungarian leadership launched an economic reform aimed at the creation of an alternative economic system. Such a deviation naturally had to be concealed and denied in all publications[1] and offset by "proper behavior" in the fields of international politics and official ideology. This deliberately hypocritical behavior of Hungarian officialdom suggests that under different conditions, that is, in absence of external constraints, the political leadership of Hungary would surely have had a different attitude to the progress of the reform. Only one telling example indicating such a possible outcome is the fact that the Hungarian party leadership intended to join the International Monetary Fund (IMF) in the mid-1960s, when it decided to start an economic reform. However, having learned of Soviets disapproval of such a move—the displeasure was personally conveyed by Soviet Prime Minister Kosygin during a bilateral meeting in the autumn of 1967—the intention was put off, although not dropped. It reappeared on the agenda in the early 1980s when Hungary was threatened by an impending default on her international payments. In 1981 it was János Kádár, the leader of the party, himself who in defiance of the Soviets personally arranged a fait accompli by secretly sending a representative to Washington with the official application for Hungary's admission to the IMF.

Thus, if we accept the Kornaian concept of the anti-reformist *"genetic program"* inherent in every CPE under mono-party regime, we should always keep in mind that the actual realization of the program takes place neither in a vacuum nor on an island. The international economic and political environment or context always plays a significant, often decisive, role both negatively and positively that is, hindering and furthering market-oriented reforms.

In the case of Hungary, a country with a highly trade-dependent economy, the promising process of economic reform was kept back perhaps not so much by any foreign political and/or ideological constraints as by the simple fact of extensive and close cooperation with the Soviet Union and other economies in the Soviet bloc. The proportion of exports or imports amounted roughly to half the Hungarian national product. About two-thirds of Hungarian foreign trade was with the CMEA/COMECON countries (more than one-third with the USSR) and only about one-third was with the rest of the world. There is no need to remind anyone how unique the CMEA market was. Both its pricing and settling of accounts were different from those common to ordinary world trade. It was nominally a multilateral, but in essence bilateral, form of barter, since, with only a few exceptions, neither the goods and services delivered nor the recompenses received could be sold on the regular international markets.

With the benefit of hindsight we can now say that the Hungarian reform could have succeeded only if parallel market-oriented reforms had also started in some other CMEA countries, including the Soviet Union, and the Hungarian government's proposal for a reform in the system of CMEA cooperation made in the late 1960s had been accepted. Neither expectation was offbase in the mid-1960s. However, in 1968, the very year when the NEM came into force, things became worse and worse in the main CMEA countries. In the spring the Communist leadership of Poland clamped down on the protest movement in the universities, and in May the Soviet leadership finally discarded the idea of any advance on the road of the so-called Kosygin reform of 1965. In August troops of the Warsaw Treaty countries, including Hungary, invaded Czechoslovakia. All hopes of the Hungarian reformers evaporated. Although in Hungary the reform was not rolled back, its progress stopped. The overall economic performance of the country, except for some sectors like agriculture, in the following years was not much better than in the other CMEA countries with which it had ties.

In the case of the Chinese reform there were no such external constraints as limited sovereignty or actual self-exclusion from the international trade and capital markets. Even if we accept that the present Chinese sociopolitical system has the same *"genetic program"* as the former Hungarian regime had, the external environment is totally different. China is a rapidly growing great power and her leadership has a high degree of freedom in its choices. Those choices can be favorably influenced and the *"genetic program"* positively modified by some promising factors absent in Hungary as follows.

1. *The pragmatic approach of the Chinese leadership.* The matter at issue is not simply the case of the proverbial black and white cats of Deng Xiaoping. The

important thing is that the reform in China did not start with the working out of a detailed blueprint and/or timetable for the desirable changes, as had happened several times in the history of the Hungarian reforms over more than four decades, when a lot of time and energy was wasted on mostly ideological discussions about the rightness of the initial assumptions and final goals. The Chinese chose instead a step-by-step tactics when looking for a way ahead. This approach was expressed by the apt phrase of Deng Xiaoping as "crossing the river by groping for stones."[2] The relatively ideology-free process of reform in China, as compared to the countries of the former Soviet bloc before the systemic change, could also be explained by the full sovereignty of the Chinese leadership. For them there was no need to prove permanently their fidelity to Marxism-Leninism and loyalty to the Soviet Union. Moreover, due to the collapse of the "socialist world system" headed by the Soviet Union the rivalry between the Soviet/Russian and Chinese Communist Parties is also over. Now neither of them is obliged to demonstrate its ideological purity.

2. *The radicalism of the Chinese reform.* The reform started in the late 1970s as a partial and limited change, namely, with the introduction of a system of contractual relations and farming households responsibility for agricultural production. However, it was a radical step of immense importance. The largest or the most populous sector of the Chinese economy was decollectivized as the communes and collective farms were dissolved.

The initiation of China's policy of external opening by establishing four special economic zones to attract foreign direct investments as early as 1980 was again something that were totally absent in the boldest blueprints of the East European reformers that time.

3. *The dynamics of the Chinese reform.* The outstanding economic performance of China during its reforms period is an indisputable success. It has outdone by this time all the economic achievements of the "new" Central and Eastern Europe. And the fact is that it is a dictatorial communist regime that carries out a successful transition to market economy. I would not like to guess how this controversy (the facts contradicting a stock phrase) can or will be solved. But as the well-known saying goes: nothing succeeds like success. And there are no evident reasons why the Chinese leadership would renounce further success.

Notes

1. For instance, a volume of readings in the history of the Hungarian economic reform edited by the present author was prohibited from publication by highly positioned party officials in 1984. Although all of the motives of the ban are not clear even now, the book was published later (Szamuely 1986) on condition that all depictions of the NEM as a third model of CPE, different from the Soviet one, should be omitted.

2. Quoted by Qian and Wu (1999). The authors used a paraphrase of Deng's metaphor in the title of their paper.

References

Brus, Wlodzimierz. 1961. *Ogólne problemy funkcjonowania gospodarki socjalistycznej*. Warsaw: PWN. [The Market in a Socialist Economy]. 1972. London-Boston: Routledge and Kegan Paul.)

Brus, Wlodzimierz, and Laski, Kazimierz. 1989. *From Marx to the Market: Socialism in Search of an Economic System*. Oxford: Clarendon Press.

Kornai, János. 1986. "The Hungarian Reform Process: Visions, Hopes and Reality." *Journal of Economic Literature* 24: 1687–1737.

Kornai, János. 1992. *The Socialist System: The Political Economy of Communism*. Oxford: Clarendon Press.

Kornai, János, and Richet, Xavier (eds.). 1986. *La voie hongroise: Analyses et expérimentations économiques* [Hungarian Voice: Economic Analysis and Experimentation]. Paris: Colmann-Levy.

Qian, Yingyi, and Wu, Jinglian. 1999. "How Far Across the River." Paper prepared for the Conference on Policy Reform in China at the Center for Research on Economic Development and Policy Reform (CEDPR), Stanford University, Nov. 18–20.

Szamuely, László (ed.). 1986. *A magyar közgazdasági gondolat fejlődése, 1954–1978*. [The Development of Hungarian Economic Thought, 1954–1978]. Budapest: Közgazdasági és Jogi Könyvkiadó.

Part II

Ownership Reform and Privatization

Anyone, capable of getting rich, may get rich first.
Any area, capable of getting rich, may get rich first.
—Den Xiaoping, December, 1978

4
SOE Reform and Privatization in Transition: China in Comparative Perspective

Katsuji Nakagane

4.1 Introduction

Reforming state-owned enterprise (SOEs) is one of the most important issues in any economy in transition. The Chinese economy has been widely recognized as a successful case of *gradualist* transition, but unexceptionally was faced with poor management and low efficiency in many SOEs. Advocates of *shock therapy* have criticized the gradualist approach, maintaining that it makes comprehensive SOE reform ineffective (Sachs and Woo 1994). Nevertheless, even in the former Soviet Union (FSU), particularly the Commonwealth of Independent States (CIS) countries, and the Central and Eastern European countries (CEECs) that took the shock therapy advice following the *Washington consensus,* the same SOE issues have persisted and some remain intractable.

As for the effectiveness of privatization of SOEs, there has been heated debate similar to the arguments like *gradualism vs. shock therapy* on transition strategies. The conventional wisdom is that if transition economies want to transform themselves from planned to market economies, ownership must change from public to private hands as well. Shock therapists strongly support this view, whereas gradualists disagree. In the light of *China's rise and Russia's fall,*[1] however, the current view generally tends to favor the gradualist approach. In particular, China specialists hold that if competitive markets are available, ownership of property rights does not matter for good corporate governance. Rawski (1994) argues that discussions of privatization should consider China's experiences as demonstrating the possibility of "growing out of the plan" as a feasible alternative to creative destruction, and that progress can be made without privatization of the SOEs. The illuminating *success* of China's SOE reform seems to have made a new gradualist view trump the conventional wisdom of shock therapy (Naughton 1995; Stiglitz 1999; Kolodko 2000).

In this chapter the following questions are asked. Is privatization necessary or effective for transformation? How is ownership reform linked with

market development and institutional evolution? What are the characteristics of privatization in China, which has been reluctant until recently to
change property rights of the SOEs? What lessons can we draw from China's
SOE reform and privatization? Next, Section 4.2 is a brief review of the performance of China's SOEs to show the background of their relative shrink-
age in the national economy. Section 4.3 presents the arguments regarding
how to reform the SOEs with a focus on three different views. There is a
theoretical argument that reformed state enterprises are not necessarily better or worse than private enterprises in terms of management and governance. Is this really relevant to the real world? Section 4.4 moves on to
the empirical evidence on the effectiveness of privatization in transition
economies. Section 4.5 examines the privatization drive in China and its
characteristics in comparison with the experiences in the CIS and CEECs.
Finally Section 4.6 draws some lessons from the experiences in the various
economies.

4.2   State-owned enterprises' performance in China

Many indicators demonstrate that SOEs in China are less efficient and profitable than other types of firms and their performance was deteriorating at
least until 1998. Figure 4.1 examines the profit rates of SOEs in comparison
with those of other non-state firms. The share of SOEs in terms of losses
was above 43 percent in 1998, and may probably have been higher than
75 percent in reality if hidden and suppressed losses had been revealed. *The
ratio of their total losses and profits* or the net amount of total losses (aggre-
gated deficits *minus* profits) showed a rising trend in the 1990s, when the
average rate of profits declined to almost zero.

Meanwhile, the SOEs' shares of industrial production and employment
declined (Table 4.1). In contrast, those of nonpublic enterprises, particularly private and foreign ones, grew rapidly by adapting themselves well to
emerging markets. As a result, they became characterized in socialist China
as the backbone of the national economy. Table 4.1 shows how flourishing
private and other nonpublic enterprises were in the 1990s.[2]

The performance of firms, however, varies not only with the type of ownership but also with other factors such as firm size, the capital/labor ratio,
type of industry, age of the firm, and employees' educational attainments.
Unless these other factors are controlled for, one cannot conclude that various types of private firms are necessarily all superior in performance to
SOEs. More simply, would privatization improve SOEs' performance? Liu
(2002) testifies affirmatively, based on regression analyses of firm-level data
for the steel industry in the 1995 census. He concludes: (1) property rights
reform (characterized as an increase in the share of non-state capital in total
fixed assets) is effective in raising productivity in former state enterprises
that adopted a new shareholding system; (2) if all of the capital were divested

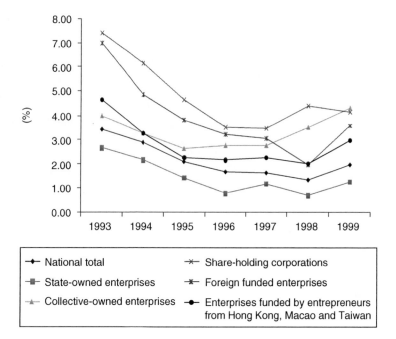

Figure 4.1   Declining profit rate of China's SOEs
Source: *Statistical Yearbook of China* (various years).

Table 4.1   Shares of state and nonpublic sectors (%)

	State sector			Nonpublic sector	
	Gross industrial output	Fixed capital investment	Urban employment	Gross industrial output	Urban employment
1978	77.6	–	78.3	–	0.2
1980	76.0	81.9	76.2	0.5	0.8
1985	64.9	66.1	70.2	3.1	3.9
1990	54.6	66.1	62.3	9.8	5.7
1995	34.0	54.4	59.0	29.4	24.5
2000	23.5	0.0	38.1	62.6	54.9

Note: Nonpublic sector means all sectors other than state and collective ones. Actually, many collectives are "red hatted," or virtually private (see text).

Source: *China Statistical Yearbook*, various editions.

by state owners to private owners, productivity would have increased by approximately 40 percent; (3) for non-state shareholding companies, an increase in corporate assets contributes to productivity growth, while an increase in state-owned capital assets has no effect on productivity.[3]

Under these circumstances, to provide relief to large and medium-size SOEs in debt, the government took several measures such as debt-equity swaps and mergers during the last three years of the 1990s and could declare in early 2001 that more than 70 percent of SOEs had succeeded in generating profits by the end of 2000. It still admits, however, that much remains to be done to improve their management, and its target is to establish the *modern enterprise system* within existing SOEs by 2010. What makes state enterprises and socialist economies so inefficient are often explained as follows.

1. *Government intervention and lack of enterprise autonomy.* It is a well-known fact that SOEs lack management autonomy. Although autonomy may have been formally provided for in several related laws, the state finds it easy to control their management directly or indirectly, whether they are formally independent shareholding corporations or not. In general, politicians and bureaucrats hold special connections with the managers of public enterprises, and can make the managers pursue their political goals (Schleifer and Vishny 1994).

2. *Soft budget constraints, that is, paternalism and protectionism by the supervising governments.* The government intervenes through the budget to ensure that no state enterprise, particularly those that are relatively large in size, would be allowed to fail as a result of SOE mismanagement. Thus no SOE is allowed to go bankrupt, even if it continues to operate at a loss in the long run.

3. *Various "historical legacies" and social burdens borne by these enterprises.* SOEs must provide medical care and retirement benefits for their employees. Pensions for retired employees are a legacy burden for state enterprises. Moreover, excessive employment characterizes SOEs as an alternative form of social security. Their workers and employees cannot be dismissed by the state.[4]

4. *Lack of market discipline.* In particular, SOEs suffer from low-quality managers who are less adaptable to a changing market environment than those in the non-state sector. SOE managers are not entrepreneurs in the true sense, but are basically bureaucrats. They are appointed by the government not according to their business ability, but according to their ranking in the bureaucratic hierarchy. Even managers of shareholding companies (and surprisingly enough, even the top leadership of a collective enterprise) are appointed and/or approved by the supervising administrative apparatus (Table 4.2). This fact illustrates how an SOE fails to ever have basic managerial independence. In fact, Ryutaro Komiya (1989) asserted in the late 1980s that no real enterprise exists in China at all. No doubt, his assertion appears

Table 4.2 Methods of appointing managers in enterprises in China (%)

	State owned	Collectives	Foreign funded	Shareholding
Appointment by government	86.0	58.4	33.2	40.4
Election by employees' meeting but with government approval	7.4	21.4	5.0	10.8
Through auction	2.2	3.1	1.5	3.0
Appointment by managerial board	2.5	14.0	58.3	43.0
Others	1.9	3.1	2.0	2.8

Source: Zhongguo Qiyejia Diaocha Xitong, "Hongguan Gaige yu Qiye Fazhan" [Macroeconomic Reform and Enterprise Development], *Guanli Shijie* [Management World], 1995, No. 1.

to be an overstatement at first sight today; nevertheless, many SOEs are still not enterprises in the sense that they do not enjoy full freedom from a variety of fetters that the state inflicts. Although many Chinese SOEs have been commercialized since the beginning of the 1990s, and can now raise their funds from relatively developed capital markets, most of them are monopolistic or oligopolistic in nature.

The Chinese leadership has not stood by and watched the SOEs market share shrink. Various policies to save and reform them have been launched periodically. For example, a corporation law was enacted, stock markets were opened, and financial aid was provided to settle nonperforming loans. Several types of SOE restructuring programs were launched to provide them with market incentives. The contract system that was widely applied in the late 1980s is one such example. However, the leadership has found that their efforts to renovate SOEs and prevent them from losing their market shares have been ineffective. Instead, their financial difficulties have aggravated, and millions of SOE workers have been laid off. Even under these circumstances, the government has strongly and officially refused to implement a broad range of privatization policies, though de facto *privatization* has proceeded. This is described below.

The term privatization remains taboo within Chinese officialdom, and the government still adheres to the traditional socialist principle of *public ownership as the basis*. China's ideological antagonism against *privatization* is fairly strong. The strategy adopted since 1995 is "retain the large, release the small" (*zhuada fangxiao*). It is a policy that compromises theory with practice, because large and important state enterprises can be retained at the economy's *commanding heights*, while small enterprises are allowed to be privatized.

This is one of the characteristics that set China's SOE reform apart from that of the FSU and CEECs where large-scale privatization was planned and implemented as an indispensable part of their economic reforms. Table 4.3 demonstrates that the more successful a country is in transition, the more widely it is privatized, although the definition of privatization remains open to question. In other words, privatization has been deeply incorporated in the economic transition process of the FSU and CEECs in contrast to China.

The European countries abandoned the socialist ownership principle as well as the ideological antagonism against privatization as a result of political democracy. Moreover, they have followed the *Washington consensus*, a package of market-based reform policies characterized by shock therapy. Privatization was also launched in China, but from below rather than from above, unlike its European counterparts. The private sector's contribution to GDP in Table 4.3 is much lower in China than in former European socialist countries. According to an International Finance Corporation (IFC) estimate, it is at least 13 percent and probably 33 percent in 1999, depending on the definition of the private sector. If agriculture is included, then this ratio rises to 51 percent (IFC 2000).

Another feature of China's SOE reform is that it is less institutional and property rights are more vaguely defined than in the European transitional economies. The vague definition also characterizes also township

Table 4.3 Development of privatization in CEECs and China (% of GDP in private sectors)

Year	1992	1993	1994	1995	1996	1997	1998
Central Europe	39.3	48.0	56.3	61.3	65.1	69.0	69.6
Southeastern Europe	24.8	34.0	39.0	45.1	54.2	59.0	59.9
Baltic states	22.9	34.6	51.8	61.9	67.1	67.2	68.6
CIS	20.3	33.2	46.4	50.6	56.0	65.4	63.7
China	n.a.	n.a.	n.a.	n.a.	n.a.	n.a.	31.0
Year	1999	2000	2001	2002	2003	2004	2005
Central Europe	70.4	73.6	76.4	76.6	76.7	76.7	76.7
Southeastern Europe	62.5	62.5	65.1	65.1	66.0	68.7	68.8
Baltic states	69.7	69.6	69.6	74.7	74.9	74.8	74.9
CIS	63.6	65.3	65.7	66.6	66.7	66.9	63.1
China	33.0	36.0	38.0	40.0	44.0	n.a.	n.a.

Note: Average percentage of private sectors in each region, weighted by GDP in the countries within the region (except for China).

Source: Figures for European transition countries are from the *Transition Report* various years. Those for China are from Garnaut et al. (2005), 10.

and village enterprises (TVEs), which have been highly praised as a success. Some authors (Weitzman and Xu 1994; Tian 2000) see a form of rationality in such an ambiguous property rights system, although it may appear irrational at first sight.[5]

Incessant waves of de facto *privatization* under the circumstances of less institutionalized and vague ownership have eroded the size and the market share of Chinese SOEs. There are two kinds of de facto privatized firms in China. One type is the so-called *red hat firm* (*hongmao qiye*). TVEs and collective enterprises fit this type in particular. They are nominally owned by the state but are in fact private. They can enjoy certain benefits from wearing a red hat such as acquiring needed loans from state banks more easily under the guise of socialist public ownership. According to a report, half of the collective enterprises are actually private in nature today. It has been said that about 80 percent of private firms wore *red hats* in Guangdong, while 70 percent of various collectives in Shanghai wore a *red hat* in 1998 (Wu 2000).

Another kind of de facto privatization occurs in the large SOEs that are managed in an autocratic way. The managers of some SOEs act as if the firm's assets were their own. They are given full authority by local governments and often act as if they are private owners. It is reported that in this way a tremendous amount of public assets is *washed away* or stripped away from SOEs by *invisible hands* in China. This kind of situation has given rise to a dynamic force toward accelerating market development, but with increasing negative effects of widening income disparity in the Chinese economy as a whole. No doubt, this sort of privatization is likely to facilitate rampant corruption by company managers and local bureaucrats in charge of such enterprises. According to official statistics in Canton City, 70 percent of the bribery cases prosecuted during 1992–94 were related to SOEs (He 1998).

4.3   SOE reform strategies: three views

The issue of SOE reform has been heatedly argued not only by the Chinese but also has attracted the attention of many China watchers worldwide. In the academic world of economics in China, there are basically two streams of thought with regard to SOEs and their reform. One is the *market school* typified by Lin and others. This school argues that if the historical burdens of social security as described above are removed, if the budget constraint facing the SOEs is hardened, and, most importantly, if a well-functioning capital market and competitive markets for goods and services are established, and competent managers are provided, then SOEs can operate as efficiently as, and with better governance, more efficiently than private firms (Lin et al. 1998). They insist that empirical evidence supports their argument by appealing to the case of Poland, which is the least developed in privatization, yet has performed the best among the postsocialist transitional economies.

The other school may be labeled as the *property rights school*, which places heavier emphasis on proprietorship, particularly ownership of enterprises. It contends that unless SOEs are privatized, they are unable to improve their management, and efficient corporate management and performance cannot be achieved. According to Zhang (1999), the state ownership system can produce no true capitalist or manager, even if these enterprises are transformed into shareholding companies. The SOEs would continue to encounter various sorts of state intervention, since the state is the single or major shareholder. Rather there must be owners who are the residual claimants to the enterprise's profits. Moreover, even if ordinary state firms were to be privatized, they would still be governed by the state's financial control, because banks are almost all state-owned. He goes on to recommend, therefore, that both financial and nonfinancial state enterprises be privatized at the same time.

These two schools simply reflect two different views on the efficient governance structure of modern firms. Since both private and individual enterprises have grown rapidly in recent years, the property rights school is now gathering momentum within Chinese academic circles. Note that the term *privatization* can be translated in two different ways in Chinese as well as in Japanese: one is *mingyinghua* (management by private persons) and the other is *siyouhua* (ownership by private hands). The latter is still a taboo in Chinese political culture today. Zhang intentionally avoids the term to argue safely and acceptably.

Besides these two schools, there is another view. Steinfeld (1998) points out through his studies on China's steel industry that property rights reform would function only when institutions protecting individual property rights are firmly established in reality. He further notes that as such institutions are either missing or underdeveloped in China and other transitional economies, property rights are hard to reform. He concludes that rather than changing the ownership structure, a policy that constrains state enterprises' activities is even more necessary to ensure their competitive behavior. Although his emphasis is placed on an aspect of institutionalization or institutional development, his recommendation resembles more or less that of the *market school* above. In the same vein and in line with the market school, he asserts that privatization in the FSU and CEECs has turned out to be an utter *failure* followed by a great deal of turmoil and disorder in those economies.

The same sort of view is shared by Jefferson, Rawski, and others to a certain extent, who argue that in China, there arose what they refer to as *endogenous reform*: that is, new institutions were generated endogenously once markets were brought in (Jefferson and Singh 1999). Regarding SOE reform, they stress the importance of markets and argue that what is required in China now is further development of markets rather than a change in property rights; that is, once a market mechanism begins to function, it will naturally create the necessary supporting institutions like property rights. Jefferson (1999) in particular defends Chinese SOEs. Declining profitability stems from increasingly keen competition with non-state enterprises, such as burgeoning foreign and private TVEs. His analysis, controlling for various factors to estimate the pure ownership effect, concludes that China's rural enterprises do not necessarily outpace SOEs in productivity.

Marketization, privatization, and institutionalization—or more precisely institutional development aside from creation of private ownership—involve trade-offs in the process of economic transition. As modern history demonstrates, these three factors are closely interwoven in the long run (Figure 4.2). First and foremost, market development interacts with institutional development. In order for a market to develop, it needs supporting institutions, which in turn facilitate further market development. Second, economic institutions have arisen and expanded as the market economy grows. For instance, private ownership has been quite effective in developing a variety of other institutions, since it requires legal institutions in order to clarify and protect the ownership of private property as well as related rights and duties. Conversely, development of institutions—such as the establishment of legal ownership rights and mechanisms to enforce these rights—helps further to promote private proprietorship.

By the same token, privatization is definitely efficient in promoting the development of markets, since ownership is clearer under private property rights than under any other type of property rights. Development of markets, on the other hand, helps to strengthen the self-interest of private owners in investing and competing in the market economy. In addition, the further markets develop, the more market-related institutions are required. As private property rights are established, contracts can be enforced to reduce transactions costs, in turn facilitating further market development,

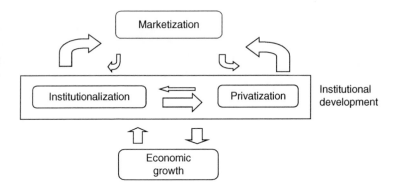

Figure 4.2 Interrelationship among marketization, institutionalization, and privatization

as North (1990) has suggested. Thus, the above three factors are interrelated to such an extent that both institutional development and private ownership are necessary for well-functioning markets. Third, as economic growth usually occurs as a result of market development, growth in turn induces institutional changes. This is what Jefferson's *endogenous reform* hypothesis implies.

The question, then, is the sequencing and relative causality among these three factors, that is, market development, privatization, and institutionalization. They probably could not occur at the same time, interact to the same degree, and proceed at the same pace. If the belief that privatization encourages market development is correct, and if institutionalization strengthens privatization as well as markets, then it seems natural to assume that privatization would be capable of further developing these other institutions. Moreover, if transition costs have to be reduced in the real transition process, such a causal chain would be realized, as marketization requires institutions, which in turn advance privatization, with the result that markets can develop further. The process of China's market development and privatization appears to have been following just such a sequence, as Jefferson and others insist. The remaining question is, then, how to accelerate this interactive process.

SOEs must be reformed either by way of privatization or through marketization even if ownership remains public, but there can be several paths or strategies to follow (Figure 4.3).[6] The first path, A, where public ownership is maintained but the market is developed, is officially deemed to be the most ideal for China. The second path, B, is the one that Jefferson and others believe to be the most appropriate process. It pursues market development in the earlier stages along Path A, but later, and in a gradual way, public property is transformed to private property. The third path, C, is considered by Zhang to be the best for China. It advocates the revision of

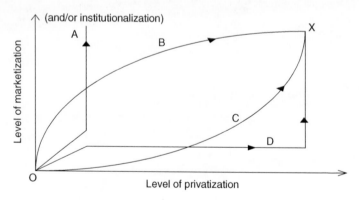

Figure 4.3   Strategies for ideal SOE reform

property rights from the beginning to keep up with market development. Privatization of SOEs is naturally recommended as an important step to follow. The final path, D, is what the so-called shock therapists believe should be applied universally to any transition economy. They insist that privatization and deregulation will be able to create a spontaneous and dynamic market mechanism. Hence, SOEs must be primarily privatized for market development.

Thus, the choice of these paths is related to the sequencing problem, and it depends on the time horizon for transition. Perspectives can differ between the short run and the long run. For example, in the short run, rapid privatization of SOEs may be unnecessary, but in the long run it is indispensable in order to establish appropriate corporate governance. Jefferson and most other *gradualists,* and probably Steinfeld as well, realize the necessity of privatizing most SOEs in the final analysis, shown as point X in Figure 4.3. In this sense, the *gradualist market school* strategy for reforming Chinese SOEs is not so different from that of the *property rights school*; only the paths to the final goal are different.

The *property rights school* maintains, however, that ownership still matters, because the financial difficulties of Chinese SOEs arises partly from the opaque character of state ownership. Certainly privatization alone is not a panacea that will dramatically improve their management. Since, however, privatizing SOEs brings about some important changes such as removing restrictions on the entry and exit of private enterprises, widening the availability of social security benefits like unemployment insurance, and introducing complementary institutions to protect private property, the management efficiency of SOEs could improve. Shirley and Walsh (2000) reviewed the empirical literature on the relative performance of public and private enterprises. They found that 32 of the 52 studies they surveyed concluded that the performances of private and privatized firms were significantly superior to those of public or state-owned firms; only five studies concluded that public enterprises performed better than private ones and the remaining 15 studies showed no significant relationship between ownership and performance.

4.4 Effects of privatization: empirical evidence

For empirical studies on privatization, two types or levels of privatization may be distinguished. The first type is the transfer of the shares of public firms partly or totally to private persons or nonpublic organizations. This means a change in ownership at the firm level. The second type means that the share of public firms in aggregate output declines, whether the public firms change their ownership structure or not. I would call the former *microprivatization* and the latter *macroprivatization*. Usually the two proceed concurrently, but macroprivatization can take place even with lagging microprivatization.

Enterprises in transitional economies can be classified broadly into the following three categories: public or state enterprises, de novo or start-up nonpublic or non-state enterprises, and privatized enterprises that were formerly public enterprises. The first question is which enterprises can deliver the best performance. Next, privatized enterprises are divided into several groups by the method of microprivatization: mass privatization, management and/or employee buyout, or privatization by an outsider whether domestic or foreign. The second question is which group can perform the best in management. The last broad question is whether microprivatization is always accompanied by social costs such as unemployment or lay-offs or not. These questions should be answered empirically rather than theoretically.

The relationship between performance and ownership of enterprises has been long debated in the West. Recent empirical studies are more or less favorable for privatization, as Shirley and Walsh (2000) above observed. Megginson et al. (1994) compared the pre- and postprivatization financial and operating performance of 61 companies in 18 countries and concluded that after privatization firms were able to increase sales, profits, capital investment, and even their workforce.

Such studies and surveys have been compiled with a focus on the CEECs and the CIS countries. Carlin (2000) provides a good summary of their main findings. Frydman and Rapaczynski (1994) find that private ownership, except for worker ownership, dramatically improves corporate performance. They also revealed that privatized firms generated significant employment gains relative to state firms, contrary to the conventional wisdom. Pohl et al. (1997) conducted comprehensive research on 6,300 industrial firms in seven CEECs and reached the conclusions that while privatized firms were able to attain productivity growth as much as three to five times higher than state firms, privatization methods like employee buyout or mass privatization did not effect such differences in productivity. Based on a series of data sets collected by the World Bank, Estrin (1998) made a comparative analysis of enterprise behavior and performance of Polish and Russian firms and obtained some important findings. For example, in Poland in 1993 privatized firms did not appear to be restructuring significantly more than SOEs, although de novo firms were performing much better. As far as output growth, employment growth, and excess employment was concerned, there was no significant difference between privatized firms and SOEs. The most striking feature of the results for both Poland and Russia was the failure of outsider-owned firms to restructure better than SOEs. These findings, however, are derived from data covering the early days in the privatization process. Estrin and Rosevear (1999) used an enterprise-level random survey of 150 firms in Ukraine and tested whether privatization improved firm performance and if specific ownership forms produced different entrepreneurial behaviors. The results refuted the hypothesis that private ownership per se improved performance. However, they found that barter is associated with lower profitability and is less common in privatized firms. Djankov (1999) investigated the relationship between ownership structure and enterprise performance in the CIS, using a nonlinear analysis of detailed survey data collected by the World Bank in 1997 and 1998. He concluded that some significant relationships existed between the two and stressed that this is consistent with theoretical propositions found for some models of corporate governance in mature economies. Grosfeld and Nivet (1997) found that large Polish privatized enterprises demonstrated clearly different behaviors from SOEs, and that the investment ratio of 85 SOEs was 4.8 percent whereas that of 27 privatized firms was 11.2 percent. This implies more active investment of privatized firms and their future growth. (Carlin 2000, 116) showed that their growth performance is not only better but is also much less influenced by sectoral output growth than the that of the SOEs.

Havrylyshyn and McGettigan (1999) reviewed privatization experiences in transitional countries and drew two important lessons. First, any privatization is better than none, regardless of whether a stable, competitive environment has been established or not. Second, start-up private companies are the best performers, followed by newly privatized firms run by outsiders, either local or foreign. The evidence may seem to support the view that the market environment is more important than the method of privatization, but the research thus far does not permit such a conclusion yet.

For the cases in China, there is no systematic empirical study comparable with the European studies to the best of our knowledge.[7] Evidence is sufficient, however, albeit indirect and weak, that privatization improves enterprise efficiency and/or profitability. For example, observe the ratio of the SOEs in an industry against the ratio of indebted enterprises in 1999 (Figure 4.4), and the higher the SOE share is, the higher the percentage of indebted enterprises. In addition, several studies exist on the performance of companies listed on the Shenzhen and Shanghai stock markets. Xu and Wang (1997) conclude that a higher state share generally worsens enterprise performance in the listed companies, and a higher concentration of share ownership has the same effect. Chen and Jiang (2000), however, applying a similar regression analysis to the listed firms in electronics, commerce, and public utilities, find the state share's negative impact on enterprise performance only in the electronics industry, where firms face a highly competitive market. They note that the state share's impact on enterprise performance varies with industry. Its effect on profitability of public utility enterprises, however, may not be positive as they conclude, because its effect on the profitability of the competitive pharmaceutical industry is positive, contrary to their findings. More importantly, the conclusions depend on the market where the firms are listed (Table 4.4). In the Shanghai public utilities market, the state share is definitely positive for the profit/revenue ratio,

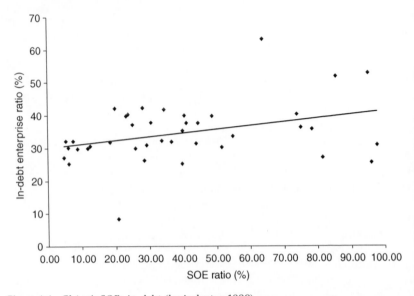

Figure 4.4   China's SOEs in debt (by industry 1999)

Source: Based on the data in the Jingji Pubao (Economic Daily), September 2, 1999.

as Chen and Jiang have found. But this is not the case for the Shenzhen market. This statistical relationship is not robust.

Contrary to expectations, the proportion of unlisted (listed) shares is not negatively (positively) correlated with profitability. This seems to imply that insiders basically control the companies in question. Unlike in Xu and Wang's conclusion, it does not seem to hold that the more concentrated a company's share, the more profitable it is. There is only a weak relation between these two variables. More importantly, such an analysis of listed companies does not strongly support the idea that privatization of SOEs has a definitely positive effect on enterprise performance, partly because the proportion of state ownership is not necessarily a good indicator of privatization. Consider, for example, two companies: in company A, the state has a 90 percent share and in company B, corporate enterprises own a 60 percent share. However, if the firms holding Company B's large shares are all state owned, then there would be no substantial difference between these two companies in terms of ownership. Moreover, shareholding itself does not guarantee good corporate governance in China today, since stockholders' meetings do not appear to be working meaningfully.

In summary, given the so-called selection bias,[8] experiences of privatization in some European transition economies indicate that the results are certainly mixed. Roughly speaking, however, privatization is conducive to an improvement in managerial performance in former SOEs in relatively

Table 4.4 Correlations of profit/revenue ratio with share structure in listed companies by industry

Category (number of samples)	Number of samples with state shares	Profit revenue ratio with state share ratio	Profit revenue ratio with unlisted share ratio	Profit revenue ratio with dominant share ratio
A. Shenzhen				
Manufacturing total (302)	203	0.106	0.036	0.132
Medicines (23)	17	0.478	0.248	0.207
Chemicals (49)	42	−0.044	0.065	−0.074
Machinery in general (93)	54	−0.133	0.098	0.110
Transport machinery (26)	20	−0.079	0.298	0.245
Metals (30)	20	−0.099	0.012	0.029
Textiles (31)	18	0.120	0.032	0.009
Energy (24)	20	0.179	0.049	0.123
Public utilities (14)	10	−0.353	0.180	−0.090
Commerce (26)	22	0.235	−0.097	0.284
B. Shanhai				
Manufacturing total (285)	194	0.095	0.001	0.047
Medicines (21)	14	0.574	0.409	0.389
Chemicals (42)	37	0.123	0.255	0.112
Machinery in general (87)	54	0.085	−0.133	0.088
Transport machinery (27)	18	0.044	0.221	0.090
Metals (24)	17	−0.161	0.141	−0.212
Textiles (32)	11	−0.178	0.033	−0.020
Energy (19)	11	0.630	0.520	0.311
Public utilities (20)	15	0.387	0.485	0.412
Commerce (56)	47	−0.013	−0.079	0.055

Notes: Dominant share ratio means a proportion of the largest marketed shares.

Source: Lin, Yixiang (ed.). *'2000 Shangshi Gonsi Fenxi* [Analysis of Listed Corporations 2000], Zhongguo Caizheng Jingji Chupanshe, 2000.

advanced countries like Poland, Hungary, and the Czech Republic, whereas its effects are not very significant in stagnant economies like Russia and Ukraine. This finding requires a revision of Lin's and Steinfeld's observations that postsocialist privatization is a failure. We need to ask why successful and unsuccessful cases occur. Based on rich and coherent analyses of privatization experiences, Frydman and Rapaczynski (1997) conclude, "unless closure is seriously contemplated, privatization is unlikely to be of much help." Moreover, given that most SOEs are "a set of white elephants in the middle of nowhere—with low quality of capital stock and an organizational structure incapable of functioning in a normal economic environment," privatization may produce nothing by itself.

Studies on CEECs give a good lesson of the effects on employment. Microprivatization may not necessarily be ineffective in securing jobs for employees. Once SOEs are restructured and privatized, they would lay off redundant workers, a proportion of whom may be absorbed by newly established private firms. Privatization and market development could offer more job opportunities. The transformation cost of privatization could be lower than many imagine in the macroeconomic sense. Social costs and benefits of microprivatization include the other aspects like increases in tax revenue, impacts on employment and wages, savings, foreign trade, and FDI, etc. It may be safe to say that privatization is particularly effective for medium and small-sized firms, and even for large-size firms, albeit to a lesser extent.[9] This evidence would be relevant even for China. The effects of different privatization types are still uncertain relative to ownership change, although firms of foreign ownership outperform domestic ones.

Using data from 218 cases of nonfinancial firms in Mexico, La Porta and Lopez-de-Silanes (1997) drew an interesting conclusion: "the additional government revenue as a result of privatization was probably large enough to offset society's cost of job losses. It would have been enough to give N\$ [New Pesos] 659,454 (US\$212,727) to each of the 550 laid-off workers from the average firm—a very large sum, given that the annual pre-privatization income of an average SOE worker is N\$ [New Pesos] 14,880 (US\$4,800)."

Finally, one should keep in mind that privatization in former socialist economies is substantially different from that in ordinary developed or developing countries. Frydman and Rapaczynski (1994) noted that it involved two objectives: depoliticization and the creation of a new institutional structure of corporate governance. Brada (1996) also stated that both objectives were necessary to establish democracy and to destroy the basis of the Communist Party's power monopoly, that is, SOEs. Privatization and transition policies must be evaluated socially and politically rather than just economically.

4.5   Characteristics of privatization in China

Macro privatization in China has been proceeding first hesitantly and then boldly since the early 1980s, as was shown by the rising trend of the private sector's share in Table 4.1. In 1999, when China's new constitution was adopted, the private sector was officially acknowledged as an "indispensable part of the national economy." Formerly, private firms had been held in contempt as "socially ostracized" or "tails of capitalism." Once they were recognized, they began to grow in size and multiply in number.

Micro privatization, nevertheless, has been proceeding until recently at a much slower pace in China than in Europe (Tables 4.1 and 4.2). After 1998, however, various types of property rights reforms were applied to SOEs. According to a survey conducted by the State Statistical Bureau in 1998, 13,726 enterprises had been *restructured*, of which 76 percent had undergone privatization through full or partial buyouts of state capital. The rate of privatization was particularly rapid in Sichuan and Shandong provinces. Yang (2000) reported: in Sichuan province the drive to reform property rights of small and county-level SOEs took place in the early 1990s. As of the end of October 1998, 81.74 percent of small firms at the city and county levels had undergone various types of property rights reforms. As a result, most of them began to perform well, changing their output structure, decreasing their debt/asset ratio, increasing employees' earnings, and raising tax revenues for the state. The case of property rights reform in Zhucheng of Shandong is well known as the *Zhucheng model*. It transformed state property into employees' collective assets and reportedly increased productivity.

Some characteristics of privatization in China may be summarized in comparison with those in the FSU and CEECs. *First*, in China privatization has been largely confined to small and medium-size enterprises, as led by the official policy of *zhuada fangxiao* mentioned above. In Europe overall privatization was carried out involving large-size SOEs. In China, at least in strategically important sectors, property rights are firmly kept in state hands, even though their relative share in output and employment continues to decline (Table 4.1). Commercialization rather than privatization is now on the agenda of large SOE reform. Many large-size state enterprises are becoming stock companies with partial offering of shares on the stock exchange.

Second, numerous nonpublic firms have mushroomed. Some disappeared quickly because of strong competition; nevertheless, they outperformed SOEs in efficiency and profitability. Property rights transformation has encountered more difficulty, since it requires a fundamental institutional change. It has been driven as an integral part of shock therapy from above in Europe rather than from below in China. As a result, there may be no selection bias in China's privatization as was seen in Europe, where relatively good enterprises tended to be sold out to individuals or corporations, either domestic or foreign. Instead in China, poorly managed SOEs were privatized often as a last resort to avoid closing them.

Third, the Communist Party of China (CPC) still holds sole political power with no concurrent depoliticization. Inclusion of party organizations is required even within foreign-funded enterprises. Even though state assets are gradually being transferred from state to private hands, the political structure within enterprises remains the same. In China the party still retains strong power in basic decisions at every corner of social life, so that depoliticization cannot be an aim of reforming SOEs here. De facto depoliticization is, however, going on notwithstanding the leadership's desires and despite their frequent political campaigns.

Fourth, de facto privatization is far ahead of de jure or formal privatization. As discussed above, SOE reform has been carried out without much development of associated institutions. Ambiguity and opacity, let alone of proprietorship, is one of the important features of the entire transition process in China. It has been a source of dynamism that pushed forward market evolution and the creation of new entrepreneurs. My view is that it has become an obstacle now to further transition of the economic system. De facto *privatization* has both positive and negative aspects. Disadvantages seem to outweigh advantages, as exemplified by rampant corruption and raging literal "privatization" of public assets by managers.[10] Private businesses should not have been discriminated against. If they had been encouraged much earlier, they would have given an even stronger impetus to the entire economy as well as to SOE reform.

Finally, implementation measures differ between China and Europe. For example, mass privatization was never carried out in China. It is not universal in Europe either. Hungary, for instance, has never tried it. Nevertheless, it has been widely adopted by many postsocialist countries. Privatization by restitution has never been considered in China, because the political leadership has been negative for ideological reasons. What it has allowed in effect is insider privatization, particularly employee buyouts, because the leadership regards this method as ideologically acceptable.

Russia resembles China, however, in some aspects of the SOE reform environment. These two large transitional countries are both underdeveloped in terms of certain institutions that protect private property rights and enforce contracts. Both have encountered serious asset stripping from firms, whether state owned or privatized. In both countries, regional governments hold special stakes in firms under their jurisdiction, and therefore intervene and draw politicoeconomic benefits from their firms' management. They are also deeply involved in protecting incumbent employees in the firms. Here again, insiders control the firm management in both countries, whether firms are privatized or not. Desai and Goldberg (2000) reported that de facto renationalization of previously privatized property had taken place among large corporations in Russia. This indicates the redirection of privatized enterprises under the poor institutional circumstances.

4.6   Concluding remarks

The overall trend of privatization will probably affect large firms in China. Macroprivatization will accelerate microprivatization. Accordingly, market development widens the area of private proprietorship and paves the way to SOE privatization, as suggested in Figure 4.2. This lesson seems to be consonant with the assertions of the market school, as voiced by Jefferson and Rawski. Their explanation narrowly pinpoints the relatively successful privatization in several CEECs and the Baltic nations, but their view is too simple to take into account the other two factors of privatization and institutional development in the model outlined above (Figure 4.2). It seems safe to draw at least three lessons from the experiences of SOE reform and privatization in the transitional economies.

First, a transitional economy should employ a more balanced approach to SOE reform than did China. Specifically, it should not focus simply on one side of the reform process, that is, market development. It is tempting to conclude that the market can solve any problem, but it requires various supporting institutions. Institutional development along with privatization as a core and long-term strategy should be simultaneously pursued. Chinese SOEs have piled up a huge amount of debt, while the leadership has hesitated to touch on basic property rights reform of them. Meanwhile, de facto privatization has proceeded to an astonishing degree, stripping many SOEs of their assets. The point is that the market cannot create new institutions by itself in the short run. Laws, regulations, rules, and norms to protect private property rights, for example, should basically be provided as a public good by the state. Changing the property structure as well as clarifying property rights is certainly a tough task, particularly for socialist economies where many people have vested interests in public property. We would argue, however, that

1. clearly defined property rights are better than vaguely defined rights; and
2. formal privatization is more effective than informal, spontaneous, and de facto privatization in promoting the transition process.

The recent trend in privatization, the difficulties encountered by both state and rural enterprises, and the various experiments of enterprise reform (*gaizhi*) in China seem to support our views, directly or indirectly. China's success in the macroeconomy does not necessarily mean its success in the micro aspects.

Second, a transition economy should not adhere to certain fixed ideological standpoints, for example, on the superiority of public ownership over private proprietorship. If China had been freed from its ideological constraints, it could have sped up its SOE reform process as well as privatization. Needless to say, this lesson cannot be applied to postsocialist economies that had already abandoned their old ideological framework when they established the current democratic regime. Other things being constant, private firms are superior on average to public firms in managerial efficiency. Therefore, as long as a transition economy retains public ownership, "opportunity loss" occurs to such an extent that there is a difference in productivity between these two types of firms. SOEs, whether in China or other countries, usually suffer from large deficits, but even if they were run more efficiently, their profits would have been lower than if they had been managed and owned by private persons. Thus they necessarily produce a certain amount of potential loss in terms of "foregone" profits.

Last, but not least, there is no single *correct* approach to SOE reform and privatization. The goal may be the same, such as point X in Figure 4.3, but the process can differ, and the time needed to reach the point vary, with the initial conditions, the political system, and the strategies adopted. As the Polish way of transition cannot be applicable to Russia, so the Chinese way of SOE reform cannot be relevant to Poland. Each has its own peculiarities that reformers must address.

Notes

1. See Nolan (1995). Of course, we can replace Russia with CEECs, FSU, Mongolia, etc.
2. Table 4.1 also shows that SOEs' industrial output has declined in relative terms, while their investment share has not changed very much. This implies that their investment efficiency has been deteriorating.
3. In my view, one of the shortcomings of Liu's analysis is that the share of private stock does not necessarily accurately measure the "privateness" of enterprises.
4. A Chinese economist, in describing the secure status of SOE workers, notes that dismissing them from their jobs is much harder than putting them in jail.
5. In my view, their arguments are not convincing. The dynamism of TVEs can be viewed as stemming from their "de facto privatized" nature.
6. This figure is a revision of Imai (2000). He insists that large enterprises cannot help but let able managers govern rather than be privatized. The challenge is how to locate and encourage the emergence of such persons. I do not believe that some success stories of SOE management (such as of Changhong, the biggest TV maker in China today and led by a strong manager), can be a typical guide for reforming state enterprises as a whole.
7. Liu's study cited above may be an exception. But his study is confined to the steel industry, and whether or not the non-state capital ratio is appropriate as an index of privatization is open to question.
8. It is often the case that well-performing firms are privatized first, leaving loss-making ones still under state ownership.
9. As far as I know, case studies on privatization effects on large enterprises are neither many nor extensive as compared to those on medium and small ones, probably because the cases are few (e.g., China) or because extensive surveys on large-scale privatized enterprises are relatively difficult.
10. De facto privatization is not the same as spontaneous privatization, which was quite popular in some postsocialist countries. The latter type of privatization took place in the process of, or in association with, a formal privatization drive.

References

Brada, Josef. 1996. "Privatization Is Transition or Is It?" *Journal of Economic Perspectives* 10(2): 67–86.

Carlin, Wendy. 2000. "Empirical Analysis of Corporate Governance in Transition." In *Privatization, Corporate Governance and the Emergence of Markets*, Eckehard Rosenbaum Frank Bönker and Hans-Jürgen Wagener (eds.). Basingstoke: MacMillan Press.

Chen, Xiao, and Dong Jiang. 2000. "Guquan Duoyuanhua, Gongsi Yeji yu Hangye Jingzhengxing" [Ownership Pluralization, Firm Performance and Industry Competition]. *Jingji Yanjiu* 388: 28–35.

Desai, Raj, and Itzhak Goldberg. 2000. "The Vicious Circles of Control: Regional Governments and Insiders in Privatized Russian Enterprises." *World Bank Working Paper*, No. 2287 (Feb.).

Djankov, Simeon. 1999. "Ownership Structure and Enterprise Restructuring in Six Newly Independent States." *World Bank Working Paper*, No. 2047 (Feb.).

Estrin, Saul. 1998. "Privatization and Restructuring in Central and Eastern Europe." In *Emerging from Communism: Lessons from Russia, China, and Eastern Europe*, Peter Boone, Stanislaw Gomulka, and Richard Layard (eds.). Cambridge, MA: MIT Press.

Estrin, Saul, and Adam Rosevear. 1999. "Enterprise Performance and Ownership: The Case of Ukraine." *European Economic Review* 43: 1125–1136.

Frydman, Roman, and Andrzey Rapaczynski. 1994. *Privatization in Eastern Europe: Is the State Withering Away?* NewYork: Central European University Press.

Frydman, Roman, and Andrzej Rapaczynski. 1997. "Corporate Governance and the Political Effects of Privatisation." In *Lessons from the Economic Transition: Central and Eastern Europe in the 1990s*, Salvatore Zecchini (ed.). Boston, MA: Kluwer Academic Publishers.

Garnaut, Ross et al. 2005. *China's Ownership Transformation—Process, Outcomes, Prospects*, Washington, DC: IFC World Bank.

Grosfeld, Irena, and Jean-François Nivet. 1997. "Wage and Investment Behavior in Transition: Evidence from a Polish Panel Data Set." *Delta Working Paper*, No. 97-17 (Oct.).

Havrylyshyn, Oleh, and Donald McGettigan. 1999. "Privatization in Transition Countries: Lessons of the First Decade." *IMF Economic Issues* No. 18 http://www.imf.org/external/pubs/ft/issues/issues18/index.htm (Aug.).

He, Qinglian. 1998. *Xiandaihua-de Xianjing* [Pitholes of Modernization]. Jinri Zhongguo Chubanshe, 93.

IFC. 2000. *China's Emerging Private Enterprises—Prospects for the New Century.* Washington, DC: International Finance Corporation.

Imai, Ken-ichi. 2000. "Ko-pore-togabanansu-no Chugokuteki Kadai" [A Task of Corporate Governance for China]. In *Gendai Chugoku-no Kozo Hendo dai2kan Keizai—Kozo Hendo to Shijoka* [Structural Transformation of Contemporary China, Vol. 2, Economy—Structural Transformation and Marketization], Katsuji Nakagane (ed.). Tokyo: Daigaku Shuppankai.

Jefferson, Gary. 1999. "Are China's Rural Enterprises Outperforming State Enterprises? Estimating the Pure Ownership Effect." In *Enterprise Reform in China: Ownership, Transition, and Performance* Gary Jefferson and Inderjit Singh (eds.). Oxford and New York: Oxford University Press.

Jefferson, Gary, and Inderjit Singh (eds.). 1999. *Enterprise Reform in China: Ownership, Transition, and Performance.* Oxford and New York: Oxford University Press.

Kolodko, Grzegorz. 2000. *Post-Communist Transition—The Thorny Road.* Rochester, New York: University of Rochester Press.

La Porta, Rafael, and Florencio Lopez-de-Silanes. 1997. "The Benefits of Privatization: Evidence from Mexico." *World Bank Working Paper*, No. 6215 (Oct.).

Lin, Justin, Fan Cai, and Zhou Li. 1998. *State-owned Enterprise Reform in China.* Hong Kong: Chinese University of Hong Kong.

Liu, Deqiang. 2002. "Kokuyukigyo Niokeru Shoyuken Kaikakuha Yuko ka?" [Does Property Right Reform Improve the Productivity of State-owned Enterprises?]. *Keizai Kenkyu* 53(1): 53–63.

Megginson, William, Robert Nash, and Matthias van Randenborgh. 1994. "The Financial and Operating Performance of Newly Privatized Firms: An International Empirical Analysis." *Journal of Finance* 49(2): 403–452.

Naughton, Barry. 1995. *Growing out of the Plan*. Cambridge, New York: Cambridge University Press.

Nolan, Peter. 1995. *China's Rise and Russia's Fall: Politics, Economics and Planning in the Transition from Stalinism*. Basingstoke, Hampshire: Macmillan Press.

North, Douglass. 1990. *Institutions, Institutional Change and Economic Performance*. Cambridge and New York: Cambridge University Press.

Pohl, Gerhard, Robert Anderson, Stijin Claessons, and Simeon Djankov. 1997. "Privatization and Restructuring in Central and Eastern Europe." *World Bank Technical Paper*, No. 368 (May).

Rawski, Thomas. 1994. "Progress without Privatization: The Reform of China's State Industries." In *Changing Political Economies: Privatization in Post-Communist and Reforming Communist States*, Vedat Milor (ed.). Boulder, CO: Lynne Rienner Publishers.

Ryutaro, Komiya. 1989. *Gendai Chugoku Keizai* [The Economy of Contemporary China]. Tokyo: Daigaku Shuppankai.

Sachs, Jeffrey, and Wing Thye Woo. 1994. "Structural Reforms in the Economic Reforms of China, Eastern Europe, and the Former Soviet Union." *Economic Policy*, Apr., 9(18): 101–145.

Schleifer, Andrei, and Robert Vishny. 1994. "Politicians and Firms." *Quarterly Journal of Economics*109: 995–1025.

Shirley, Mary, and Patrick Walsh. 2000. "Public versus Private Ownership: The Current State of the Debate." *World Bank Working Paper*, No. 2420 (Aug.).

Steinfeld, Edward. 1998. *Forging Reform in China: The Fate of State-Owned Industry*. Cambridge and New York: Cambridge University Press.

Stiglitz, Joseph. 1999. "Whither Reform? Ten Years of the Transition." Paper presented for the Annual Bank Conference on Development Economics, Washington DC, Apr. 28–30.

Tian, Guoqiang. 2000. "Property Rights and the Nature of Chinese Collective Enterprises." *Journal of Comparative Economics*. 28: 247–268.

Weitzman, Martin, and Chenggang Xu. 1994. "Chinese Town ship-Village Enterprises as Vaguely Defined Cooperatives." *Journal of Comparative Economics* 18: 121–145.

Wu, Junping. 2000. *Minikui Chugoku Shonin* [Ugly Chinese Merchants]. Translated by Takeo Kakehi. Sososha..

Xu, Xiaomin, and Yan Wang. 1997. "Ownership Structure, Corporate Governance and Firms' Performance: The Case of Chinese Stock Market Companies." *World Bank Policy Research Working Paper*, No.1794 (May).

Yang, Gang. 2000. "Zhongxiaoxing Guoyou, Jitiqiye Chanquanshidu Gaige Fenxi" [Analysis of Property Rights Reform in Medium and Small Sized State and Collective Enterprises]. Presented at an international workshop held by the Institute of Developing Economies, Chiba, Jan. 27.

Zhang, Weiying. 1999. *Qiye Lilun yu Zhongguo Qiye Gaige* [Firm Theory and Enterprise Reform in China]. Beijing: Daxue Chupanshe.

5
Vietnamese Gradualism in the Reform of State-Owned Enterprises: The First Phase of Doi Moi

Tran Van Tho

5.1 Introduction

In any planned economy the state owned enterprises (SOEs) are a major factor in stagnant growth and macroeconomic instability.[1] Reforming them is extremely difficult because of the social burdens normally imposed upon them. They provide the employees with social welfare for expensive items like medical care, pension benefits, etc. and guarantee employment. The SOE workers regard themselves under a kind of lifetime employment system. Since social safety nets, social welfare, and employment opportunities elsewhere are lacking, they resist very strongly reform programs that may lay them off.

The SOEs are the mainstay in *the socialist market economy* in China and *the socialism-oriented market economy* in Vietnam, so any reform substantially reducing state ownership seems inconceivable in the foreseeable future. The difficulty is also partly caused by the markets initially being underdeveloped, so transition requires their buildup particularly for factors of production. Next, legal and other institutional frameworks must be set up. Thus, transition is a long-term process (Ishikawa 1990). As Vietnam follows China in adopting gradualism, the following steps have been taken.

1. Along with market development, the government provides autonomy to management and then hardens the budget constraints on the SOEs, aiming at improving their efficiency without an immediate change in ownership.
2. The government simultaneously encourages the private sector by permitting new private enterprises to increase employment opportunities. This will generate new fiscal resources, which in turn permits the government to further the reform. This approach seems to achieve *macroprivatization* eroding gradually the share of SOEs in the national economy with no

immediate *microprivatization* of SOEs. Then, the economy as a whole is de facto gradually privatized.[2]

Section 5.2 overviews the reform process, growth performance, and the position of SOEs in the Vietnamese economy. Section 5.3 discusses the reform measures adopted inside the SOEs to improve efficiency without changing ownership. Section 5.4 focuses on privatization issues. Section 5.5 offers a theoretical assessment of SOE reform. Finally, Section 5.6 summarizes the major conclusions.

5.2   The Vietnamese economy in the transitional process: SOE-led growth

In January 1981, a number of initial reform measures were launched. They included the introduction of a product-based contract system in agriculture and the institutionalization of partial autonomy for management of the SOEs. In December 1986, a comprehensive reform policy known as *doi moi* (renovation) was set out. It was conceived of as a decision to shift from a socialist model of planning and ownership to a regime based on the market mechanism, an international division of labor, and non-state ownership. In the context of this *doi moi* policy, the Foreign Investment Law was promulgated in 1987, providing the legal framework for foreign firms to operate in Vietnam. The *doi moi* policy has subsequently been realized in the areas of agriculture and its pricing system. Reforms have been directed toward reducing the role of cooperatives and increasing the autonomy of households.

The earlier partial reform of 1981, as evidence increasingly shows, was not effective, because it was designed within the framework of collectivization, giving few incentives to farmers. In 1988 the Vietnamese leaders decided to give substantial autonomy to farming households. Since then, they have been considered officially as basic units of production, and the basis of Vietnamese agriculture has shifted from collectively operated cooperatives to individual household farms.

As far as the pricing system is concerned, in March 1989 drastic measures were adopted to overcome the crisis of hyperinflation and stagnating production. They included the deregulation of the price of most commodities except 12 selected items, the devaluation of the exchange rate to the black market level, a substantial rise in interest rates to generate positive real rates, and the reduction of fiscal subsidies to zero. As will be seen later, these drastic reforms resulted in macroeconomic stability and a substantial increase in production.

Reforms in other areas, however, particularly ownership change, have been carried out very cautiously. Changes in the ownership structure are seen in two forms. One is the privatization of SOEs as such, which is called *microprivatization* and is treated in detail in Section 5.4. The second is *macroprivatization*, which can be further divided into two: development of the indigenous or local private capitalist sector and that of the foreign capitalist sector. For simplification, hereafter the former will be called the private sector. Regarding this sector, the Law on Companies and the Law on Private Business were promulgated in 1990. The first provided the basis for establishing limited liability and shareholding companies, whereas the second allowed the private sector to be formally involved in business activities. But it has taken a long process of trial and error to implement these laws. In June 1991, the National Congress of the Communist Party of Vietnam reconfirmed the necessity of developing the private sector and encapsulated that policy into the long-term strategy of development characterized as a *planned development of a multisector commodity economy*. The term *planned development* does not imply central planning before *doi moi*. Instead the term just emphasizes the important role of the state in providing public goods (including law, security, defense, and other institutions and infrastructure) necessary for economic development. The term *multisector commodity economy* means a market economy in which non-SOE sectors are developed side by side with SOEs. Recognition of a multisector commodity economy was formally indicated in the new Constitution in 1992. In 1994, the Law for Promotion of Domestic Investment was amended to encourage domestic entrepreneurs to undertake investment in the non-state sector. This law plays a role complementary to the Law of Foreign Investment, which encourages investment and business activities by the foreign private sector.

In fact, however, the private sector took a long time to show any substantial development. The reasons are: (1) some related laws have been amended, but the quality of legal system and law enforcement has been poor; (2) there has been discriminatory treatment favoring the SOEs over the private sector in land-use rights, access to financial and other resources, etc.; and (3) complicated administrative procedures for setting up new businesses and the complex supervision and regulation of private businesses by the multiple strata of local authorities have hindered the operation of private firms, discouraged their development, and resulted in rent-seeking activities. As Reza (1999) and others noted, the inadequacies and complexities in the legal and administrative system increased transactions costs and posed disincentives for the growth of the private sector. Mass de novo entry into the private sector (Kornai 2000, 7), one of main characteristics of gradualist strategies, was prohibited.

The Foreign Investment Law provided tax exemptions and other incentives to attract foreign capital but at the same time imposed many regulations and requirements upon foreign investors. In addition to the overall underdevelopment of the legal system, they made Vietnam less attractive than neighboring countries. From the early 1990s, therefore, the laws were revised substantially in June 1990, December 1992, November 1996, and May 2000.

FDI flows into Vietnam, however, were substantial, except for 1997–99, the years of the Asian financial crisis. The most important reason was that most FDI projects were undertaken jointly with SOEs. The legal and administrative environment forced foreign firms to choose SOEs as their partners. This helped them avoid the private firms' disadvantages and enjoy reduced transaction costs.

The Vietnamese economy has performed fairly well through the 1990s. The success in agricultural reform appeared in 1989, a year after the shift from a cooperative to a household farming system. The World Bank (1991) cited the export performance of the agricultural sector as a good example of the relationship between institutional reforms and export competitiveness. Most other sectors also performed well. As Table 5.1 shows, from the early 1990s, GDP grew more than 8 percent per annum except in the years of the Asian financial crisis, and the hyperinflation of the early stage of reforms

Table 5.1　Trends in major economic indicators of Vietnam

	GDP growth	Growth by sector			Retail price changes	Investment ratio (I/Y)	Saving ratio (S/Y)
		A	I	S			
1986	2.8	3.0	10.9	−2.3	387.2	n.a.	n.a.
1987	3.6	−1.1	8.5	4.6	301.0	n.a.	n.a.
1988	6.0	3.7	5.0	8.8	308.2	n.a.	n.a.
1989	4.7	7.0	−2.6	7.9	74.3	11.4	−0.1
1990	5.1	1.0	2.3	10.2	36.4	14.4	2.9
1991	5.8	2.2	7.7	7.4	80.0	15.0	10.1
1992	8.7	6.9	12.8	7.6	17.5	17.7	13.6
1993	8.1	3.3	12.6	8.6	5.3	25.1	14.8
1994	8.8	3.4	13.4	9.6	14.0	25.5	15.0
1995	9.5	4.8	13.6	9.8	12.7	27.3	17.0
1996	9.3	4.4	14.5	8.8	4.5	27.9	16.7
1997	8.2	4.3	12.6	7.1	3.7	27.6	20.1
1998	5.8	3.5	8.3	5.1	9.2	29.0	21.5
1999	4.9	5.2	7.7	2.3	0.1	27.6	24.6
2000	6.7	4.0	10.1	5.6	–	29.5	27.0

Note: A, I, and S stand for Agriculture, Industry including construction and Service.

Sources: GDP growth and growth by sector: General Statistical Office.
Retail price changes: 1986–94: World Bank (1994); 1995–99: *Kinh te 1999–2000* (Thoi bao Kinh te Vietnam), January 2000.
I/Y, S/Y: Central Institute of Economic Management.

was overcome. Substantial improvement of savings and investment as ratios of GDP were also noteworthy.

Manufacturing industries were the leading sector in economic growth in this period. From 1992 to 1997, manufacturing's growth rate was 4 to 5 percentage points higher than that of total GDP. As a result, the composition of the country's GDP changed remarkably with the share of the secondary sector expanding at the expense of the primary sector (Table 5.2). The secondary sector is composed of mining, manufacturing, and public utilities (manufacturing accounted for 80 percent of total industry in 1997), and all these subsectors expanded in the period under discussion.

Other main factors for rapid growth may be summarized. First, domestic reforms and an open-door policy made the international environment surrounding Vietnam increasingly favorable, so that official development assistance (ODA) and other resources were provided steadily from advanced countries and international financial institutions from 1993 onward. This not only facilitated the construction of infrastructure and provided intellectual inputs for further reforms but also reduced the uncertainties for the investment atmosphere in Vietnam. Second, the Vietnamese economy has been increasingly interwoven with the dynamic Asian Pacific region since the early 1990s. Until the late 1980s, almost 70 percent of Vietnamese exports were to the former USSR and other European socialist countries, all far away from Vietnam, but from this time the same share is accounted for by the exports to the Asian Pacific region. The same countries accounted for more than 70 percent of FDI inflows to Vietnam in the 1990s.

Table 5.2 Structure changes in the Vietnamese economy

	1991	1992	1993	1994	1995	1996	1997	1998	1999	2000
Shares in GDP (%)										
Primary sector	40.5	34.9	29.1	27.4	27.2	27.8	25.8	26.0	25.4	24.1
Secondary sector	23.5	23.7	28.6	28.9	28.8	29.7	32.1	32.7	34.5	36.9
Tertiary sector	36.0	41.4	42.3	43.7	44.0	42.5	42.1	41.3	40.1	39.0
Share in employment										
Primary sector	73.3	73.2	72.0	70.8	69.7	69.2	68.8	68.3	69.0	63.1
Secondary sector	12.4	12.3	12.4	12.8	13.3	12.5	12.5	12.7	12.1	13.2
Tertiary sector	14.3	14.5	15.6	16.4	17.0	18.3	18.7	19.0	18.9	23.8

Source: General Statistical Office, government of Vietnam.

Improved external relations provided both important financial resources and markets for Vietnam. In the first half of the 1990s, FDI and ODA accounted for 25 percent and 11 percent of total investment respectively. In the second half of the decade, the respective figures were 23 percent (US$ 10 billion) and 14 percent (US$ 6 billion). The expansion of exports was also noteworthy: the exports to GDP ratio rose from 29 percent in 1991 to about 40 percent in 1999.

The change in the performance of SOEs in an increasingly open economy may also be observed. Before *doi moi*, the economy was run by three types of firms: SOEs (state ownership), cooperatives (collective ownership), and household units of production or service. Cooperatives were seen mainly in agriculture and, to a lesser extent, in traditional handicrafts and services. With *doi moi*, other types of firms, that is, private firms and foreign-owned enterprises, emerged, but until the early 1990s such firms were small in number. FDI flows started in 1988, but a substantial amount of spending was recorded only after 1992. In the later stage of the *doi moi* process, such firms emerged increasingly in two forms, the individually owned company (sole proprietor enterprises) and shareholding companies (with multiple ownership). Table 5.3 records the share of each of six types of firms in the 1990s. This table shows that the share of the traditional household companies was quite large and remained roughly constant at around one-third of GDP. Foreign-owned firms showed an increasing share, but the share of private firms (single owner and mixed ownership companies) remained unchanged at a low level during this period.

The position of the state sector rose during the reform process (Table 5.4) to build up a multisector economy. While the industrial sector's share of GDP rapidly changed (Table 5.2), the collective sector declined, but the state (SOEs) and the foreign-related sectors increased. The state sector chiefly has

Table 5.3   Structure of GDP by type of ownership (GDP = 100)

	1995	1997	1999
State sector	40.2	40.5	39.5
Collective sector	10.1	8.9	8.6
Single owner	3.1	3.6	3.4
Household	36.0	34.3	33.1
Mixed	4.3	3.8	3.6
FDI-related	6.3	8.9	9.8

Note: Mixed type is composed of private multi-owner limited liability companies and shareholding companies.

Source: *Statistical Yearbook 1999*, General Statistical Office, 2000.

Table 5.4 Position of SOEs in the Vietnamese economy (% of SOEs in each category)

	1991	1995	1997	1999
Total GDP	22.2	30.3	31.4	30.4
	(31.1)	(40.0)	(40.5)	(38.7)
Agriculture GDP	4.3	4.5	n.a.	n.a.
Manufacturing GDP	67.2	66.5	49.1	n.a.
Total employment	6.5	5.1	5.2	4.8
	(10.1)	(8.7)	(8.8)	(9.0)

Note: Figures in parentheses are share of all state sector (including SOEs and others).

Source: Central Institute of Economic Management.

monopoly powers in public utilities, transport and communications, and banking and insurance.

They all developed rapidly during the 1990s and increased their share in the economy. In manufacturing, the SOEs' share declined (Table 5.4) mainly as a result of the rising share of foreign capital, which accounted for about 23 percent in 1997 (Table 5.5). The shares in office machines, radio and television, cars and motorcycles in particular reached as high as 70–100 percent. The foreign sector's share is also especially high in mining (Table 5.6) because of the discovery of petroleum in the late 1980s and its exploitation since the 1990s. This has been carried out by a joint venture with the former Soviet Union (FSU). The SOEs' share remained high, however, in heavy industries like chemicals, metals, paper, and nonferrous metals as well as some others like machines, electric and electronic products, cigarettes, and textiles.

However, the SOEs share, as recorded in Tables 5.3 through 5.6 may be underestimated, since almost all FDI projects have been undertaken jointly with SOEs and also in most cases, the SOEs' contribution in these joint ventures has been 30 percent, and was made providing a fixed asset, mainly land. If, therefore, the SOEs' contribution in the FDI-related firms was taken into account, the SOEs share would be higher than reported in Tables 5.3 through 5.6. Such an adjustment is attempted in Table 5.7. Towards the end of the period discussed, the adjusted SOE share in industrial production rose to 54–57 percent, about 9–10 percentage points higher than nonadjusted shares in this sector.

In fact, the effect of FDI on the development of SOEs has been stronger than the figures in the tables suggest. By exclusively having undertaken investments and joint operations with foreign firms, SOEs had advantages in supplying inputs to the joint ventures and access to foreign markets and technologies.

Table 5.5   The structure of the manufacturing sector in Vietnam (1997)

	Total turnover (VND billions, 1994 prices)	Share of indigenous capital enterprises (%)			Share of foreign-owned enterprises (%)
		Total	SOEs	NonSOEs	
Total	107,662	77.1	49.1	28.0	22.9
Food and drink	34,015	79.0	47.5	31.5	21.0
Cigarette	4,400	99.2	99.1	0.2	0.8
Textiles	7,261	79.9	55.4	24.6	20.1
Clothes	4,325	79.5	34.5	45.1	20.5
Leather products	6,614	53.9	30.1	23.7	46.1
Wooden products	3,146	89.9	21.5	68.3	10.1
Papers	2,644	85.2	56.7	28.5	14.8
Printing, publishing	1,620	97.5	89.0	8.5	2.5
Oil refining	84	100.0	0.0	100.0	0.0
Chemicals	7,223	79.5	69.7	9.8	20.5
Rubbers and plastics	3,528	81.5	36.5	45.0	18.5
Nonferrous metals	12,223	87.5	65.0	22.5	12.5
Metals	4,000	67.6	59.2	8.4	32.4
Metal products	3,559	75.0	13.2	61.8	25.0
Machines, equipment	1,674	90.9	66.6	24.3	9.1
Office machines	38	0.0	0.0	0.0	100.0
Electric, electronic products	1,650	74.5	60.9	13.6	25.5
Radio, television	3,278	24.8	22.1	2.7	75.2
Medical equipment	239	64.4	24.3	40.2	35.6
Cars and motorcycles	1,629	29.0	12.2	16.8	71.0
Other transport equipment	1,815	66.1	43.2	22.9	33.9
Furniture	2,564	80.0	8.8	71.1	20.0
Others	133	100.0	0.0	100.0	0.0

Source: General Statistical Office, *Results of Survey on Industry 1998*, Statistical Publishing House 1999.

Table 5.6 Vietnam's industrial production by type of firms (1997)

	Production value (in VND billions, 1994 prices)	Share in industry total (%)	Share in sub-sector (%)
Industry total	134,420	100.0	–
SOEs	64,474	48.0	
Foreign-owned	38,878	28.9	
Other	31,068	23.1	
Mining	18,314	13.6	100.0
SOEs	3,206	2.4	17.5
Foreign-owned	14,239	10.6	77.7
Other	869	0.6	4.7
Manufacturing	107,662	80.1	100.0
SOEs	52,864	39.3	49.1
Foreign-owned	24,606	18.3	22.9
Other	30,192	22.5	28.0
Public utilities	8,444	6.3	100.0
SOEs	8,404	6.3	99.5
Foreign-owned	33	0.0	0.4
Other	7	0.0	0.1

Source: General Statistical Office, *Results of Survey on Industry 1998*, Statistical Publishing House 1999.

Table 5.7 Industrial production by ownership

	1995	1997	1999
A. Production value (billion dongs)			
Total	103,375	134,420	166,965
SOEs	51,991	64,474	72,604
Adjusted SOEs	59,771	76,137	90,010
Foreign capital	25,933	38,878	58,019
Adjusted foreign capital	18,153	27,215	40,613
Non-state (domestic)	25,451	31,068	36,342
-collective	650	751	n.a.
-households	18,191	19,704	n.a.
-single owner Ltd. Co.	2,277	3,224	n.a.
-mixed	4,333	7,389	n.a.
B. Share in total industrial production (%)			
SOEs	50.3	48.0	43.5
Adjusted SOEs	57.8	56.6	53.9
Foreign capital	25.1	28.9	34.7
Adjusted foreign capital	17.6	20.2	24.3
Non-state (domestic)	24.6	23.1	21.8
-collective	0.6	0.6	n.a.
-households	17.6	14.7	n.a.
-single owner Ltd. Co.	2.2	2.4	n.a.
-mixed	4.2	5.5	n.a.

Note: Mixed type is composed of private multi-owner limited liability companies and share holding companies. Adjusted by moving 30% of production value made by foreign capital to SOEs (see text).

Source: Compiled from *Statistical Yearbook 1999*, General Statistical Office, 2000.

5.3   SOE reforms without privatization

Reform in this period was limited to management and restructuring, first, to improve efficiency by giving autonomy but hardening budget constraints, and second, to increase the scale by merging small SOEs or liquidating badly managed and financially weak SOEs. In 1990 there were 12,000 SOEs, of which about 3,000 large and medium-size enterprises were under the jurisdiction of the central government, whereas remaining 9,000 medium and small-size enterprises were under local jurisdiction of provincial or city governments.[3]

5.3.1   Initial reforms

Reforms began in 1981 by with the introduction of the *three part planning system*. This system required each SOE to set out three plans: the first to fulfill the quota given by the government, the second to deal with the products left free for the firm, and the third to allocate assets and other resources to some areas for best use.

After 1986 *doi moi* policy progressed, particularly from 1989, and managerial autonomy was granted to SOEs to allow them to freely set output targets and prices, disburse bonuses, and retain some profits for intra-firm social services. Mitsui and Wada (1998, 82) conducted a survey of 200 Vietnamese SOEs in the manufacturing sector in 1996 and 1997 and reported that almost 90 percent of management had autonomy throughout the 1990s. Traditionally, the government allocated intermediate goods and other inputs to SOEs which fulfilled a given quota by supplying the products to the government. In the new system such transactions were switched to a contract basis, taking market prices into account, and direct subsidies to SOEs were greatly reduced. After 1990, SOEs had to borrow from banks to finance their investment instead of this being supplied from government funds.

Budget constraints on SOEs became increasingly hard from 1989 when a wide range of prices were deregulated. After 1991 transactions with FSU shifted from planned soft conditions for Vietnam to competitive markets. Trade liberalization since the early 1990s increased competition and tightened budget constraints by limiting the prices SOEs could charge for outputs. Under these circumstances, the weakness of Vietnamese SOEs in domestic and world markets was easy to recognize, given their small scale. Most of them were very fragile in their financial, managerial, and organizational aspects. As in other transitional economies, they were overstaffed and also had the function of providing social welfare and security. Yet the Vietnamese *socialism-oriented market economy* demanded that they play the leading role in nation-building. It was absolutely necessary, therefore, to restructure and reorganize them somehow into strong groups of firms.

5.3.2 Restructuring and reorganizing SOEs

In 1991, the government issued a decree requiring all SOEs to reregister according to new criteria, which allowed only financially viable and potentially profitable enterprises to exist. This sharply decreased the number of SOEs from 12,084 in 1990 to 6,544 in 1993 (Tran 1996) and around 6,000 in 1994–96 (Table 5.8). In this way, more than 3,500 firms were merged with others and about 2,500 were closed or disbanded. The SOEs that merged or closed were mainly firms controlled by local authorities. In contrast, the number of SOEs administered by central government agencies increased. Nevertheless, most SOEs were small and weak. Those with fewer than 100 employees accounted for 47 percent of the total (6,544 firms), and only 4 percent of SOEs had more than 1,000 employees in 1992.

Then, the strength of business groups in Japan or the *chaboel* in Korea inspired the Vietnam leadership to adopt in 1994 a program for establishing large-scale groups of corporations and strengthening international competitiveness through concentration and autonomous management. The Prime Minister issued *Decision 90* and *Decision 91* which called for the grouping of about half of the SOEs under a number of holding companies known as *general corporations* (GC). Decision 90, issued on March 7, 1994, created 76 GCs, usually called *GC90*, each with at least five voluntary members and a minimum legal capital of VND 100 billion, whereas Decision 91 called for much larger corporations with at least seven SOE members and a minimum capital of VND 1,000 billion, resulting in only 17 GCs called *GC91*. In total the GC91 and GC90 combined had 1,392 SOEs, accounting as a proportion

Table 5.8 Number of state-owned enterprises (SOEs) in Vietnam

	SOEs	SOEs which have been		
		Equitized	Sold	Transferred
1989	12,000	0	0	0
1992	6,545	0	1	0
1993	6,264	0	4	0
1994	6,019	0	5	0
1995	5,962	5	6	0
1996	6,025	5	8	0
1997	5,873	18	8	0
1998	n.a.	57	12	0
1999	5,700	370	12	1
2000	5,280	451	20	5

Note: SOEs which have been equitized, sold, and transferred are on a cumulative basis. Figures for 2000 are data by August.

Source: Central Institute of Economic Management (Vietnam).

of all SOEs in number, capital, and employees[4] 24 percent, 66 percent and 55 percent respectively.

From 1995, SOE reforms were carried out through implementation of the Law on State Enterprises, aimed at gradually abolishing the supervision of line ministries and experimenting with the separation of GC91 from the government. The aim is that SOEs remain in the state ownership but operate as entities exposed to competition in the market with other types of firms. However, SOEs and their reform continues to encounter a number of problems.

1. Ambiguity of real ownership among many of the organizations involved undermines corporate governance as it leaves open the responsibility for monitoring managers. Since 1995, the SOEs' capital and assets have been under control of the Ministry of Finance, but the operation is still supervised by their respective line ministry or local government, and their directors are still constrained by regulations of many organizations. In addition, with the establishment of GCs, member firms in each GC are gradually losing their previous autonomy and are forced to transfer it to the GC Board of Directors.

2. With increasing autonomy but without a controlling system, directors have tended to privatize national assets in their own enterprises. However, nobody including the government as owner is well informed of the financial conditions of the SOEs.

3. Budget constraints turned from *soft* to *hard* but then tended to return to *soft* again, particularly for large SOEs. The reason is that the Asian financial crisis of 1997 caused financial difficulties to many SOEs. The government extended assistance to protect the large SOEs that had to play a leading role in the socialist-oriented economy. In a survey carried out in 1997, Mitsui and Wada (1998) also showed that as the financial difficulties increased, SOEs tended to depend on government assistance, and that government intervention strengthened again.

5.4   Reforms with privatization

In the early 1990s, a program to reform the SOEs and to develop a multisector economy was launched to transfer or diversify SOE ownership as well as to encourage development of the private sector. However, until the 1990s neither microprivatization nor macroprivatization had progressed smoothly in Vietnam.

5.4.1   *Equitization* of SOEs

With Cabinet Decision No. 143 of May 1990, the government decided to undertake a pilot plan of *equitization* for several SOEs. The term *equitization* is used to express a concept equivalent to *privatization* for two reasons. First, in many cases the state still holds the majority shares in SOEs. Until relatively recently, full privatization has been very rare in Vietnam and China. The meaning of the term equitization is broader in order to cover all cases of SOE ownership reforms. Second, the term is acceptable to conservative leaders in Vietnam since it implies the continuing control by the state. Its real meaning may be understood as the "transfer of SOEs to a stock company." In 1992, seven SOEs were selected as objects for this pilot plan. In 1993, the government formally encouraged other SOEs to prepare for *equitization* to improve efficiency by renewing the management and working atmosphere and to raise funds for investment. On this policy, three observations may be made. First, its pace has been slow. Although the decision came in 1990, by 1997 only 18 firms had been equitized (Table 5.8). Second, only small SOEs have been chosen for equitization. Third, the scope of individuals and organizations who can buy the shares of equitized SOEs has been expanded step by step. Initially only their employees could buy the shares, then later outsiders, still limited to Vietnamese residents, could do so. More recently any parties, including foreign-related firms, can buy. In fact, however, the state or internal employees and managers usually hold the majority shares.[5]

Until 1996, equitization was realized on a voluntary basis. Only the SOEs that accepted it registered with the government and took the necessary procedures. After 1997 the Prime Minister gave quotas to line ministries or provincial and city authorities to select a target number to equitize, but only 57 firms had been equitized by 1998 (Table 5.8). The reasons for this slow pace are as follows.

1. Directors and managerial staff tend to protect their vested interests. Given the lack of a social safety net or other social security measures, employees resist any drastic change in ownership, because unemployment is a very serious social problem in Vietnam. Despite high economic growth throughout the 1990s, the industrial and service sectors did not generate enough employment opportunities to absorb redundant labor in both rural and urban areas. During this period, nearly 70 percent of the labor force was still in agriculture with low productivity (Table 5.2). The unemployment rate in the urban areas reached 20 percent. SOEs employed about 1.6 million workers, accounting for about 4 percent of the total labor force or about 34 percent in the secondary sector. (Table 5.4). In the reregistration and restructuring in the early 1990s, many SOEs were merged or disbanded and sharply decreased the share of SOE workers in total employment (Table 5.4). Most of them were so small and located in such local areas that they could not resist restructuring. In existing SOEs, the rate of overstaffing was estimated to be in the range of 20–30 percent (World Bank 1998).[6]

2. The formation of the security market took more time than anticipated. The preparation started in 1994, but the market only opened in July 2000

and the impact of this market on SOE reforms was initialy almost negligible. By the end of 2000, only four firms, originally SOEs but equitized, were listed in the market.

3. Barely any information on any SOE is disclosed. Nobody including the government is well informed of the financial state of SOEs. The problem is so serious that one of the ODA programs provided by the Japanese government was devoted to investigate financial and various other management problems in 100 selected SOEs and diagnose them in preparation for new reforms in this sector.

From 1998, equitization and other measures for diversifying ownership were rapidly introduced. Prime Ministerial Order No. 20/1998/CT-TTg issued on April 21, 1998 classified SOEs into two groups in the following way. Group I was composed of important SOEs for which 100 percent state ownership was to be maintained. These SOEs were to be strengthened in terms of management, organization, financial capacity, and operations and were to play a leading role in the modernization and industrialization. This group included major public service enterprises as well as the firms that did not at that time meet the conditions for equitization.[7]

Group II comprised the SOEs whose ownership could be changed. They could be reclassified into several subgroups according to the extent to which the state would relinquish its share. The first subgroup was the small SOEs with capital less than VND 1 billion. The government decided to transfer partially or entirely their ownership to non-state interests, contract out the management, or lease the assets to private managers.

In order to speed up the equitization of SOEs, the Prime Minister requested the line ministries, local authorities, and GC91 to select some SOEs to be equitized and no longer be under dominant ownership of the state. This group was large and consisted of at least 20 percent of SOEs under their jurisdiction. With these strong policies and efforts, the number of SOEs equitized in 1998 and 1999 jumped substantially and those sold or transferred also showed a marked change (Table 5.8).

The reasons for the rapid microprivatization after 1998 are as follows.

1. Restructuring carried out since the early 1990s had not strengthened the SOEs' structure or improved their efficiency. Firms with losses still accounted for a large percentage, and those within each GC tended to increase the burden and prevent the efficient operation of GCs as a whole. These trends were been more pronounced after the 1997 financial crisis.

2. The integration into the world market put increasingly strong pressure on the SOEs in the late 1990s and forced Vietnam to speed up rationalization programs for all of them. A member of the Association of Southeast Asian Nations (ASEAN) since 1995, Vietnam joined the Asian Free Trade Area

(AFTA) in 1996 and had to fulfill its duty of free trade with other ASEAN members by 2006. In addition, negotiations with America to sign a trade agreement had been underway since 1998, and the Vietnam-U.S. Bilateral Trade Agreement was signed in July 2000. The prospect of WTO membership, which was realized in late 2006, brought about many challenges for SOEs in addition to intensifying domestic competition.

As regards the reemployment of the employees made redundant after equitization, in 1998 the government set up the National Target Program on Employment for 1998–2000 and National Fund for Employment Promotion to facilitate the equitization program by providing financial support. The Three Year SOE Reform Program, launched in 1999, set up the Special Fund for Reorganization and Equitization to support the program by issuing separation allowances and helping to retrain the laid-off workers. This proves that the SOE reforms required the changes in institutions. The lack of such changes deterred microprivatization.

5.4.2 Development of the private sector

The role of indigenous private capital still remained marginal in this period even though the Law of Companies was promulgated in 1990 to permit various forms of private ownership. By 1995, there were only about 1,800 joint-stock limited companies in manufacturing. They accounted for only 8 percent of the total registered capital. Sole proprietary ownership, which is the most numerous form (5,030) in manufacturing, accounted for about 3 percent of registered capital (UNIDO and MPI 1997, 63).[8] From 1995 to 1998, private firms increased, but their role in the economy was still limited. The main reason was that the economic environment remained significantly biased against the private sector vis-à-vis the SOEs. The bias was manifested in discriminatory incentives of both financial and institutional nature.

The slowdown in growth in 1998, however, pushed Vietnam to promote the private sector by removing regulations and promulgating the Enterprise Law, which came into effect in January 2000, replacing the Company Law and the Private Enterprise Law of 1990. If implemented effectively, it is intended to improve the climate for private enterprises and increase employment. In 2002, only about 1 million or 3 percent of the total number of employees (36 million) were working in the private corporate sector.

There was skepticism about the effectiveness of the new law. For instance, according to the World Bank's *East Asia Quarterly Brief,* published on January 31, 2000, it would take another two to three years before the new law could operate effectively, since some of the key supporting legislation was still missing, and there were numerous laws and regulations inconsistent with the new law and in need of abolition or amendment. However, combined with the removal of more than a hundred business licensing requirements, the law generated a strong response from the domestic private sector. In the first five months of 2000, the number of registered non-SOE firms rose to 5,100 with a breakdown as follows: 2,652 sole proprietor enterprises, 2,244 limited liability companies, and 204 joint-stock companies. By August 2000, the total number rose to more than 7,000 companies and by December of the same year, about 14,000 new firms were registered. In addition, the deregulation of export activities since July 1998 resulted in a jump in the number of non-state export firms. It seems that 1998 was a turning point in the reforms in Vietnam. While SOEs have to continue further reforms in efficiency improvement, both micro- and macroprivatization are being promoted.

5.5 The Vietnamese experience from a theoretical perspective

5.5.1 The performance of SOEs in Vietnam

The reforms so far had brought about high growth for the economy as a whole and SOEs themselves. In order to make a more accurate evaluation of the performance of SOEs, examination of the following questions may be desirable. Have SOEs improved their technical efficiency in the reform process? What market conditions have they faced after being granted management autonomy? Due to limited data, however, thorough analysis is not possible. The following analysis relies on the findings of some field surveys and other sources of information.

A survey of 208 manufacturing firms (148 SOEs and 60 private firms) in Hanoi and Ho Chi Minh City was conducted by the Vietnamese State Planning Committee (currently the Ministry of Planning and Investment, MPI) and the Overseas Economic Cooperation Fund (OECF) of Japan in late 1994. Its findings were recorded and analyzed in Ohno (1996) and showed that during the 1991–94 period, many SOEs improved the performance in their capacity utilization rate, changes in nominal profitability, the ratio of redundant labor to total labor, and the competitiveness of their outputs with other firm's domestic products and imports. The study also suggested that the ownership pattern had not influenced the performance of the firms surveyed. The factors specific to each enterprise such as managerial autonomy and the size and the degree of competition were more strongly associated with performance. The study's findings supported the *gradualist* approach; *that is*, reforms without changing ownership.

More recent surveys and information suggested the deteriorating performance of SOEs. Mitsui and Wada (1998) reported on a survey of 200 SOEs in the manufacturing sector by the OECF and the Central Institute of Economic Management (CIEM) of MPI between 1996 and 1997, covering the period of 1991–95 and showed several findings:

1. the SOEs experienced a steady increase in labor productivity, attributable to the steady rise in the capital-labor ratio as a result of the expansion of investment;
2. most SOEs were only competitive in protected domestic markets—where they have superiority in facilities, technology, and skilled labor compared to other types of firms in Vietnam—but not so in international markets; and
3. although sales and other indicators showed a substantial increase, the profitability of most SOEs had deteriorated considerably.

As for the financial performance of SOEs, there has been no comprehensive data since the mid-1990s, but various sources of information have warned foreign and Vietnamese observers to watch out for their inefficiency. Most SOEs were operating with obsolete machinery and equipment, resulting in low productivity and quality. Thus, many SOEs had to borrow capital from other state enterprises, the banking sector, and other sources, creating a complex maze of cross-subsidization and indebtedness (Kokko 1998, 320–321). Dapice (1999) quoted a World Bank source as saying that only 37 percent out of 5,800 SOEs were profitable in 1997; their debts amounted to VND 170 trillion at the end of that year, more than half of the annual GDP; and fully 45 percent of the debts were overdue for repayment. In addition, three-fifths of the SOEs surveyed were unprofitable and had the debts of about double the value of their state capital.

According to a survey by the Vietnamese Ministry of Finance and the IMF, about 40 percent were profitably run in 1997,[9] but a more recent report by the Ministry of Finance showed that at the end of 1999 only 20 percent of them were operating efficiently and generating profits and demonstrating a capacity to maintain their capital and assets, paying debts, and contributing to the government budget. My own interview with the Central Committee for Renovation of Enterprise Management in Hanoi in January 2000 also confirmed the deterioration in the performance of SOEs.

Regarding market conditions, it is possible to divide SOEs into three types facing different market conditions. The first type is the monopolist SOE in the nontraded sectors such as telecommunication, transportation, construction, and public utilities. These firms enjoy monopolistic market power and are reportedly very profitable since the prices they charge are very high. International telephone charges in Vietnam are among the highest in the world. The second type is in capital-intensive heavy industries such as steel, cement, metals, and machinery. Until the mid-1990s they were monopolistic or oligopolistic in domestic markets but have been increasingly exposed to competition with imports due to trade liberalization under the AFTA regime as well as being under stronger pressure from domestic users. These two types are mainly controlled by the central government. The third type is the small and medium-size SOE, principally controlled by local government. They are in labor-intensive industries in sectors where this gives Vietnam a comparative advantage but because of their outdated technology and financial weakness many can not compete with imports.

The second type of SOE as well as the first type, such as construction firms, have long enjoyed a privileged position as regards access to government credit and expanded rapidly during the reform process. This fact is consistent with the observations by many observers of Vietnamese economic reform and development that the Vietnamese economic growth in the 1990s was characterized by increasingly capital-intensive industrialization, import substitution bias, and thus inefficient investments (World Bank 1996; Sachs *et al.* 1997; World Bank 1997; Kokko 1998). A steady rise in the incremental capital-output ratio (ICOR) for the economy as a whole partially supports these observations.

With these qualifications, the expansion of the SOE sector and the growth of the economy as a whole may be similar to the East Asian *input-driven* case of growth (Krugman 1994). He argued that East Asian growth has not been driven by technical improvement, since total factor productivity growth there has been low.[10]

5.5.2   SOE reforms and the theory of gradualism: a tentative view

The characteristics of SOE reforms in Vietnam may be summarized.

1. Along with agriculture, SOEs have been the targets of reforms since the early stage of transition. SOE reforms started with giving autonomy to the management, then hardening the budget constraints as well as restructuring and grouping, to create larger and stronger SOEs to enable them to compete more effectively in the market economy.
2. Privatization of SOEs has been conducted in the later stage of transition and has been confined to small SOEs.
3. The development of non-SOEs or macroprivatization has been formally promoted in the reform and development strategy but during the period under review did not show any substantial performance, except for the foreign invested sector strongly associated with SOEs.
4. The position of SOEs has been strengthened in the reform process, and the Vietnamese economy so far has shown a good performance in growth and stability. This is after all the most important feature of the reforms in Vietnam.

These characteristics may be attributed to two factors. One is the ideological principle of building a socialism-oriented market economy with SOEs as keystones. This principle means that the government tended to allocate resources to the SOEs by providing various financial supports and administrative favors. Ishikawa (1999, 319) points out: during the reform process budget constraints were hardened for small SOEs but not necessarily for larger ones. From 1998, as a result of the downturn of the Vietnamese economy, SOEs encountered more severe market conditions, and this situation tended to make the government further soften the budget constraints on them. Another factor is that the institution-building essential to develop the non-SOE sectors has been undertaken at a slow pace. In particular, efforts at setting up a legal framework have been made on a long trial-and-error process, so that the investment environment for non-SOE sectors has not been stabilized. In addition, because of the legacy of war, Vietnam lacks the necessary human resources to construct an institutional framework and an efficient administrative mechanism.

The conventional view of gradualism or the two track approach to economic reforms suggests that the reform of SOEs should be undertaken in the long run, and that reform strategies should treat the SOE sector differently from the rest of the economy. For SOEs, because of the low level of market development and political and social sensitivity, the initial reform strategy is to improve the efficiency of the firms without privatizing their ownership but hardening budget constraints and granting autonomy to the management. On the other hand, efforts are made to expand the non-SOE sectors in order to generate employment and build an institutional framework. The two approaches prepare the essential preconditions for further reforming the SOE sector in the next stage. Figure 5.1 illustrates such reform path. With deregulation in the non-SOE sector, this sector expands at a faster speed than that of SOEs. SOEs remain almost the same size as before, but their relative position declines in the reform process. In the case of Vietnam, as seen above, even though the two track approach was adopted and the economy performed well in the reform process during the period under review, the

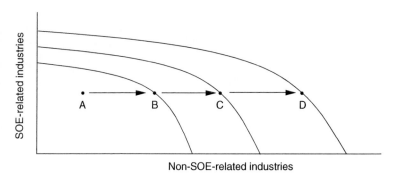

Figure 5.1 Conventional path of gradualism: non-SOE-biased shift of production possibility frontier

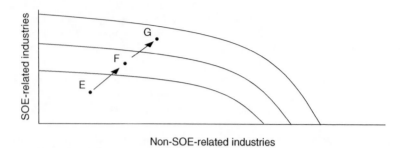

Figure 5.2   Vietnamese path of gradualism: SOE-biased shift of production possibility frontier

SOE sector expanded in both absolute and relative terms. The reasons have been explained above. This case may be illustrated by Figure 5.2. Note that in this case, all production points (E, F, and G) lie inside the frontiers.

5.6   Concluding remarks

SOEs in Vietnam have gone through a long process of reform. The first stage, reforms without privatization, was aimed at improving the efficiency of SOEs by granting them partial autonomy (1981) and later giving more substantial autonomy (1987) to their management, followed by hardening budget constraints (1989–91), restructuring (1992) and grouping of SOEs (1994). Microprivatization had been postponed until the late 1990s and macroprivatization was not substantial until the late 1990s except for in the foreign investment sector, which was been strongly associated with SOEs.

The Vietnamese economy had thus far shown a remarkable performance and the role of SOEs was significant in this process. In this way, Vietnam had taken a path of gradualism, although this seemed to bring about some misallocation of resources. With the constraints of institutional resources and political factors, however, such a path could be judged as inevitably the second best way. However, in the second stage of reforms which can be marked as a period beginning at the late 1990s, Vietnam needed to move to the conventional path of gradualism with the expansion of the non-SOE sector and development of comparative advantage industries and the increasing pressures of globalization might speed up that process.

Notes

1. See Lavigne (1999), pp. 33–35, for example, for a discussion of basic characteristics of SOEs.
2. See also the paper by Nakagane in this volume. The terms *macroprivatization* and *microprivatization* are borrowed from his earlier paper, Nakagane (2000).

3. The size of SOEs here refers to the relative meaning in the Vietnamese context. By international standards, most SOEs in Vietnam are small. In 1992, even after the launch of the restructuring policy which resulted in a sharp reduction in the number of SOEs due to merger and liquidation, only 255 out of 6,544 SOEs had 1,000 employees or more. See Tran (1996), Tables 4–5, p. 74.
4. *Kinh te va du bao,* March 1999.
5. Vu Dinh Bach and Ngo Dinh Giao (1996), 171 recorded the structure of new ownership for five equitized SOEs.
6. According to the survey on 195 SOEs, conducted in 1999 by the Central Institute of Economic Management (CIEM), a research organ of the Vietnamese government, the average rate of overstaffing was 14.6 percent. CIEM (2000).
7. According to the document of the Central Committee for Renovation of Enterprise Management, quoted in *Thoi bao kinh te Saigon,* May 4, 2000, there were 732 public service enterprises (out of 5,280 SOEs) in mid-2000.
8. According to Vietnamese law, a limited liability company has more than two owners or more than one organization, a sole proprietor company is a small-scale one-owner unlimited company, and a shareholding company was determined from 1990 to 1999 as a company having more than seven shareholders with a minimum legal capital but since January 2000, under the newly promulgated Enterprise Law, the only requirement is more than two shareholders.
9. Reported in *Thoi bao kinh te Saigon,* May 4, 2000.
10. This view has been controversial and is not necessarily convincing. My comments on this point are recorded in Tran (2001). However, for the reasons just cited, the input-driven growth hypothesis seems to be relevant to the case of Vietnam.

References

Dapice, David O. 1999. "Vietnam's Economy: Responses to the Asian Crisis." Harvard Institute for International Development (mimeo).

Ishikawa, Shigeru. 1990. *Kaihatsu Keizaigaku No Kihon Mondai* [The Basic Problems of Development Economics]. Tokyo: Iwanami Shoten.

Ishikawa, Shigeru. 1999. "Kokuei Kigyou Kaikaku" [SOE Reforms]. In *Vietnam Shijo Keizaika* [Vietnam's Transition to a Market Economy], Shigeru Ishikawa and Yonousuke Hara (eds.). Tokyo: Toyokeizai-Shinposha.

Kokko, Ari. 1998 "Vietnam: Ready for Doi Moi II?" *ASEAN Economic Bulletin* 15(3) (Dec.): 319–327.

Kornai, János. 2000. *Ten Years After the "Road to a Free Economy: The Author's Self-Evaluation."* Annual Bank Conference on Development Economics, World Bank. Washington, DC, Apr.

Krugman, Paul. 1994. "The Myth of Asia's Miracle." *Foreign Affairs* 73 (Nov./Dec.): 62–68.

Lavigne, Marie. 1999. *The Economics of Transition from Socialist Economy to Market Economy.* 2nd Edn. Hampshire and New York: Palgrave.

Mitsui, Hisaaki, and Yoshio Wada. 1998. "Analysis of Reform of State-Owned Enterprises in Vietnam." *Journal of Development Assistance* (OECF RIDA) 4(1): 68–103.

Nakagane, Katsuji. 2000. "Privatization in China and Other Transition Economies—A Note on Several Theoretical and Empirical Issues." Paper presented at a workshop on transition economies in Kitakyushu, Mar. 30–31.

Ohno, Izumi. 1996. "Ownership, Performance, and Managerial Autonomy—A Survey of Manufacturing Enterprises in Vietnam." *Journal of Development Assistance* 1(2) (Mar.).

Reza, Sadrel. 1999. "Institutional Aspects of Privatization—The Case of Vietnam." *ADB Institute Working Paper*, No. 5. (Dec.).

Sachs, Jeffrey et al. 1997. *Development Strategies for Vietnam: Challenges to Prosperity.* Cambridge, MA: Harvard Institute for International Development (HIID), Harvard University. (Sep.).

Tran Van Tho. 1996. *Betonamu Keizai no Shintenkai* [New Development of the Vietnamese Economy]. Tokyo: Nihon Keizai Shinbunsha.

Tran Van Tho. 2001. "Gijutsu-Iten to Shakaiteki Noryoku" [Technology Transfer and Social Capacity]. In *Ajia Keizai no Tassei* [Achievement of the Asian Economy], Toshio Watanabe (ed.). Tokyo: Toyokeizai-Shinposha.

UNIDO, and MPI. 1997. "Vietnam: A Medium Term Industrial Strategy." Hanoi, Vietnam: UNIDO and MPI.

Vu Dinh Bach, and Ngo Dinh Giao (eds.). 1996. *Phat trien cac thanh phan kinh te va cac to chuc kinh doanh o nuoc ta hien nay* [Development of the Multi-sector Economy and Businee Organizations in Vietnam]. Nha xuat ban chinh tri quoc gia.

World Bank. 1991. *World Development Report: The Challenge of Development.* Oxford: Oxford University Press.

World Bank. 1996. *World Development Report: From Plan to Market.* Oxford: Oxford University Press.

World Bank. 1997. "Vietnam, Deepening Reform for Growth." An Economic Report, Document of the World Bank, Oct. 31.

World Bank. 1998. "Vietnam: Rising to the Challenge." An Economic Report of the World Bank, Consultative Group Meeting for Vietnam, Dec. 7–8.

6
From Public to Private Savings: Decline of State Ownership in the Chinese Corporate Sector

Chunlin Zhang

6.1 Introduction

At the outset of the reform in 1978, state-owned enterprises (SOEs) completely dominated the corporate sector in China and accounted for nearly 80 percent of the gross value of industrial output. By 1998 this figure had dropped to 28 percent (NBS 1999, 423). In September 1999, the Communist Party of China (CPC) made further strategic decisions in the Fourth Plenum of the Central Committee on state ownership to *withdraw* the state from most industries and enterprises except for a few of strategic significance. This chapter provides an account of this decline in state ownership, adopting corporate finance as an analytical framework. Before the reform, the SOEs were financed by public savings, but market-oriented reform combined with the part privatization of agriculture shifted their reliance from public to private savings. Reform efforts forced the state to withdraw from the corporate sector. The liabilities that the government incurred in financing the SOEs would drive the reform toward further transformation of ownership.

Section 6.2 looks back to the pre-reform era and explains how the corporate sector was financed with public savings generated by pricing instruments in central planning. Section 6.3 discusses how the foundation of this system was undermined by reform and how private savings were generated. Section 6.4 describes the reform of the corporate sector that reduced state ownership. Section 6.5 discusses the fiscal implications of corporate sector reform and examines policy options for further withdrawal of state ownership with reference to reform strategies implemented and undertaken during recent years. Finally, Section 6.6 provides some concluding remarks on the implications of further reform.

6.2   Financing the corporate sector with public savings

How can the state raise capital to finance investment in and the operation of SOEs? State, with full control over national income distribution,
has two options: finance them with either private savings or public savings. When national income is completely distributed among households,
people will save out of their incomes, and then the state transfers the savings from the household sector by taxation, public borrowing, or issuing
shares. Alternatively, the state can generate public savings by retaining part
of the national income and distributing the remainder to households. This
is known as the *deduction* approach in China, following Karl Marx's design
(1989, 81–90) for an ideal socialist economy, one of the theoretical blueprints of the centrally planned economy.

Financing of the SOEs was basically accomplished through a *deduction*
method. The government manipulated household incomes to keep them at
a low level so as to minimize private savings and maximize government savings for financing investment in and the operation of SOEs primarily through
the state budget (Table 6.1).

During the period 1950–80, *capital construction* (largely fixed investment),
working capital, and *technical improvement* of SOEs accounted for 48.6 percent
of total budget expenditure (Ministry of Finance 1995, 395). Private savings were negligible. In 1978, per capita bank deposits, by far the dominant
form of noncash private financial assets then, were only RMB (renminbi)
21.9 (PBC 1992, 29) or equivalent to the price of 55 kilograms (121 pounds)
of rice. The state banking system played only a trivial role in financing
about 18.7 percent of their assets, including through bank loans in 1980
(Wu 1995). An important question is how the *deductions* were made; that is,
how the government manipulated income distribution to keep household
income at a sufficiently low level. Lack of data makes it difficult to draw a
detailed and complete picture,[1] but some qualitative observations may be
offered based on widely recognized facts.

Table 6.1   The role of the state budget in financing the state sector investment
in China, 1953–78 (sum of the period, in RMB billion)

Indicator	Amount or percentage
1. GDP	4,844.26
2. Government revenue	1,687.1
3. As a percentage of national income (2/1)	34.8%
4. State sector investment in fixed assets	764.4
5. Of which financed by budgetary appropriation	542.7
6. As a percentage of the total investment (5/4)	71.0%
7. As a percentage of government revenue (5/2)	32.2%

Source: NBS, 1998a: 55; 1997b: 21–24.

First, taxation was not a significant instrument. Virtually no tax was imposed on households at that time. Tax revenues were just enough to finance expenditure outside the SOE sector. During 1950–80, tax revenue accounted for only 47 percent of total revenue, while 51.4 percent of budget expenditure was spent on items other than SOEs (Ministry of Finance 1995, 395–405).

Second, a major vehicle for transferring savings from the rural household sector to the industrial sector was the relative prices of agricultural products.[2] As Lardy (1983, 101) noted, the government set these prices largely to generate industrial profit and thus government revenue. During the period 1950–77, agricultural procurement and retail price policies enabled the government to generate through light industry's profits revenues amounting to as much as 29 percent of the entire state budget (Lardy 1983, 126–127). The low relative prices of food grains meant lower labor costs and higher profits in the entire SOE sector (Lardy 1983, 114–119).

Third, the low wage rate in the state sector contributed to government savings. Workers received very low wages that were almost never adjusted upward (Table 6.2), so they were unable to make long-term savings.

The government collected the proportion of national income to be distributed to and saved personally by workers, in the form of profit remittances from the SOEs and increased its budget revenue and savings. Needless to say, the government and SOEs provided various social services. This system served to maximize government savings, since it enabled the government

Table 6.2 Salaries and wages of staff and workers of state-owned units, 1952–97

Year	Total wage bill (RMB billion)	Average wage per person (RMB yuan)	Total wage bill (% of gross value of industrial output of SOEs*)	Bonus** % to total wage bill
1952	6.75	4.46	44.6	–
1957	15.64	6.47	41.4	–
1962	21.36	5.92	26.4	–
1865	23.53	6.52	18.6	–
1970	27.75	6.09	15.0	–
1975	38.61	6.13	14.8	–
1978	46.87	6.44	14.3	2.4
1980	62.79	8.03	16.0	9.7
1985	106.48	12.13	16.9	14.5
1990	232.41	22.84	17.8	19.1
1995	608.02	56.25	19.5	16.8
1997	721.10	67.47	24.8	15.7

Notes: *The total wage bill and wage are those of staff and workers of all state-owned units, including nonindustrial SOEs and other state agencies, institutions, and organizations.
**Including extra payments for above-quota performances under the piece-rate system.
Source: NBS, 1998b: 37, 38, 43; NBS 1998a: 433.

to control the level of expenses for social services effectively and to keep the expenses as low as politically feasible.

6.3   Financing the corporate sector with private savings

6.3.1   The emergence of private savings

The market-oriented reform in the late 1970s inevitably ran the danger of undermining China's socialist foundations, but it proceeded step by step as follows. In the early years of the reform agricultural prices were substantially raised, while many other prices were liberalized later. Agricultural production was privatized through what is known as the *family contracting responsibility system*. Privatization was partial because the land was still collectively owned. Nonetheless, farming households were granted control rights and residual claims similar to the two key elements of enterprise ownership. These reforms led to rapid growth of output and increase in farmers' incomes. Between 1978 and 1988, agricultural prices rose 1.45 times and the average income tripled (Guo and Han 1991, 130–133).

In the urban economy, government softened substantially its control over the effective wage rate (the formal wage *plus* bonuses and various benefits) because of the increase in living costs and SOE reform in the 1980s and aimed to "delegate more power, including the one to give bonuses to workers, and concede more benefits" to managers and workers. As bonuses and other payments for above-quota performance under the piece-rate system became an increasingly large component of the total wage bill, more of the income generated by the industrial sector was distributed to workers (Table 6.2). Government budget revenue from SOEs, however, fell, making its share of fiscal revenue in GDP decline sharply. From 1978 to 1995, it fell from 31.2 to 10.7 percent of which about 15 percent was attributable to the decline in income from SOEs (NBS 2000, 256–257).

Consequently, the share of rural and urban households in national income grew steadily at the expense of those of government enterprises (Guo and Han 1991, 99). This change was of fundamental significance and became more evident when it translated itself into the new pattern of the national savings. One statistical study shows (Figure 6.1) that the share of government in national savings dropped from 38.5 to 1.7 percent during 1978–95, whereas that of households increased from 11.6 to 56.3 percent, emerging as the main source of national savings.

6.3.2   Adjustments of the corporate sector

Despite the increasing importance of private savings, the government rejected any possibility of a major-scale privatization. Instead, it tried to maximize state ownership and its control in the corporate sector. It imposed, however, some constraints on SOEs. One severely tightened in the last two decades of the twentieth century was that even SOEs had to pay or at least to

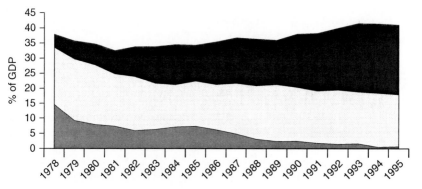

Figure 6.1   Change in the structure of national saving in China, 1978–95
Note: Black=households, white=enterprises, gray=government.
Source: Wu *et al.* (1998: 207–208).

commit themselves to pay for almost all of their inputs. Another constraint was that the government could not force households to deposit their money with state banks. These constraints and other factors led to the following four consequences and brought about a decline in state ownership.

First, a dynamic non-state sector emerged. The state can allocate funds only under the control of the state budget, state banks or SOEs. The second constraint above made it possible for private households to invest private savings directly, or indirectly through township and village collectives, in non-state firms. Private and other non-state enterprises, together with firms funded by FDI or township and village enterprises (TVEs), became the most dynamic in the corporate sector. From 1978 to 1997, the gross value of industrial output increased 14 times, while that of industrial SOEs increased only fourfold (NBS 1998a, 433).

Second, many SOEs were over indebted or *decapitalized*. An evaluation of assets by the government in the mid-1990s found that nearly 40 percent of the 302,000 nonfinancial SOEs were *empty shells* in the sense that their debts exceeded the assets even in terms of book value, and the value of state equities in them had been completely wiped out (Wu *et al.* 1998, 26). This percentage would certainly be much higher if assets were recorded in terms of market value and off-balance-sheet liabilities were taken into account. This was clearly a result of their adjusting to the emergence of private savings. Nevertheless, the government did not give up ownership and control of SOEs but began instead to channel private savings into SOEs through the state-owned banking system. Thus the state banks became the central institutions for channeling funds from private households to SOEs. Bank debt finance replaced fiscal finance and became the main source of finance to SOEs. This circumstance rapidly increased per capita household bank deposits and the indebtedness of SOEs. From 1978–95, per capita household bank deposits soared from RMB 21.9 to RMB 1,829.4 (PBC 1992, 6, 29; NBS 1997a, 622), while the average debt-to-assets ratio of SOEs went from less than 20 percent to 66 percent (China State Owned Assets Yearbook Editorial Group 1997, 446). Thus, bank debt finance temporarily kept the SOEs running and expanding with little equity investment from the budget, but this proved to be unsustainable. As indebtedness rose and operational losses eroded owner equity, more SOEs were virtually *decapitalized*. A substantial number of large SOEs were built with bank loans in 1985–95 and as a result became *zero-equity enterprises* from the very beginning. The state government was able to maintain its control rights in a large number of such enterprises with zero or negative net worth only because the major creditors were also state-owned and the rules and enforcement of bankruptcy law failed to protect non-state creditors properly.

Third, some SOEs were capitalized with non-state equity investments, and their ownership was diversified. Given the shortage of state equity investment and the nonsustainability of bank debt finance, some SOEs in better shape turned to non-state equity investment, with the support of the government. Two forms of such investment were introduced. One was overseas equity investments mainly by forming joint ventures; another was the one through the stock markets. In 1997, joint ventures and joint-stock companies together accounted for 21 percent of industrial output (NBS 1998a, 444, 456). When SOEs are transformed into joint ventures or listed on the stock exchange, the existing state equity holdings are typically not sold but diluted.[3]

Fourth, some nonviable SOEs were liquidated. Before the reform very few were bankrupted, since more than 80 percent of the assets were typically financed by state government grants as *free funds*. They became increasingly dependent on bank loans, however, and as funds from banks are not free and they had to be recorded as liabilities, even if these liabilities were calculated at a low administrative rate of interest. Thus, the government could monitor the risk to the banking system imposed by inefficient SOEs. In the mid-1990s the government decided to eliminate these gradually through bankruptcy procedures. Since 1994, the government has organized bankruptcy experiments in selected cities and sectors all over the country and liquidated about 3,470 SOEs,[4] including some very large ones. More SOEs were liquidated outside the experimental areas. Data from the Supreme People's Court show 22,471 cases during 1997–2000, of which 12,181 were SOEs.[5]

6.3.3   A financial system with the state as primary intermediary

The financial system in relation to the state government, the corporate sector, and households is summarized in Figure 6.2. Five main channels transfer financial resources from the household to the corporate sectors.

Channel 1: Part of the national income to be distributed to households is retained by the state and becomes budget revenue. It is invested in enterprises

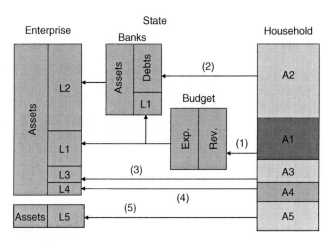

Figure 6.2 A financial system with the state as a primary intermediary

and results in state-owned equity (L1), which is essentially assets owned by the state on behalf of all Chinese citizens (A1).

Channel 2: Households deposit their savings with state banks and become holders of debt claims against the banks (L2), which are their private assets (A2).

Channel 3: Households invest part of their savings in equities of enterprises that are transformed from wholly state-owned enterprises into joint-stock companies (L3); these equity holdings become their private assets (A3).

Channel 4: Overseas investors participate in the ownership structure of former SOEs (L4) by acquiring shares or forming joint ventures (A4).

Channel 5: Households invest their savings in private firms, TVEs, acquire small SOEs, and turn them into joint-stock cooperatives in which all employees hold shares. These investments are recorded as equity on the balance sheets of such non-state enterprises (L5) and become another form of private assets (A5).

Channels (1) and (2) are explicitly monopolized by the state and have been the main sources of finance for the SOE sector. Channels (3) and (4) are also under heavy government intervention. For example, only the SOEs selected by the government can be listed on stock exchanges or form joint ventures with overseas investors. Evidently the allocation of capital continues to be dominated by the state, although in the case of China the situation is much more market-friendly than before the reform. A key to the corporate sector reform is the role of the state serving as a primary intermediary between the household and the corporate sectors.

6.4   Maintaining government solvency

The most important consequence of this financial system is the liabilities that the state incurs in raising funds for SOEs from the household sector. They are critical for two reasons. First, they represent one of the major constraints on China's corporate and financial sector reform. Second, efforts to maintain government solvency and social stability are likely to lead to a further withdrawal of the state from the corporate sector. This section explains what these liabilities are and why they can influence reform options and policies.

6.4.1   Explicit and implicit liabilities of the state

The state's liabilities under the bank debt finance system are explicit. There are binding contracts between state banks and household depositors specifying the obligations of the banks, which are effectively liabilities of the state. As Sheng (1996, 9) noted, the international experience of bank restructuring since the 1980s shows that irrespective of public or private ownership of banks, commercial bank losses in excess of capital must be borne by the state and thus are de facto quasi-fiscal deficits. This is particularly true in China because the state-owned banks have never been an independent means of administering capital allocation, and there has been an implicit state guarantee of the repayment of deposits.

The liabilities that the state incurred in raising funds for SOEs under the fiscal finance system are not obvious, since the part of national income that became state capital was retained before being distributed to households, and there is no binding contract specifying how much a household has contributed to the formation of state capital and so how much it is entitled to have returned. Since, however, households were left with too few savings to meet the financial needs of housing, pension, unemployment, medical services, education, etc., presumption of the state's responsibility to provide such services was inevitable. It made economic sense, therefore, to consider the state sector as a kind of comprehensive social security fund to which workers were forced to contribute part of their incomes before it was distributed to them, and in return, they were entitled to receive certain kinds of social services. The government's responsibilities in provision of such social services to government employees are, therefore, liabilities that the state incurs in raising funds through administratively determined low wage rates.

6.4.2   Settlement of state employees

There are two major categories of liabilities on the part of the state sector to its employees: pensions and unemployment insurance. As noted in a World Bank report, China's pension system faced an immediate and urgent problem, that is, a pension crisis in the SOE sector (World Bank 1996b, ix), which had been financed on a pay-as-you-go basis. When it was founded in the early 1950s, there were more than 400 workers for each retiree and the SOEs' contribution to the pension fund, which was equal to 3 percent of the wage bill, was sufficient to fund the system (World Bank 1996b, 3). At the outset of the reform, there were only 30 workers contributing to the pension system for each retiree. By 1995, this figure had dropped to five (Lardy 1998, 44). Many factors were responsible for this trend apart from the aging population, including the slow growth of employment in the state sector, which was obviously related to the rapid expansion of the non-state sector. One consequence of this crisis was the slowing down of SOE reform and restructuring. The bankruptcy or sale of an SOE raises the difficult issue of how the commitment to pensioners, along with other social welfare obligations of the enterprise, will be honored. "When alternative arrangements for pensions and other social services are not available, enterprise reform halts in its tracks since liquidations, joint ventures, or mergers cannot proceed smoothly until the social obligations of SOEs are assigned elsewhere" (World Bank 1996b, ix).

While the system was surely unsustainable, a transition to a sustainable funding system would be costly to the state, because additional financial resources would be needed to pay the current pensions and the accrued pension rights of workers who had contributed before the transition, referred to as the "implicit pension debt" of the state. According to an estimate by the World Bank, this amounted to 46–69 percent of GDP in 1994 (World Bank 1996b, 26).

Similarly to the pension system, the approach to coping with potential unemployment also became unsustainable. From the early 1950s, open unemployment in the state sector was suppressed mainly through a policy of job sharing, better known in China as a policy of *low wage and high employment*, meaning *five persons share three persons' work*. This approach became unsustainable for a number of reasons. One reason was that there was an absence of pooling in the sense that each enterprise bore the cost of its own potentially redundant employees. It follows that this approach would work only when every enterprise had sufficient cashflow. As the rise of non-state enterprises intensified competition and the reform hardened budget constraints, more SOEs found themselves in a poor financial situation and unable to support redundant employees. This has been particularly true over recent years since the government required banks to commercialize themselves and reduced administrative intervention in bank lending from local governments by centralization of the control in the banking system shortly after the Asian financial crisis. As a result, an increasing number of employees lost their income and work and became *xiagang* or laid-off workers. Although they were not called unemployed in official statistics because they remained employees of their enterprises in legal terms, the difference is not that significant. According to official statistics, which may have understated the scale of layoffs, 24.14 million employees were laid off in the SOE sector in 1997–99, and 17.64 million were *reallocated* or reemployed, leaving a stock of laid-off employees of 6.5 million at the end of 1999.[6]

China began to build an unemployment insurance system in the 1980s. It is funded by the contributions of enterprises, however, and far from capable of accommodating the potential unemployment. Only individuals officially classified as *urban registered unemployed*, whose numbers remained at around 5.7 million in the late 1990s, for example (NBS 2000, 115), can claim unemployment benefits from the formal unemployment insurance system. To cope with the pressure under SOE restructuring and World Trade Organization (WTO) accession, there was a requirement for the government to make available sufficient financial resources to raise the capacity of the formal unemployment insurance system.

6.4.3   Recapitalization of state banks

As state-owned commercial banks (SOCBs) have been the major vehicle used by the state to channel private savings to SOEs' investment and operations since the reform, the deterioration of the quality of their portfolio is unsurprising.

Reflecting the financial distress in the SOE sector and the weak position of the fiscal sector, SOCBs have been riddled by a huge amount of nonperforming loans (NPLs) for many years. After the establishment of four asset management companies (AMCs) in 1999, a total of RMB 1.3 trillion of NPLs was carved out from the big four SOCBs, but this figure was only part of the NPLs made before the end of 1995, and the total was obviously higher. Chinese banks were severely undercapitalized by international standards and since it was not an option for the government to default on household depositors, the need for a major recapitalization of SOCBs with public money was beyond any doubt. In addition, a large number of state-owned non-bank financial institutions such as Investment and Trust Companies (ITICs) were also in a poor financial condition. With an assumption of a 15 percent average recovery rate of NPLs under Asset Management Companies (AMCs), the head of the research department of the Peoples Bank of China (PBC) indicated that the total cost of restructuring the entire financial sector could reach RMB 2.5 trillion or 31 percent of 1999 GDP.[7]

6.4.4   Financial resources available

The main implication of the existence of implicit and explicit state liabilities is that corporate sector reform and restructuring could not succeed before the state made sufficient resources available to meet its financial obligations. The key question, therefore, was where the state could find the needed financial resources. There seemed to be at least five potential sources.

1. Tax revenue could be increased further. In 1999, tax revenue accounted for only 13 percent of GDP (NBS 2000, 257).

2. More government bonds could be issued. China had an unusual advantage in that its ratio of government debt to GDP was quite low. Besides, rapid growth would enable the government to sustain a high ratio of debt to GDP.
3. The government owned a large stock of housing assets which could be sold to employees in the state sector at discounted prices, compensating for their low wages in the past. The state could still expect to get back some revenue.
4. The state and SOEs could sell the land use rights in the market.
5. There was a huge stock of state-owned assets in the SOE sector. Their book value totaled RMB 9,096 billion in 1999, including RMB 5,330 billion of equity holdings in SOEs.[8] Although the return on assets had been very low, implying a large difference between book value and potential market value, this still represented the bulk of financial wealth of the state.

To summarize, the challenges and the policy options available can be outlined in a stylized balance sheet of the state (Table 6.3). Underlying is the notion that the state sector—comprising the fiscal sector, the financial sector, and the SOE sector should be regarded as one super company. Since the state could still reallocate resources among the three sectors, the binding constraint was the solvency of the entire state sector rather than one or another component. For instance, for the Chinese banking system (which

Table 6.3 A stylized balance sheet of the state

Assets	Liabilities
1. Present value of future non-debt revenue such as tax	1. Present value of non-debt expenditure obligations, including unemployment benefit, environmental cleanup
2. Net worth of SOEs, including market value of state equity holdings in joint-stock companies, joint ventures, and other enterprises	2. The outstanding stock of government internal and external debts
3. Net worth of state-owned financial institutions with nonperforming assets calculated at book value	3. The implicit pension debt
4. The market value of state-owned housing assets and other nonbusiness assets	4. The potential loss of nonperforming assets of state-owned financial institutions
5. The market value of state-owned land use rights	5. Other claims of non-state entities against the state sector
6. Other claims of the state sector against non-state entities	6. Net worth of the state, or the difference between the sums of assets and liabilities listed above

is hardly independent of the state budget), what mattered would be the solvency of the state rather than that of the banks themselves.

6.4.5   Financial difficulty of the state can drive ownership transformation

While inadequacy of funding often prompts the government to postpone or abort fundamental reform such as ownership transformation and corporate restructuring, it may also become a driving force for reform, because the potential insolvency of the state and the associated risks of social unrest and financial crisis would also be vital threats that the government could not afford to ignore. Given the constraints highlighted in Table 6.3, the government would find it hard to avoid ownership transformation to fulfill its financial obligations.

Chinese economists had been proposing the financing of the transition through the disposal of state-owned equity since the early 1990s. This idea was not accepted by the CPC and the government until the Fourth Plenum in 1999, which made the political decision to sell some of the state-held shares in listed companies to finance the social security system. In April 2000, explicitly admitting the nonsustainability of the existing system, the government revealed its determination to take more fundamental actions including sale of state equities. The Chinese Premier made it clear[9] that the government was prepared to solve the funding problem by significant means including the issuing of long-term government bonds and sales of state assets. A National Social Security Fund was set up to manage the proceeds of the sale of state-owned assets, and a detailed implementation plan was submitted to the CPC Central Committee for approval at the end of 2000. The system of reemployment centers based on a cost-sharing arrangement was recognized to be unsustainable and this recognition was to be followed by changes to the unemployment insurance system, eventually to take care of all laid-off workers, requiring more expenditure.[10]

As regards the banking sector, no sustainable alternative appeared to exist. When taking over the NPLs at their face value, AMCs are supposed to pay the bulk of their bills with their own bonds carrying a 2.25 percent interest rate, and the bonds are supposed to be guaranteed by the Ministry of Finance. Thanks to the growth in households' deposits, the replacement of NPLs with AMC bonds would be unlikely to push banks to the limit of their liquidity constraints. The potential risk of a banking crisis would not be alleviated by any measure, however, unless AMCs serviced their bonds properly and the Ministry of Finance honored its obligations. This would require a large amount of cash flow of AMCs which could only be generated by sales of assets, including debt-converted equities in SOEs, in the market. The state would eventually face a choice: to give up some of its ownership stakes and control in some SOEs or bear the same financial risk in the banking sector as it had before the establishment of the AMCs. The difficult position of the state budget and the challenge of WTO entry to the banking sector seemed to be sufficient for the government to accept the former, as was the case of the social security system.

6.5 Policy options

If the decision of *withdrawal* by the CPC in 1999 was to be fully implemented, the immediate question was how to withdraw. The structure of the system (as depicted in Figure 6.2) implied four possible paths of withdrawal:

1. privatization, that is, to sell or give away the state equity holdings of SOEs to non-state entities;
2. debt-equity swap followed by equity sale, that is, conversion of the debts of SOEs into equities and their sale in the market to non-state entities;
3. capitalization with transfer of control, that is, introduction into SOEs of non-state shareholders and the transfer of corporate control to them; and
4. liquidation, that is, the sale of the assets of SOEs to non-state entities in the market.

The central policy issue was then what path should be taken by what kind of enterprise. To analyze this issue, it is useful to categorize SOEs into four types.

First, SOEs can be divided into two groups: group I with positive net worth and group II with zero or negative net worth. Net worth here should be measured in terms of market value. Only group I enterprises can be privatized, while group II enterprises have no state equities to sell or give away.

Second, group II enterprises can be divided: IIA, viable enterprises and IIB, nonviable ones. Debt-equity swap and equity sale is meaningful only for type IIA, whereas type IIB is suitable only for liquidation.

Third, we can divide group I into *large* and *small* enterprises or type IA and type IB. If an enterprise is so large that it is unlikely to avoid a separation of ownership and control, it should be classified as a *large* or type IA enterprise. All others are *small* or type IB. This distinction is important because the privatization of the small or type IB enterprises involves much less complexity in terms of corporate governance and institutional backup.

6.5.1 Liquidation and restructuring

The Chinese government began to deal with group II enterprises systematically in 1994 in a pilot program of bankruptcy and merger (Zhang 1998). The primary constraint was identified as a lack of financial resources to settle with the laid-off and retired employees and compensate banks for their loss. Within the limits defined by the availability of financial resources, liquidation was implemented with the intention of providing an orderly exit to those nonviable SOEs, that is, type IIB enterprises. The primary targets for mergers were the enterprises that were in financial distress but still perceived as viable, that is, type IIA enterprises.

The Asian financial crisis and the prospect of WTO accession generated a large stock of nonperforming loans in the banking system, which was a most urgent issue for the government. In late 1998, a decision was finally made to clean up the banking system by following a good-bank-bad-bank approach and setting up four AMCs for the four major state banks in order to take over and dispose of their NPLs. The AMCs are authorized to conduct a wide range of transactions, including the sale of equity and debt holdings to domestic and overseas investors *in accordance with relevant regulations of the state.*

Since more than 40 percent of SOEs in China were effectively decapitalized, the main battlefield of any fundamental reform in the corporate sector had to be the liquidation and restructuring of SOEs, in all probability initiated by the AMCs. This battle would determine the probability of the reoccurrence of nonperforming loans in the banking system as well as the success or failure in restructuring the banks and reducing the burden on the fiscal system. The planned withdrawal of state ownership from these enterprises was thought likely by many to be the primary form of privatization in China, at least in the short term, which would be no surprise with full recognition of the significance of the emergence and accumulation of private savings during the last two decades of the twentieth century when the non-state sector and the entire economy enjoyed an unprecedented high rate of growth.

6.5.2   Privatization, incorporation and capitalization

Although the government ruled out any possibility of privatization as a solution to corporate sector reform, an exception was admitted with small SOEs. Since the Thirteenth National Congress of the CPC in 1987, the official stance had been that *some* small SOEs could be *sold* to private owners. There were not many such sales until the mid-1990s, when the then leadership proposed a strategy of *grasp the big and let go the small*. During 1995–97 a substantial number of small SOEs were sold to insiders under the name of *joint-stock cooperatives*. The authority regarded them as a variant of collective ownership in which workers owned their enterprise as shareholders. Typically shares were distributed to insiders either equally or with a bias in favor of the management at preferential prices. Outsiders also acquired minority shares in some cases.

The Fifteenth Communist Party National Congress in the autumn of 1997 was perceived by local governments as giving a green light to more open privatization not only of small but also medium and even large SOEs. More cases of insider privatization of small, medium, and large SOEs then took place. It is, however, worth noting that small and medium SOEs were on average in much worse shape than large ones and there would not be many enterprises of type IB left after the privatization of the previous years.

It was the relatively better performing large SOEs, that is, type IA, that would be the most challenging part of the reform, with at that time several good reasons to postpone more fundamental reform of these SOEs to a later stage. First, such firms are typically the leaders of their industries and the backbone of the economy. They are often of strategic importance because of their fields of industries and their contributions to the budget. Privatization of them would be in most cases politically unacceptable to the CPC. Second, the opportunity cost of privatizing them in the short term would be too high. The urgency of corporate sector reform stemmed from the heavy burden group II enterprises imposed on the financial and fiscal system, not from type IA enterprises. If the problems of group II enterprises could be resolved quickly and the sector of small and medium enterprises (SMEs), including privatized small and medium SOEs, could develop well, economic efficiency and stability could be substantially improved. The rational sequence of reform, therefore, seemed to be concentrating on group II and type IB before turning to type IA later on for more fundamental reform.

This was of course not to say that nothing should be done for type IA enterprises. Incorporation with participation of non-state investors can do a lot in improving performance, and this is indeed what the government has been doing. All large and medium-size SOEs are required to be incorporated with the participation of multiple, presumably non-state, investors. Even those *extremely few* SOEs that are not open to non-state investors must be held by *multiple* state entities. For those with expansion potential, capitalization is obviously a good way to incorporate. At the end of the period under discussion, some large SOEs were planning to enter the international capital market through Initial Public Offering (IPO), and more were shortly expected to be listed in the domestic stock market.

6.5.3 Corporate governance and institutions

By the end of the 1990s, it was much clearer than ten years earlier that private ownership leads to economic efficiency in large corporations only when corporate governance is sound and institutional backup is adequate (Frydman et al. 1996; Nellis 1999). Private ownership can be created relatively easily in the sense of residual claim, for example, by giving away state assets to citizens through a voucher program, but the privatization of corporate control is the critical part of any privatization program. This has certainly been true in the case of China's corporate sector reform and restructuring, with reallocation of corporate control being the critical issue wherever the state withdraws. Since almost all existing SOEs would need restructuring that was often *global* rather than *marginal* (Frydman et al. 1996) and the success or failure of restructuring is largely determined by the controlling party that implements the restructuring, reallocation of corporate control would be key for translating the reform into competitiveness, profitability, and efficiency. Similarly to what is found in other economies (LaPorta et al. 1999), China would face more or less the same set of options: widely dispersed ownership with insider control, family control, state control, institutional investors' control, or foreign company control. In the following years, corporate sector reform in China would have to cope with the challenge of corporate control reallocation. In particular, the pace of state withdrawal would be constrained by institutional developments such as improvement in investors' protection for a better-functioning dispersed ownership model; promotion of small and medium private enterprises as the basis of family control; the rules, institutions and human capital accumulation required by an active role of institutional investors in corporate control; and foreign direct investment through merger and acquisition.

6.6   Concluding remarks

By the end of the 1990s, state ownership in China's corporate sector had clearly declined with no large-scale privatization except for the agricultural sector. The shift from public savings to private savings played a key role in generating this trend. The mismatch between private savings in the household sector and state ownership in the corporate sector resulted in a sharp rise of indebtedness and decapitalization in a large fraction of SOEs and a fragile banking system riddled with a huge amount of NPLs. The household sector had accumulated a large number of claims over the state which struggled to collect funds to finance the SOE sector. The high financial and political risks associated with the banking, social security, and the fiscal systems forced the government to take actions that would eventually lead to privatization of most SOEs. Private savings also gave rise to a fast-growing non-state sector, including joint-stock companies and joint ventures as a result of capitalization of SOEs These in turn contributed to the accumulation of private savings. A shortage of equity investment and the need to change corporate governance would force more SOEs to be capitalized with non-state investment and a transfer of control in some cases. The privatization of small and medium SOEs and government support for other SMEs would further accelerate the growth of the non-state sector. The combination of these developments would create a much larger and more-developed private sector in the following years, further extending the rapid growth. This larger and more developed private sector combined, with a healthier financial and fiscal system, can provide the financial and entrepreneurial resources to absorb the remaining state sector and eventually complete the transition, making China's transition look like a movement characterized by *one step by the left foot, another step by the right foot.*

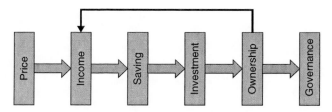

Figure 6.3   China's corporate sector reform: the logical path

Major risks would lie in three aspects; first, how well the government could manage potential fiscal risks with the high-level state liabilities; second, how well the government could manage the social aspects of corporate restructuring; and third, how efficient the reallocation of corporate control would be.

From the perspective of international comparison, there seems to have been a logical path underlying the reform in the Chinese corporate sector, as summarized in Figure 6.3. It was possible with many China-specific factors, such as a large rural sector before reform, FDI from an overseas Chinese community, etc. It may nonetheless illustrate the existence of one unique approach by which a state-owned corporate sector has been reformed.

Notes

The author wishes to thank Klaus Lorch of the World Bank for stimulating discussions on a number of issues involved in this paper, and Ari Kokko of Stockholm School of Economics for excellent comments. The author has also benefited from comments received from the participants of the International Workshop on Transitional Economics in Central-Eastern Europe and East Asia held in Budapest on November 24–25, 2000, and Bruno Dallago, in particular, as well as a seminar at the University of Washington held on February 1, 2001. The views expressed in the paper are entirely those of the author and should in no way be interpreted as the views of the World Bank.

1. Nambu (1970) tried to determine the source of capital accumulation in China for the First Five-Year Plan period, for which more data were available.
2. Also see World Bank (1997), p. 9.
3. Ownership transformation of this kind shares certain common features with the reform that took place in Bolivia in the 1990s, known as *capitalization* rather than traditional privatization (Pierce 1997).
4. A speech made by an official of SETC in a World Bank workshop on March 19, 2001.
5. A speech made by an official of the Highest People's Court in a World Bank workshop on March 19, 2001.
6. *People's Daily*, February 29, 2000.
7. *South China Morning Post*, October 24, 2000.
8. *People's Daily*, August 1, 2000.

9. *People's Daily,* April 27, 2000.
10. As of February, 2008 the proposal of proceeds of state-owned equities to finance social security system remains a proposal under discussion. However, the pension system has undergone a range of reforms, starting with an experiment in the three northeastern Provinces in 2001–04. The system of reemployment centers was ended during 2004–05. All laid-off workers are now taken care of by the formal unemployment insurance system.

References

China State Owned Assets Yearbook Editorial Group. 1997. *China State Owned Assets Yearbook 1996.* [In Chinese.] Beijing: China Economic Science Publishing House.

Frydman, Roman, Cheryl W. Gray, and Andrzej Rapaczynski. (eds.). 1996. *Corporate Governance in Central Europe and Russia.* Budapest: Central European University Press.

Guo, Shuqing, and Han Wenxiu. 1991. *The Distribution and Use of GDP in China.* [In Chinese.] Beijing: China People's University Press.

LaPorta, Rafael, Florencio Lopez-de-Silanes, and Andrei Shleifer. 1999. "Corporate Ownership around the World." *Journal of Finance* 54: 471–517.

Lardy, Nicholas. 1983. *Agriculture in China's Modern Economic Development.* New York: Cambridge University Press.

Lardy, Nicholas. 1998. *China's Unfinished Economic Revolution.* Washington, DC: Brookings Institution Press.

Marx, Karl. 1989. "Critique of the Gotha Programme." In *Collected Works,* Vol. 24, Karl Marx and Frederick Engels. Moscow: Progress Publishers.

Ministry of Finance. 1995. *Finance Yearbook of China, 1995.* [In Chinese.] Beijing: China Finance Journal (Zhongguo Cai Zheng Zazhi).

Nambu, Minoru. 1970. "The Sources of Socialist Accumulation in Communist China." *Kobe University of Commerce Working Paper,* No. 6, Kobe, Japan.

NBS. 1981. *China Statistical Yearbook 1981.* Beijing: China Statistical Publishing House.

NBS. 1997a. *China Statistical Yearbook 1997.* Beijing: China Statistical Publishing House.

NBS. 1997b. *China Statistical Yearbook on Investment in Fixed Assets, 1950–95.* Beijing: China Statistical Publishing House.

NBS. 1998a. *China Statistical Yearbook 1998.* Beijing: China Statistical Publishing House.

NBS. 1998b. *China Labor Statistical Yearbook 1998.* Beijing: China Statistical Publishing House.

NBS. 1999. *China Statistical Yearbook 1999.* Beijing: China Statistical Publishing House.

NBS. 2000. *China Statistical Yearbook 2000.* Beijing: China Statistical Publishing House.

Nellis, John. 1999. "Time to Rethink Privatization in Transition Economies?" *Finance and Development* 36(2): 16–19.

PBC. 1992. *China Financial Statistics, 1953–91.* Beijing: Financial Publishing House.

Peirce, Margaret H. (ed.). 1997. *Capitalization: The Bolivian Model of Social and Economic Reform.* Florida: Woodrow Wilson Center and North South Center of University of Miami.

Sheng, Andrew. 1996. *Bank Restructuring: Lessons from the 1980s.* Washington, DC: World Bank.

World Bank. 1996a. *The Chinese Economy, Fighting Inflation, Deepening Reforms.* Washington, DC: The World Bank.

World Bank. 1996b. *China: Pension System Reform*, Report No. 15121-CHA. Washington, DC: The World Bank.

World Bank. 1997. *China: 2020.* Washington, DC: The World Bank.

Wu, Jinglian, Zhang, Junkuo, Liu Shijin. (eds.). 1998. *Strategic Restructuring of the State Sector.* [In Chinese.] Beijing: China Development Publishing House.

Wu, Xiaoling. 1995. "Debt Restructuring Between SOEs and State Banks in China." *Comparative Economic and Social Systems* 3: 2–9. [In Chinese.]

Wu, Xiaoling. (ed.). 1998. *China's Finance in the New Round of Reform.* Tianjin: Tianjin People's Publishing House. [In Chinese.]

Zhang, Chunlin. 1998. "Debt Reduction, Bankruptcy and Enterprise Restructuring in Chinese State-Owned Sector." Paper presented at The Australian National University, Canberra, Feb.

Part III

The Role of the State and Market in Transition

Anybody may get rich before anybody else.
Don't be afraid of growing too fast.
Market economy may be promoted
in the Socialist system.
　　　　　　—Den Xiaoping, January, 1992

7
The Social Safety Net in China

Shoichi Ito

7.1 Introduction

The Chinese GDP growth rate was 9.2 percent in 1991; above 10 percent in 1992–95 and after a slight decline in 1996–2001, again above 10 percent from 2002–07. But along with such high growth rates, unusually its unemployment rate rose steadily until 2003. Unemployment has been the most serious issue in China in the second half of 1990s and the early twenty-first century. This problem includes the issue of laid-off workers,[1] because the number is as large as that of unemployed workers. An examination of both issues shows that the unemployment rate is very high in the age groups below 25 years, that in the age groups of 25 years and above has increased, and that of female workers is higher than that of male workers. University graduates have had difficulties in finding new jobs in recent years. Among laid-off workers, female workers of age 30 and above face more difficulties than male workers of comparable age. The rates of unemployment and laid-off workers differ from one region to another.[2]

Workers facing the possibility of layoff may resort to labor disputes to protect their living. A rapid increase in the number of labor disputes in the 1990s (Ito 1999b) was closely related to the increase in layoffs (Ito 2000). The size of payment given by the employer companies is very limited (Ito 2000). According to *1997 Survey of Chinese Workers Situations: the Volume of Statistics*, 73 percent of laid-off workers in the sample received payment below 200 yuan per month, and only 44 percent of them could derive their major financial source for their livelihood from their employer companies.[3] The aging of the population also has serious implications for the social safety net. According to Ou (2001), the share of the population of age 65 and above in 1990 was 5.6 percent, and is projected to rise to 8.2 percent in 2010, 15.3 percent in 2030, and 20.6 percent in 2050, and the ratio of the same group to the age group of 15–64 was 0.101 in 1995 and 0.109 in 1998,[4] but will be as high as 0.171 in 2030.[5] Clearly an aging population with the rising cost of medical insurance will pose serious problems soon. This chapter aims to discuss the social security system as a safety net mainly for urban workers and then examine the issues involved in broader provision of social security in China.

7.2   A brief history of the social security system in China

Substantial research on the Chinese social security system was undertaken in the 1990s.[6] Those studies include old-age insurance and unemployment insurance, consisting of four parts:

1. social relief for poor people,
2. social insurance for workers and employees,
3. social welfare for all the people, and
4. improvement of social treatment for military and related personnel.

The social insurance system in China consists of maternity insurance, medical insurance, unemployment insurance, old-age insurance, and labor-injury insurance. In addition, the government now has a basic system for securing living standards for laid-off workers and the employees of state-owned enterprises (SOEs).[7] The social security system has been established in urban and rural areas since the foundation of the People's Republic of China (PRC) in 1949. In rural areas the People's Commune System was responsible for the security of rural households and the land holdings. In September 1949, at the end of its general meeting, the People's Political Consultative Conference made a decision in the temporary constitution on "the Common Principle of People's Political Allies Conference of China," which included Article 23: "the gradual enforcement of a Labor Insurance System." On October 27, 1950, the draft of the Labor Insurance Regulations was made public. On February 26, 1951, the Labor Insurance Regulations were officially enforced. In January 1953, they were somewhat modified. The regulations were applied to all regular workers of state-owned, joint state and privately owned, and privately owned enterprises and their owners' family members.

The provisions of the insurance were mainly divided into two categories: labor insurance and welfare benefits for workers. The funds for the insurance came from the enterprises, and the amount of funding was equal to 3 percent of the total wage bill. Funds were deposited in particular national banks: 30 percent in the accounts of the All Chinese Trade Unions, and 70 percent in the accounts of enterprise trade unions. In the 1950s, various regulations and directions were announced concerning the social welfare for regular workers at various enterprises and organizations. In rural areas, in June 1956, high level agricultural cooperative societies were organized to help the farmers and other people with various types of difficulties. This social security system had no basic change from 1957 through 1983, despite many small modifications. But the Cultural Revolution seriously damaged it especially as regards the collection of funds.

7.3 The social safety net before 1995

The proportion of workers for whom the social safety net fully covered their cost of living was very small, and the difference in the benefits for urban and rural workers very large. Urban workers enjoyed unemployment insurance and public and enterprise's subsidy of medical care costs and other items, whereas rural workers were supposed to get support from the government and their communities for various aspects of social welfare. In fact, however, an individual rural worker might obtain help from the community if he/she had financial difficulties. Only if the community could not do so, could he/she get help from the government. In reality, the majority of rural workers remained outside the coverage of such a social safety net. Zhou Yong Shen Ge (1995) points out that according to 1990 statistics, only 29.5 percent of workers enjoyed social security, and, among them, only 1.9 percent of rural workers enjoyed the old-age insurance and help which was provided to really poor people with no family nor relatives. Rural workers were basically not covered under the social safety net.

According to the same study, public expenditure on medical care expanded rapidly from 2,700 million yuan in 1978 to 18,340 million yuan in 1988 and 31,500 million yuan in 1991. The reasons were the increase in the number of patients who enjoyed free medical services, the improvement in medical conditions, the price increase of medicines, and other problems in the Chinese medical care system that provided free medical services.[8]

7.4 The background and the structure of the social safety net in the 1980s and 1990s

Zhou Yong Shen Ge (1995) pointed out that in 1984 the government shifted the emphasis of reform from rural to urban areas and caused four issues: (1) limited coverage, (2) limited amount of social security funds, (3) inefficient management, and (4) the low level services of the social security system. In any case, social security was then integrated into the social development reform plans of central and local governments. Two new regulations were promulgated: (1) for old-age insurance for workers of various enterprises including SOEs and collectively owned enterprises and (2) for labor-management relations in foreign enterprises including the social insurance system. Funding was dependent on the payments to be made by individual workers, enterprises, and government.

A brief history of Chinese unemployment insurance in the 1990s is given by Guo Wuyan et al. (1999). When the PRC was founded, the most serious economic issue was the existence of innumerable unemployed workers.

The State Council authorized the labor department to promulgate the "Temporary Regulation of Relief of the Unemployed Workers." It established an early version of the unemployment relief system and contributed to the stabilization of the turmoil.

To improve the system, in July 1986 the State Council promulgated four regulations on employment: the "Temporary Regulation for the Waiting Job Insurance for the workers and employees of state-owned enterprises." In 1993, this regulation was modified so as to cover a larger range of workers and make some changes in the method of collecting insurance fees. In January 1999, the State Council promulgated the "Regulation of Unemployment Insurance" which became a part of the social security system under the market economy. The difference between the 1999 unemployment insurance and the 1993 regulation consists of the following:

1. unemployment insurance coverage became wider than before, when unemployment insurance was targeted at workers and employees of SOEs and collective-owned enterprises,
2. the unemployment insurance fees were raised; that is, to enterprises on a flexible ratio of between 0.6 percent and 1.0 percent to 2 percent and to individual workers to 1 percent,
3. the collection of unemployment insurance fund was leveled up,
4. the standard of unemployment insurance payments was improved,
5. the terms of expenditure of unemployment insurance were clearly specified in order to secure the unemployment insurance fund,
6. the system of monitoring and control of labor, public finance, and banks and the system of practicing control over both revenue and expenditure was established, and
7. the socialization of the administration for the provision system was regulated.[9]

According to Table 7.1, the employment structures of urban and rural workers have changed since the early days of economic reform in 1979. In urban areas, the number of SOE workers kept increasing until 1995 but began to decline after then, especially so after 1997, when it declined sharply. The number of workers in collectively owned units peaked in 1991 and then began to decrease. After 1997 it declined drastically and in 1999 became below half the level of 1991. On the other hand, the numbers of workers in private enterprises and self-employed individuals expanded rapidly in the 1990s. In rural areas, the number of workers in township and village enterprises (TVEs) was 28.27 million in 1978 and kept increasing, except in 1989 and 1990, until 1992, when double-digit growth rates started. This began declining soon after 1997, but numbers of workers in private enterprises and self-employed individuals showed an increasing trend in the 1990s. In 1999

Table 7.1 Number of employed persons at yearend by residence in urban and rural areas (10,000 persons)

Year	Urban area					Rural area			
	Sub-total	State-owned units	Collective-owned units	Private enterprises	Self-employed individuals	Sub-total	TVEs	Private enterprises	Self-employed individuals
1978	9,514	7,451	2,048	–	15	30,638	2,827	–	–
1980	10,525	8,019	2,425	–	81	31,836	3,000	–	–
1983	1,746	8,771	2,744	–	231	34,690	3,235	–	–
1984	12,229	8,637	3,216	–	339	35,968	5,208	–	–
1985	12,808	8,990	3,324	–	450	37,065	6,979	–	–
1986	13,293	9,333	3,421	–	483	37,990	7,937	–	–
1987	13,783	9,654	3,488	–	569	39,000	8,805	–	–
1988	14,267	9,984	3,527	–	659	40,067	9,545	–	–
1989	14,390	10,108	3,502	–	648	40,939	9,367	–	–
1990	17,041	10,346	3,549	57	614	47,708	9,265	113	1,491
1991	7,465	10,664	3,628	68	692	48,026	9,609	116	1,616
1992	7,861	10,889	3,621	98	740	48,291	10,625	134	1,728
1993	18,262	10,920	3,393	186	930	48,546	12,345	187	2,010
1994	18,653	11,214	3,285	332	1,225	48,802	12,017	316	2,551
1995	19,040	11,261	3,147	485	1,560	49,025	12,862	471	3,054
1996	19,922	11,244	3,016	620	1,709	49,028	13,508	551	3,308
1997	20,781	11,044	2,883	750	1,919	49,039	13,050	600	3,522
1998	21,616	9,058	1,963	973	2,259	49,021	12,537	737	3,855
1999	22,412	8,572	1,721	1,053	2,414	48,982	12,704	969	3,827
2000	23,151	8,102	1,499	1,268	2,136	48,934	12,820	1,139	2,934
2001	23,940	7,640	1,291	1,527	2,131	49,085	13,086	1,187	2,629
2002	24,780	7,163	1,122	1,999	2,269	48,960	13,288	1,411	2,474
2003	25,639	6,876	1,000	2,545	2,377	48,793	13,573	1,754	2,260
2004	6,476	6,710	897	2,994	2,521	48,724	13,866	2,024	2,066

Source: China Statistical Yearbook, 1994: 84–85; China Statistical Yearbook, 1996: 87; China Statistical Yearbook, 2005: 120–121.

they reached 9.69 and 38.27 million respectively. Thus in rural areas in the 1990s nonagricultural labor expanded, but agricultural labor declined.

The social security system in the 1990s was targeted at the workers in SOEs and the collectively owned sectors in urban areas. But numbers of workers kept expanding in nontraditional sectors there and in nonagricultural sectors in rural areas as well, and the social security system did not cover them. Its coverage had to be expanded.

7.5 Revenue and expenditure on social insurance

The social security system consists of old-age insurance, occupational injury insurance, medical insurance, maternity insurance, and unemployment insurance. Table 7.2 shows that the balance of funds continued to expand until 1997 and declined from 1997 to 1998.

In the same manner, the outlay from the total balance of social insurance continued to expand until 1997 and declined from 1997 to 1998. The net revenue of the total balance of social insurance rapidly expanded from 1993 to 1996 and declined rapidly from 1996 to 1998, especially in 1998.

If one compares the amounts of revenue of the various types of insurance, old-age insurance is in absolute terms the most important. It explains the changing pattern of the total balance of social insurance. The revenue, outlay, and net revenue of old-age insurance show the same patterns as those of the total balance. However, the net revenue of old-age insurance declined from 1996 through 1998 and even became negative in 1998. This change may indicate an uncertain future balance of funding for old-age insurance. Since the aging population problem will worsen soon, the negative net balance implies serious problems for China.

The second most important type of social insurance is medical insurance. Its revenue has expanded rapidly, and its outlay and net revenue also rapidly expanded from 1993 through 1998. It has no serious problem currently, although its future remains uncertain. Liu (1999) examines the future of the funds and expenditures of the Chinese social security system and concludes that his simple calculation guarantees its capacity to sustain national urban unemployment insurance including medical insurance.

We shall examine old-age insurance funded by state-owned, urban collectively owned, and other enterprises. According to Table 7.3, the ratio between retired workers and employees and the total number of workers and employees continued to increase from 21.63 percent in 1992 through 32.18 percent in 1998. If the ratios are examined sector by sector, large differences are observed among those ratios for three types of enterprises. The ratios of state-owned, collectively owned, and other enterprises were 20.48 percent, 28.76 percent, and 6.25 percent in 1992, respectively; and 32.26 percent, 38.34 percent, and 12.63 percent in 1998, respectively.

Table 7.2 The balance of social insurance funds (100 million yuan)

	Total					Medical insurance			
Year	Revenue	Outlay	Net revenue	Surplus at yearend	Year	Revenue	Outlay	Net revenue	Surplus at yearend
1993	526.1	482.2	43.9	303.7	1993	1.4	1.3	0.1	0.4
1994	742.0	680.0	62.0	365.7	1994	3.2	29	0.3	0.7
1995	1,006.0	877.1	128.9	516.8	1995	9.7	7.3	2.4	3.1
1996	1,252.4	1,082.4	170.0	696.1	1996	19.0	16.2	2.8	6.4
1997	1,458.2	1,339.2	119.0	831.6	1997	52.3	40.5	11.8	16.6
1998	1,623.1	1,636.9	-13.8	791.1	1998	60.6	53.3	7.3	20.0
1999	2,211.8	2,108.1	103.7	1,009.8	1999	89.9	69.1	20.8	57.6
2000	2,644.5	2,385.6	258.9	1,327.5	2000	170.0	124.5	45.5	109.8
2001	3,101.9	2,748.0	353.9	1,622.8	2001	383.6	244.1	139.5	253.0
2002	4,048.7	3,471.5	577.2	2,423.4	2002	607.8	409.4	198.4	450.7
2003	4,882.9	4,016.4	866.5	3,313.8	2003	890.0	653.9	236.1	670.6
2004	5,780.3	4,627.4	1,152.9	4,493.4	2004	1,140.5	862.2	278.3	957.9

	Old-age insurance					Occupational injury insurance			
Year	Revenue	Outlay	Net revenue	Surplus at yearend	Year	Revenue	Outlay	Net revenue	Surplus at yearend
1993	503.5	470.6	32.9	258.6	1993	2.4	0.4	2.0	3.1
1994	707.4	661.1	46.3	304.8	1994	4.6	0.9	3.7	6.8
1995	950.1	847.6	102.5	429.8	1995	8.1	1.8	6.3	12.7
1996	1,171.8	1,031.9	139.9	578.6	1996	10.9	3.7	7.2	19.7
1997	1,337.9	1,251.3	86.6	682.8	1997	13.6	6.1	7.5	27.7
1998	1,459.0	1,511.6	-52.6	587.8	1998	21.2	9.0	12.2	39.5
1999	1,965.1	1,924.9	40.2	733.5	1999	20.9	15.4	5.5	44.9

Continued

Table 7.2 Continued

Old-age insurance

Year	Revenue	Outlay	Net revenue	Surplus at yearend
2000	2,278.1	2,115.5	162.6	947.1
2001	2,489.0	2,321.3	167.7	1,054.1
2002	3,171.5	2,842.9	328.6	1,608.0
2003	3,680.0	3,122.1	557.9	2,206.5
2004	4,258.4	3,502.1	756.3	2,975.0

Occupational injury insurance

Year	Revenue	Outlay	Net revenue	Surplus at yearend
2000	24.8	13.8	11.0	57.9
2001	28.3	16.5	11.8	68.9
2002	32.0	19.9	12.1	81.1
2003	37.6	27.1	10.5	91.2
2004	58.3	33.3	25.0	118.6

Unemployment insur-ance

Year	Revenue	Outlay	Net revenue	Surplus at yearend
1993	17.9	9.3	8.6	40.8
1994	25.4	14.2	11.2	52.0
1995	35.3	18.9	16.4	68.4
1996	45.2	27.3	17.9	86.4
1997	46.9	36.3	10.6	97.0
1998	72.6	56.1	16.5	133.4
1999	125.2	91.6	33.6	159.9
2000	160.4	123.4	37.0	195.9
2001	187.3	156.6	30.7	226.2
2002	215.6	186.6	29.0	253.8
2003	249.5	199.8	49.7	303.5
2004	291.0	211.0	80.0	386.0

Maternity insurance

Year	Revenue	Outlay	Net revenue	Surplus at yearend
1993	0.8	0.5	0.3	0.8
1994	1.5	0.8	0.7	1.4
1995	2.9	1.6	1.3	2.7
1996	5.5	3.3	2.2	5.0
1997	7.4	4.9	2.5	7.5
1998	9.8	6.8	3.0	10.3
1999	10.7	7.1	3.6	13.9
2000	11.2	8.3	2.9	16.8
2001	13.7	9.6	4.1	20.6
2002	21.8	12.8	9.0	29.7
2003	25.8	13.5	12.3	42.0
2004	32.1	18.8	13.3	55.9

Source: China Labour Statistical Yearbook, 2003: 553; China Labour Statistical Yearbook, 2005: 573.

Table 7.3   Ratio between number of retired workers and employees and workers

Years	Total	State-owned enterprises	Urban collective-owned enterprises	Other enterprises
1992	21.63	20.48	28.76	6.25
1993	22.97	22.01	28.51	12.76
1994	24.48	23.79	29.71	11.47
1995	25.65	25.06	31.30	10.77
1996	26.93	24.94	32.08	13.27
1997	29.22	28.81	35.38	11.77
1998	32.18	32.26	38.34	12.63
1999	31.40	34.03	38.57	–
2000	32.36	–	–	–
2001	31.30	–	–	–
2002	32.42	–	–	–
2003	33.14	–	–	–

Source: China Labour and Social Security Yearbook, 1999: 535; China Labour and Social Security Yearbook, 2000: 661; China Labour and Social Security Yearbook, 2004: 557.

According to Table 7.4, the revenue and outlay of old-age insurance for SOEs both increased rapidly until 1997 and declined from 1997 to 1998. Net revenue increased rapidly until 1996 and started to decline in 1997 and became negative in 1998. In the case of collectively owned enterprises, both the revenue and outlay of old-age insurance increased from 1993 through 1998, except for a fall in revenue in 1997. However, net revenue was always negative from 1993 through 1998, its balance at the yearend became negative in 1995, and its negative value rapidly expanded from 1995 through 1998. On the other hand, revenue, outlay, net revenue, and balance at the yearend of old-age insurance of other enterprises continued to increase. In this sense, the important issue is how in future to compensate for the negative balance of old-age insurance of both SOEs and collectively owned enterprises.

There may be two ways in which to compensate for the negative balance of old-age insurance of such enterprises. One way is for the government to support them financially. The other way is to utilize the net balance of other enterprises to compensate for the negative balance of the SOEs and collectively owned enterprises or by combining them. The government has recognized the importance of expanding the coverage to various types of workers, including rural workers in urban areas, individual workers in urban areas, and workers of the TVEs.[10] Furthermore, the accumulated amount of insurance fees not paid rose to 38.3 billion yuan in the first half of 1999, which accounts for 24 percent of annual payments of old-age insurance. This is another important problem to be solved.[11] The net revenue of old-age insurance has expanded rapidly since 1999, because the growth rates of average nominal wage of staff and workers has exceeded 10 percent since 1999. This has expanded the yearend balance.

Table 7.4 The balance of enterprises' total old-age insurance funds

Old-age insurance funds

The balances of enterprises' total

Year	Revenue	Outlay	Net revenue	Balance at yearend
1993	5,035,402	4,706,303	329,099	2,585,889
1994	7,074,245	6,610,902	463,343	3,047,662
1995	9,500,507	8,476,087	1,024,420	4,298,338
1996	11,717,639	10,318,689	1,398,950	5,785,604
1997	13,379,100	12,513,300	865,800	6,828,500
1998	11,251,300	11,395,200	-143,900	5,874,100

Year	Revenue	Outlay	Net revenue	Balance at yearend
1993	737,853	760,869	-23,016	131,676
1994	912,068	1,022,695	-110,627	24,636
1995	1,112,733	1,181,729	-68,996	-25,493
1996	1,392,106	1,510,317	-118,211	-160,932
1997	1,362,500	1,675,300	-312,800	-486,500
1998	1,501,000	1,931,500	-430,500	-917,700

State-owned enterprises

Year	Revenue	Outlay	Net revenue	Balance at yearend
1993	4,121,355	3,824,911	296,444	2,373,503
1994	5,986,280	5,514,963	471,317	2,839,742
1995	8,025,770	7,162,391	863,379	3,904,164
1996	9,686,402	8,618,486	1,067,916	5,067,942
1997	11,308,500	10,585,900	722,600	5,987,700
1998	8,798,000	9,168,600	-370,600	4,570,200

Other enterprises

Year	Revenue	Outlay	Net revenue	Balance at yearend
1993	51,466	15,900	35,566	80,710
1994	175,897	73,244	102,653	183,284
1995	362,004	131,967	230,037	419,667
1996	639,131	189,886	449,245	878,594
1997	708,100	252,100	456,000	1,327,300
1998	952,100	295,600	656,500	1,931,800

Source: China Labour Statistical Yearbook, 1999: 515.

Consider unemployment insurance by region (Tables 7.5 and 7.6). The average ratio of the number of workers and employees contributing to unemployment insurance to the total number in 1996 and 2004 was 0.561 and 0.637, respectively. In this manner, the coverage of unemployment insurance increased from 1996 to 2004. The provinces that had high ratios in 1996 were Shanghai at 0.801, Tianjin at 0.764, Jiangsu at 0.716, Zhejiang at 0.671, Hebei at 0.665, Sichuan at 0.603, and Shaanxi at 0.594. These provinces and

Table 7.5 Data on unemployment insurance by region 1996

	A Number of workers and employees	B Number of contributors to unemployment insurance	C Number of beneficiaries unemployment insurance	B/A (%)	C/B (%)
National	148,453,000	83,330,573	3,307,884	56.1	4.0
Beijing	4,606,000	2,160,370	31,000	46.9	1.4
Tianjin	2,840,000	2,169,313	70,931	76.4	3.3
Hebei	6,962,000	4,632,411	62,329	66.5	1.3
Shanxi	4,649,000	2,352,760	100,584	50.6	4.3
Inner Mongolia	3,797,000	1,532,679	12,607	40.4	0.8
Liaoning	9,977,000	7,966,544	208,224	79.8	2.6
Jilin	5,133,000	2,935,110	27,254	57.2	0.9
Heilongji-ang	8,146,000	4,369,100	621,056	53.6	14.2
Shanghai	4,568,000	3,660,070	224,611	80.1	6.1
Jiangsu	9,055,000	6,482,984	116,503	71.6	1.8
Zhejiang	4,953,000	3,322,310	102,028	67.1	3.1
Anhui	5,025,000	2,017,921	83,922	40.2	4.2
Fujiang	3,505,000	1,326,542	52,378	37.8	3.9
Jiangxi	4,120,000	1,830,319	42,088	44.4	2.3
Shangdong	9,307,000	5,252,644	156,660	56.4	3.0
Henan	8,421,000	4,510,580	429,227	53.6	9.5
Hubei	7,380,000	3,928,877	118,747	53.2	3.0
Hunan	5,968,000	3,068,200	341,657	51.4	11.1
Guangdong	9,041,000	4,326,143	89,484	47.9	2.1
Guangxi	3,445,000	1,656,952	12,962	48.1	0.8
Hainan	1,028,000	410,820	5,173	40.0	1.3
Sichuan	9,874,000	5,953,577	154,943	60.3	2.6
Guizhou	2,316,000	872,028	19,573	37.7	2.2
Yunnan	3,154,000	1,355,315	6,657	43.0	0.5
Tibet	167,000	34,748	63	20.8	0.2
Shaanxi	3,980,000	2,362,329	54,814	59.4	2.3
Gansu	2,516,000	1,275,504	144,611	50.7	11.3
Qinghai	656,000	294,530	2,823	44.9	1.0
Ningxia	727,000	317,723	6,593	43.7	2.1
Xinjiang	3,136,000	952,170	8,402	30.4	0.9

Source: China Labour Statistical Yearbook, 1999: 522; China Labour Statistical Yearbook, 1997: 139.

Table 7.6   Data on unemployment insurance by region 2004

	A Number of workers and employees	B Number of contributors to unemployment insurance	C Number of beneficiaries of unemployment insurance	B/A (%)	C/B (%)
Total	166,139,000	105,839,000	4,190,000	63.7	4.0
Beijing	7,236,000	3,082,000	38,000	42.6	1.2
Tianjin	2,462,000	1,951,000	510,00	79.2	2.6
Hebei	6,444,000	4,790,000	110,000	74.3	2.3
Shanxi	4,531,000	2,865,000	54,000	63.2	1.9
Inner Mongolia	3,434,000	2,223,000	58,000	64.7	2.6
Liaoning	8,678,000	6,162,000	817,000	71.0	13.3
Jilin	4,446,000	2,822,000	122,000	63.5	4.3
Heilongji-ang	6,800,000	4,758,000	97,000	70.0	2.0
Shanghai	5,643,000	4,878,000	159,000	86.4	3.3
Jiangxu	10,549,000	7,971,000	436,000	75.6	5.5
Zhejiang	8,397,000	4,284,000	113,000	51.0	2.6
Anhui	5,424,000	3,711,000	264,000	68.4	7.1
Fujian	5,060,000	2,664,000	95,000	52.6	3.6
Jiangxi	4,344,000	2,266,000	72,000	52.2	3.2
Shandong	11,855,000	7,475,000	306,000	63.1	4.1
Henan	8,695,000	6,816,000	223,000	78.4	3.3
Hubei	7,115,000	3,913,000	170,000	55.0	4.3
Hunan	6,481,000	3,805,000	98,000	58.7	2.6
Guangdong	13,714,000	10,058,000	234,000	73.3	2.3
Guangxi	4,038,000	2,264,000	98,000	56.1	4.3
Hainan	1,165,000	579,000	21,000	49.7	3.6
Chongqing	3,279,000	1,934,000	92,000	59.0	4.8
Sichuan	7,295,000	3,986,000	126,000	54.6	3.2
Guizhou	2,658,000	1,299,000	12,000	48.9	0.9
Yunnan	3,714,000	1,732,000	105,000	46.6	6.1
Tibet	291,000	67,000	–	23.0	–
Shaanxi	4,592,000	3,255,000	72,000	70.9	2.2
Gansu	2,638,000	1,610,000	43,000	61.0	2.7
Qinghai	785,000	331,000	12,000	42.2	3.6
Ningxia	882,000	364,000	12,000	41.3	3.3
Xinjiang	3,494,000	1,924,000	77,000	55.1	4.0

Source: China Labour Statistical Yearbook, 2004: 13, 584.

municipalities are located in the coastal region or the urban centers of northeast and southeast China. The provinces in interior regions, however, have relatively low coverage ratios. A similar pattern is observed in 2004.

The ratio of the number of workers receiving unemployment insurance to those contributing to unemployment insurance averaged 0.040 in both 1996 and 2004. The provinces whose ratios exceed 0.10 are Heilongjiang at

Table 7.7 Balance of unemployment insurance by region 1996 (10,000 yuan)

	Revenue	Outlay	Relief	Net revenue	Balance at yearend
National	452,491.1	272,896.6	138,704.0	79,594.5	863,802.6
Beijing	25,106.6	8,521.0	2,074.0	16,585.6	42,485.0
Tianjin	11,094.6	8,394.7	7,207.0	2,699.9	17,592.7
Hebei	21,459.5	15,758.6	807.0	5,700.9	34,428.9
Shanxi	11,276.8	5,477.3	859.0	5,799.5	27,733.2
Inner Mongolia	6,443.9	3,753.9	1,956.0	690.0	15,723.2
Liaoning	24,387.2	17,711.3	10,977.0	6,675.9	50,700.3
Jilin	9,905.3	5,256.7	2,671.0	648.6	24,786.7
Heilongjiang	14,404.4	9,102.2	4,870.0	5,302.2	40,026.9
Shanghai	40,753.0	21,999.0	12,987.0	8,754.0	38,825.0
Jiangsu	37,565.2	25,608.3	15,379.0	11,956.9	67,246.7
Zhejiang	29,511.0	15,773.5	8,134.0	13,737.5	41,310.5
Anhui	13,727.3	8,444.7	5,070.0	5,282.6	23,074.8
Fujiang	10,009.0	6,527.0	580.0	482.0	22,443.0
Jiangxi	8,084.2	3,264.3	825.0	4,819.9	22,667.7
Shandong	27,287.1	18,643.0	797.0	8,644.1	51,091.6
Henan	19,725.9	13,502.3	6,448.0	6,223.6	33,826.3
Hubei	16,760.2	11,103.2	429.0	5,657.0	38,815.5
Hunan	18,172.7	13,364.7	6,294.0	808.0	32,958.1
Guangdong	28,648.7	18,046.0	9,350.0	10,602.7	60,865.0
Guangxi	8,392.7	4,423.5	1,403.0	3,969.2	20,461.7
Hainan	2,741.0	1,193.5	322.0	1,547.5	6,022.2
Sichuan	26,419.9	13,352.9	6,426.0	13,067.0	59,068.9
Guizhou	3,457.9	1,393.3	1.0	2,064.6	9,752.7
Yunnan	7,914.4	4,210.4	172.0	3,704.0	14,254.2
Tibet	219.4	60.6	6.5	158.8	903.8
Shaanxi	11,977.0	10,221.0	845.0	1,756.0	21,908.0
Gansu	6,859.5	3,451.2	1,680.0	3,408.3	20,158.8
Qinghai	1,474.7	565.3	55.0	909.4	4,548.7
Ningxia	1,217.2	607.4	169.0	609.8	3,672.9
Xinjiang	7,494.8	3,068.8	209.0	4,426.0	16,449.6

Source: China Labour Statistical Yearbook, 1999: 522.

0.142, Hunan at 0.111, and Gansu at 0.113, all of which are located in the interior regions. The province that exceeds 0.10 in 2004 is only Liaoning at 0.133, and the ratios of Anhui and Yunnan are 0.076 and 0.061. Liaoning province has faced the serious difficulty of SOEs, while Anhui and Yunnan are located in interior region. This may indicate that SOEs and collectively owned enterprises faced serious competition with other enterprises and also had to face unemployment issues.

Next, Tables 7.7 and 7.8 show the balance of unemployment insurance by regions. Their revenue and outlay increased from 1996 to 2004 with positive

Table 7.8   Balance of unemployment insurance by region 2004 (10,000 yuan)

	Revenue	Outlay	Relief	Net revenue	Balance at yearend
National	2,907,797.1	2,112,764.1	374,983.1	795,033.0	3,857,680.8
Beijing	55,597.0	108,344.0	60,461.0	7,253.0	161,852.0
Tianjin	64,578.7	30,629.7	24,932.4	33,949.0	67,303.1
Hebei	101,162.7	61,976.6	35,522.0	39,186.1	212,914.2
Shanxi	42,521.9	25,796.5	12,834.9	16,725.4	107,594.5
Inner Mongolia	36,494.5	25,404.7	19,431.1	11,089.8	57,353.6
Liaoning	255,648.5	295,303.0	268,829.3	–39,654.5	–79,099.9
Jilin	56,447.0	35,632.0	25,838.0	20,815.0	65,606.0
Heilongjiang	82,964.6	46,162.2	36,072.3	36,802.4	193,321.2
Shanghai	295,110.6	294,345.9	66,653.3	764.7	84,507.9
Jiangxu	266,936.2	211,320.5	147,296.1	55,615.7	272,100.8
Zhejiang	157,718.8	66,315.9	56,617.4	91,402.9	242,689.1
Anhui	80,319.3	81,869.8	61,449.4	–1,550.5	28,257.1
Fujian	70,022.4	42,153.7	33,358.9	27,868.7	124,384.6
Jiangxi	36,655.9	31,166.1	14,772.6	5,489.8	75,592.8
Shandong	205,434.0	132,163.0	99,286.0	73,271.0	306,523.0
Henan	98,724.6	79,599.5	55,480.6	19,125.1	208,680.6
Hubei	77,454.0	57,933.8	40,128.1	19,520.2	82,719.0
Hunan	67,888.3	60,950.3	29,574.1	6,938.0	25,982.8
Guandong	279,832.0	124,691.0	98,531.0	155,141.0	556,151.0
Guangxi	56,081.6	33,873.6	28,983.5	22,208.0	139,091.9
Hainan	16,252.0	6,943.3	6,183.6	9,308.7	38,020.8
Chongqing	36,372.5	27,963.4	24,791.2	8,409.1	23,068.8
Sichuan	90,719.9	73,607.0	30,663.6	17,112.9	145,687.1
Guizhou	36,169.3	8,492.3	3,528.6	27,677.0	137,073.9
Yunnan	52,492.4	51,020.8	34,157.3	1,471.6	95,447.3
Tibet	4,378.1	595.7	3.4	3,782.4	17,680.4
Shaanxi	64,191.5	31,524.3	20,730.1	32,667.2	95,078.2
Gansu	31,223.5	23,731.1	11,872.8	7,492.4	64,055.3
Qinghai	10,002.1	3,658.6	1,927.1	6,343.5	21,473.7
Ningxia	8,726.1	4,366.4	3,122.4	4,359.7	23,649.5
Xinjiang	69,677.6	35,229.7	21,951.1	34,447.9	162,920.6

Source: China Labour Statistical Yearbook, 2004: 587–589.

balance, except for two provinces, Liaoning and Anhui that have negative balance in 2004. The unemployment situation may be worse in Lioaning in 2004 than 1996.

The proportion of workers and employees of SOEs and collectively owned units has become below that of the other enterprises especially in some coastal provinces and municipalities (Table 7.9). It shows the shares of workers and employees contributing to unemployment insurance by region in 2004. The national average share of workers and employees' contributions to unemployment insurance is 39.98 percent. Table 7.9 shows the high shares of provinces such as Shanghai (86.44 percent), Tianjin (79.24 percent), Henan (78.39 percent), Jiangsu (75.56 percent), Hebei (74.33 percent), Guangdong (73.34 percent), Liaoning (71.01 percent), mostly in coastal regions. The shares of provinces and autonomous regions in the North-West and South-West are very low. Regional divergences are very clear.

Workers' and employees' contributions to unemployment insurance show large differences among SOEs, collectively owned and other enterprises, including foreign-funded enterprises. The shares of the first two are 43.69 percent and 10.09 percent respectively in 2004, and that of other enterprises is 23.21 percent. As a trend. the shares of the first two have declined, whereas that of others has increased. The latter contributions have expanded. This is a good trend, especially with private and individual enterprises, for the future sound funding of unemployment insurance.

7.6   Concluding remarks

Ito (1999c) pointed out that a large number of rural workers who immigrated into cities were laid off by SOEs and urban collectively owned enterprises. This is the most critical issue in the Chinese economy under reform. The employment structures of urban and rural areas are changing drastically, so that the social security system originally targeted at the traditional sectors no longer covers the workers in nontraditional urban sectors as well as the rural workers in nonagriculture and agriculture. Bai Jie (2000) briefly described reforms of the social security system for rural workers. For example, various related government organizations like the public health and agriculture departments jointly promulgated a draft regulation concerning medical services based on the rural cooperatives in December 1979.

On January 3, 1992, the public service department promulgated the rules of a prefecture level rural social old-age insurance fund. On October 19, 1995, the State Council promulgated its opinion concerning further improvement of the rural social old-age insurance system. It is still at the formative stage to be completed later.

Wu (1999) introduced three basic principles of the social security system included in *The decision of some problems concerning establishment of the market economy system under socialism* by the Third Party Plenum (1993). These

1. established a total, simultaneous, and multilevel social security system,
2. put the old-age insurance system for urban workers and employees on a contribution basis, establishing individual accounts that would be borne by employers and employees, and
3. separated the social security administration from the management of social welfare funds.

Table 7.9 Urban employment and unemployment insurance by region 2004

				Urban Employment		
	Total	State-owned enterprises	Collectively owned enterprises	Other enterprises	Private enterprises, individuals	Total
Total	26,476.0	6,709.9	897.2	3,491.8	5,515.0	10,583.9
Beijing	723.6	99.5	28.2	275.2	220.8	308.2
Tianjin	246.2	92.1	12.5	89.3	52.3	195.1
Hebei	644.4	360.8	40.2	93.1	150.3	479.0
Shanxi	453.1	258.4	37.5	66.0	91.1	286.5
Inner-Mongolia	343.4	166.6	13.5	62.9	100.3	222.3
Liaoning	867.8	309.0	45.6	148.0	365.1	616.2
Jilin	444.6	199.0	25.5	60.2	159.9	282.2
Heilongjiang	680.0	328.5	47.1	130.6	173.8	475.8
Shanghai	564.3	149.3	17.0	164.8	233.1	487.8
Jiangxu	1,054.9	293.0	43.8	270.1	448.0	797.1
Zhejiang	839.7	179.1	35.9	241.5	383.1	428.4
Anhui	542.4	215.6	35.3	90.5	201.0	371.1
Fujian	506.0	151.3	22.0	204.4	128.3	266.4
Jiangxi	434.4	202.2	18.7	50.5	163.1	226.6
Shandong	1,185.5	492.5	68.8	230.8	393.4	747.5
Henan	869.5	408.8	96.1	191.0	173.6	681.6
Hubei	711.5	320.9	38.2	150.8	201.6	391.3
Hunan	648.1	298.6	32.7	62.3	254.5	380.5
Guangdong	1,371.4	374.3	72.3	384.1	540.7	1,005.8
Guangxi	403.8	200.5	21.8	53.9	127.5	226.4
Hainan	116.5	58.1	3.9	12.6	41.9	57.9
Chongqing	327.9	123.6	17.2	0.7	114.3	193.4
Sichuan	729.5	317.1	45.6	137.4	229.3	398.6
Guizhou	265.8	147.1	13.6	41.9	63.3	129.9
Yunnan	371.4	178.0	13.6	54.3	125.4	173.2
Tibet	29.1	16.3	0.5	0.8	11.7	6.7
Shaanxi	459.2	251.3	23.9	56.4	127.6	325.5
Gansu	263.8	157.6	14.9	21.1	70.2	161.0
Qinghai	78.5	34.1	2.3	6.1	36.0	33.1
Ningxia	88.2	38.4	1.9	20.1	27.7	36.4
Xinjiang	349.4	188.2	6.9	48.5	105.9	192.4

Source: China Labour Statistical Yearbook, 2004: 13, 585–586.

(10,000 persons)

	Contributors at end of yearend					
	Enterprises					
	State-owned enterprises	Collectively owned enterprises	Other Enterprises	Foreign-funded enterprises	Institutes	Others
8,148.4	4,624.4	1,067.7	2,456.4	784.5	2,255.9	179.5
236.7	92.8	12.8	131.1	32.1	71.5	–
162.8	95.7	18.5	48.6	32.0	32.2	–
354.7	237.0	43.8	73.9	19.8	122.9	1.3
240.5	212.6	25.7	2.2	1.0	45.6	0.4
157.5	92.4	12.1	53.0	5.2	62.3	2.5
467.3	214.0	120.7	132.5	38.3	108.8	40.2
233.0	189.4	20.5	23.1	3.2	48.5	0.6
425.5	322.5	71.8	31.2	13.9	49.8	0.4
365.3	99.4	35.6	230.3	68.3	63.4	59.0
640.9	242.9	122.2	275.8	102.2	141.6	14.6
321.7	70.4	34.8	216.5	36.1	93.0	13.8
281.3	170.0	53.3	58.0	6.3	88.7	1.1
216.7	67.9	21.6	127.2	60.6	47.4	2.3
152.4	132.3	10.6	9.6	1.6	74.0	0.1
586.2	382.7	97.1	106.3	39.9	158.8	2.5
508.9	336.9	93.9	78.2	10.0	167.8	4.9
284.3	222.5	30.3	31.5	10.7	105.7	1.3
255.4	204.1	26.4	24.8	7.1	123.0	2.1
883.6	226.7	81.6	575.3	268.8	101.3	20.9
139.0	102.3	12.8	23.9	4.0	87.1	0.3
43.6	32.6	3.1	7.9	2.7	12.8	1.5
154.4	114.3	28.1	2.0	4.0	36.4	2.7
270.6	160.5	21.1	89.0	8.3	126.5	1.6
89.3	77.1	5.3	6.9	1.6	40.6	0.1
117.0	73.0	15.4	28.6	1.4	55.0	1.1
2.8	2.8	–	–	–	3.9	–
251.9	198.0	28.8	25.1	3.2	71.3	2.3
120.6	98.4	13.4	8.8	1.1	39.9	0.4
21.6	16.7	0.7	4.2		11.1	0.3
25.9	22.9	1.2	1.8	0.1	10.4	0.2
137.0	113.5	4.5	19.0	1.2	54.5	0.9

Wu (1999) also points out that the unfunded liabilities for the retired workers and employees are the major issues of the social security system in China. Thus, old-age insurance is the most important in the amount of funds. In 1998 its net revenue happened to be negative but has become positive ever since and expanded. perhaps as a result of the increase in the wage rates in various enterprises. In the immediate future, this trend will overcome the rising ratio of retirees to workers in the urban labor force, but the retirees to workers ratio will keep on expanding as a result of the one child policy and may tip the future balance of not only old-age insurance but also social insurance as a whole. Preparation for such a future situation is an urgent priority. As for medical insurance, for instance, its revenue, outlay, and net revenue expanded from 1993 onwards so it currently seems to have no serious problems. But the aging population will tip the balance of its funding in the future. In the 1990s, the proportion of groups of workers and employees who contributed greatly to the unemployment insurance system started to decline, whereas those of the other groups whose contributions were very low began to increase. It is essential, therefore, to find ways and means to raise the contributions of groups of workers and employees outside SOEs and collectively owned enterprises for the future balance of unemployment insurance.

Notes

1. XiaGang in Chinese was translated into English as *displaced workers* in *China Labour Statistical Yearbook, 1998* but as *laid-off workers* in *China Labour Statistical Yearbook, 1999*.
2. Ito (1999a) shows the various aspects of unemployment and laid-off workers in China.
3. Ito (1999b), pp. 562–565 and Ito (2000), pp. 16–19.
4. Ou (2001), pp. 17–18.
5. Li, Cheng (2000), p. 272.
6. Bai Jie (2000), pp. 102–118.
7. *Ibid.*, pp. 94–102.
8. Zhou Yong Shen Ge (1995), pp. 90–91.
9. State Council, Office of Law System, Labor Security Department, and Labor & Social Security Ministry, Law System Department (1999), pp. 85–86.
10. He Xiao Yi (1998), pp. 56–57.
11. Ou (2001), p. 43.

References

Bai Jie. 2000, "Chongguo Shehui Baozhang Lirung Yanzhu ye Zhide Bianqian" [The Theoretical Research of Social Security of China and Changes in System]. In *Chongguo Shehui Baoxhan Dhixi Gaige ye Wansheng* [Reform and Improvement of Social Security System of China], Cheong Su Wei (ed.). Beijing: Democracy and Construction Publisher. [In Chinese.]

Guowuyan Fazhi BangongShi Chengfa Raodong Baozhang Su ye Raodong he
Shehui Baozhangbu Fazhi Su [State Council, Office of Law System, Labor Security
Department and Labor & Social Security Ministry, Law System Department] (ed.).
1999. *Shehui Baoxianfei Zhongji Jianxin Diaoli he Shehui Baoxian Diaoli Xieye* [The
Interpretation of Temporary Regulation for Collecting the Social Insurance Costs
and the Regulation for Unemployment Insurance]. Beijing: The China's Labor and
Social Security Publisher. [In Chinese.]

He Xiao Yi. 1998. *Zouxiang 21Shiji De Zhongguo Shehui Baoxian* [China's Social Insurance
Toward the 21st Century]. Beijing: China's Labor Publisher. [In Chinese.]

Ito, Shoichi. 1999a. "Chugoku ni okeru Shitsugyo Mondai" [The Unemployment Issues
in China]. *Osaka Gakuin University, Economic Review* 13(1, 2): 1–41. [In Japanese.]

Ito, Shoichi. 1999b. "Chugoku niokeru Roudousougi" [The Labor Disputes in China].
Kwansei Gakuin University, Economic Review 52(3): 561–585. [In Japanese.]

Ito, Shoichi. 1999c. "The Characteristics of Transition in the Chinese Economy."
In *Recent Lessons From Transition and Privatization, Proceedings of the Third ECPD
International Round Table*, Negoslav P. Ostojic and Norman Scott (eds.). Belgrade:
European Center for Peace and Development (EPCD) of the University for Peace
established by the United Nations.

Ito, Shoichi. 2000. "The State-owned Enterprises' Reform and its Impact on Labor
Market in China." Presented at ICEAD, Transitional Economies—Comparison
of Transition in Central-Eastern Europe and East Asia, Kitakyushu, Japan, Mar.
30–31.

Li, Cheng et al. 2000. "Yanglao Shehui Baoxian de Pingheng Wenti Fenxi" [The
Analysis of the Balance Problem of Old Age Social Insurance]. In *Zhongguo Shehui
Baozhan Tixi Gaige yu Wanshang* [The Reform and Improvement of China's Social
Security System], Cheon Suwei (ed.). Beijing: Democracy and Construction
Publisher. [In Chinese.]

Liu, Shaojia. 1999. "Chongguo shi Feinong Yongyou Yige Wanshen de Quanguo
Dongshou de Chengzhen Shiye Shehui Baozhang Tishi" [Can China Have a Perfect
National Unemployed Social Security System?]. In *Chongguo Shehui Baozhang Dizhi
Gaige* [Social Security Reform in China], Dianqing Xu, Jason Yin, and Tuxin Zheng
(eds.). Beijing: Economic Science Press. [In Chinese.]

Ou, Bunryou. 2001. *21Seiki ni mukeru Chugoku no Shakaihosho* [The China's Social
Security for the 21st Century]. Saitama: Nihonkyouhou. [In Japanese.]

Wu, Jinglian. 1999. "Chongguo Shehui Baozhang Dizhi Gaige: Wenthi he Chure"
[Reforming the Social Security System-Problems and Perspectives]. In *Chongguo
Shehui Baozhang Dizhi Gaige* [Social Security Reform in China], Dianqing Xu, Jason
Yin, and Tuxin Zheng (eds.). Beijing: Economic Science Press. [In Chinese.]

Zhou Yong Shen Ge. 1994. *Shehui Furi de Bianzao-Chongguo Shehui Baozhang Wendi*
[Variation of Social Welfare—The Social Security Issues of China]. Beijing: Chong
Gong Chong Yang Publisher. [In Chinese.]

8
The State and the Transformation of Economic Systems

Bruno Dallago

8.1 Introduction

Most Central and Eastern European countries (CEECs) did not properly recognize the role of the state in the transformation process, and so the conditions needed to realize an orderly and productive transformation were missing. They could not undertake political reform of the state before economic transformation. Their policies mostly disregarded the differences in political, social, and economic conditions, institutions, and their respective perspectives. This chapter purports to offer a classification of these differences and suggest how the role of the state should be adapted to these differences. Although it is desirable that the proper reform of the state precedes privatization and stabilization, the cases of some countries that confronted the economic transformation without the preceding political reform are also discussed.

In 1989 the CEECs were in great turmoil. A long historic era of the greatest social, political, and economic experiment involving two to three generations was ending as an apparent failure. Few scholars and policymakers have been truly concerned with the legacy of that experiment. Various scholars and policymakers thought, however, that it was high time for a new, grand experiment. Some named themselves the *new Bolsheviks* or *market-Bolsheviks*. They took over the economies and societies torn down by the *wrong-Bolsheviks* to restore the *normal* life. As the Polish stressed with their usual bitter humor, they tried to convert fish soup into an aquarium, after their predecessors had attempted to convert an aquarium into fish soup.

Anatoly Chubais, the leading figure in Russian privatization, is credited with having answered a question on his role as privatization minister between 1992 and 1994. "Chubais conceded that his privatization efforts could be characterized as *Bolshevik style*—lacking public support and quickly executed. His strategy was to privatize as quickly as possible, using every minute of the day to privatize. 'I did not speak, I privatized', Chubais proclaimed."[1]

In a similar fashion, Yegor Gaidar, the Minister of Stabilization and Privatization in 1992, stresses that "the gradualist approach to transforming a communist economy is the strategy of a communist or totalitarian regime trying to adapt to new realities. But shock treatment is usually the only alternative for a postcommunist government coming to power after the strategy of the previous regime or bad luck has led to the failure of the gradualist approach."[2]

Clearly these are extreme examples in the sense that the authors proclaim themselves *extremists* and Russia was certainly on the extreme of the transitional countries' spectrum. It was an outlier in economy, society, and politics but other countries faced definitely more moderate and less problematic situations largely as a result of pretransition reforms. The old debate on shock therapy *vs.* gradualism vanished without contributing much to the theoretical and practical clarification of the issue.[3] As Kornai stresses, the question in the debate was badly put:

> I am convinced that speed, while important, is not the primary measure of success. Excessive emphasis on speed leads to impatience, aggressiveness and arrogance. The expression *mass privatization* used as a synonym of give-away and voucher schemes is the inverse of the *mass collectivization* familiar in the history of Stalinism. I do not want to exaggerate the comparison. Nonetheless, there were similarities: the subordination of the ownership reform to political and power purposes, the horror of gradual change, the impatience, and the obsession with speed.[4]

Gaidar acknowledged also the power dimension. "In adopting a universal approach [to privatization], however, we somehow had to take into account the interests of the various social groups that had the power to block the implementation of the privatization procedures: for instance, the managers of the State enterprises, the working collectives, and the regional centers of power."[5]

Both sides in the debate and many critics overlook an important question: the consequences of the chosen transformation and stabilization strategies. There are some aspects to this question, of which output's drop or recovery is one, but not the most important, aspect. More crucial aspects are the distribution process and the features of the developing economic system. Again Kornai writes,

> The transition from socialism to capitalism has to be an organic development. It cannot be done otherwise. It is a curious amalgam of revolution and evolution. It is a trial-and-error process, which retains or liquidates old institutions, and tries out, accepts or rejects new ones. Each element in the process might be very rapid, fairly rapid or slow. Each has its own

appropriate speed. Some episodes call for a one-stroke intervention. Many other processes advance by incremental changes.[6]

I can only agree with this position, which theoretical considerations and nearly two decades of experiences strongly support. An ensuing analysis should clarify when, where, and under which conditions one or the other transformation approach should prevail. Transformation is not simply a technical problem or a process that is independent of the nature, character, and goals of actors. It also depends on the initial conditions and those that arise during transformation. Implicit in Kornai's statement is the Schumpeterian idea of *creative destruction*. It was indeed a strong idea from the beginning of transition and was proposed by economists in the Austrian and evolutionary traditions.[7] Yet, *creative destruction* during transformation is jeopardized by exactly what it is all about: changing institutions and the coordination of institutions and decisionmaking. If coordination fails at any moment—and it must fail for a while for the very success of transformation—there will be only destruction with no creation. This opens up great opportunities for actors and actions that jeopardize the success of transformation.[8] Therefore, an important problem is how to reduce the danger and consequences of the void of institutions and coordination. This missing link is, I contend, the state.

Another quotation will make the point clearer. Stanley Fisher and Ratna Sahay (2000), reviewing ten years of experiences, concluded,

> The countries that have done best are those who have pursued their reform agendas most consistently; they are also those who seemed from the start most committed to reform. By and large, they are also the countries closer to Western Europe, and those who had spent the least time under communist rule.

This amounts to saying that "the extent of reform has been strongly correlated with the initial conditions."[9] It is a trivial conclusion for any historian. Important questions are what were the factors that produced this path-dependent outcome? Could it have happened in a different way?

The same Stanley Fisher spoke of Russia, the best-known case of transformation failure up to the 1998 financial crisis.

> It cannot be overlooked, however, that many if not most of the proposed measures have already been part of government programs in the past— they have just not been implemented. Why? The poor record reflects fundamentally a failure to overcome fierce resistance from vested interests in the face of weak government consensus.[10]

Philip Hanson shares this view. "In most ex-communist countries the consistent pursuit of reform policies has so far not happened. In this sense, there is nothing special about Russia: like most ex-communist countries, it has floundered."[11] Again the question arises of why this was so. Was it by chance due to adverse coalitions in transformation, or the very transformation policies and measures that were implemented?

The next section, Section 8.2 explains why state reform has been the missing link between transformation policies and sustainable development. Section 8.3 deals with the particular nature of policies during transformation. Section 8.4 sketches the features of the state before transformation. Section 8.5 discusses the nature of transformation, the danger of rent-seeking outcomes, and why reforming the state should have priority over the standard components of transformation. Section 8.6 presents a matrix of the state to show that the size and the role of the state depend on different factors. Section 8.7 concludes.

8.2 The missing link

The questions in point are: was it really possible to implement and sustain reform measures? Were their comprehensive effects, including spillover, really positive? There are various reasons to maintain that the answers have not been affirmative, and that both shock therapists and gradualists were equally right and wrong. After two decades of intensive debate, experimentation, policymaking, and adaptation, however, the situation has become rather different to the one before transformation. Any analysis must start from this new circumstance.

Speed may be necessary in well-defined fields and cases: "a well-compiled package of correctly calibrated measures is capable of restoring equilibrium in several important dimensions of the macroeconomy at once, or at least bringing the economic state much closer to a tolerable degree of equilibrium."[12] The processes of transformation, however, need a long time to materialize, for example, the change of institutions, development of markets and market infrastructure, fostering the new actors, formation of new ways of market coordination, accumulation of private capital, and development of individual and organizational capacities. In these matters speed plays a negative or only modestly positive role.

This debate shaded another relation between macroeconomic stability and creative destruction. The important idea here is creation without destruction. The government can realize macroeconomic stability through determination, but it imposes a sometimes substantial cost upon the economy. Without creation, the economy cannot sustain stability in the long run. The case is similar with creative destruction. A determined government can privatize and allow individuals to establish market organizations or it can do so directly. Then, private individuals or groups can confiscate capital by *privatizing* state assets. In the case of such destruction with no substantial creative activities, no balanced macroeconomic stability can be maintained.

Then, there is no guarantee that the new economic system is viable in the long run, not to speak of its efficacy.[13]

Failures in CEECs offer the clearest evidence of the above arguments. Their output fall was the longest and deepest of the past century. Predictably, the outcome did not coincide with its blueprint. There have been only a few good episodes,[14] such as the fair performance of some state-owned enterprises (SOEs) and domestic management, particularly in Poland, and the strong inflow of foreign direct investment, particularly in Hungary and later in Poland, the Czech Republic, and the Baltic states. Yet most surprises have been negative. The costs proved to be much higher than anticipated, the processes took much longer, and generally the emerging economic system was less, sometimes much less, satisfactory than envisaged at the start.

One crucial reason was that destruction was not followed by sufficient creation largely because of the drastic measures for stabilization and hasty privatization of SOEs. Particularly in some countries like Russia, the new small and medium-size enterprises (SMEs) were underdeveloped, barely viable, and far from compensating the devolution of large companies.[15] Entrepreneurship has not been fostered sufficiently[16] and too much energy and resources have been invested into rent-seeking activities. The main reason for all these disappointing outcomes was, this author believes, first the devolution of the state and later the neglect of the state. The state is the missing link between transformation policies and their success. To argue on this point, the following three propositions are prepared.

1. The state has been too strong and impatient where it should have been more flexible, in particular in hurrying with privatizing the state sector. It was too weak and slow where it should have been more supportive, in particular in the case of SMEs and in developing the market capacities.
2. Failures in promoting a competitive market economy were ironically a result of the success of stabilization and privatization policies. The capture of the state by special interests of private groups was the consequence of those successful strategies.
3. In a transforming economy, creation is more important than destruction and needs entrepreneurship. But destruction, like the speedy privatization of SOEs, does not require productive entrepreneurs but stimulates some privileged individuals or groups for rent-seeking and a passive attitude in most other actors.

Thus, the crucial conclusion is that reforming and strengthening the state should receive a high priority from the very beginning. If, however, the state is weakened or seized by special interest groups, this reform may be very difficult. In such a case, some alternatives must be conceived. In preparing such policies two considerations should not be forgotten. One is the effect of policy announcement,[17] and the other is the capabilities of new markets and economic actors in transforming economy. Initially the external conditions rapidly and dramatically change, and their effects must be examined more in detail, because *the Washington consensus* has not properly considered them in its context.[18] In three areas the transforming economies differ from the ones implicit in the *consensus* hypotheses: (1) the features of economic actors; (2) the nature of markets and equilibrium; and (3) the response of aggregate supply in the short run and its long-term perspectives.

1. Economic actors can not be like representative businessmen in a mature market economy. Privatization and liberalization need devices to produce new actors and change their pattern of behavior and decisionmaking. In the new system, they can naturally have neither the knowledge nor the capabilities for adopting market-type optimizing behavior. Economic institutions and the coordination mechanism must also be changed, so that there may not be any established optimizing behavior. What well-informed actors can adopt may be only a bounded rational behavior. Yet bounds are severe on knowledge and information, and calculation is even harder because of floundering institutions and coordination. With no perfect knowledge, the market mechanism cannot work well enough to erase opportunism. It can easily cause socially undesirable consequences.

2. Competitive equilibrium does not naturally prevail in markets at the beginning. More exactly, there are no self-equilibrating markets. Firms are often monopolistic producers. The announcement of transformation changes the goals of economic actors from implementing plan targets to private gain, but not their behavior for reasons like deficient knowledge of markets, lack of credibility of government policies, unpredictable reactions of other actors, and tardy reform of institutions. Business uncertainty is bound to follow. Under these circumstances new actors behave in the crucial time between the disrupted old system and the new one to be stabilized and determine their *starting conditions and positions* in the new system.

3. The old economic structure regulated by administrative decisions must radically change, including altering working conditions and labor skills. Aggregate supply of goods and services is likely to fall in the short run, because many of the old products disappear as they no longer satisfy market standards and previous production links are disorganized and disrupted. Price liberalization may allow monopolists to exploit their market position without increasing production. Consequently, labor demand in liberalized markets is likely to be well below the level compatible with any natural rate of unemployment. Weak competition among firms, however, perhaps supports employment at the expense of labor productivity. *Transitional depression* is likely to be deep, and unemployment exceeds the *equilibrium* level, because actors cannot make any long-run calculations. A long process of learning by trial and error is unavoidable before a new normality is established. Meanwhile actors pursue only short-run goals.

What would be *righteous policies* then? *The Washington consensus* holds that good economic performance requires liberalized trade, macroeconomic stability, and getting prices right.[19] Since the transitional circumstances do not satisfy the theoretical presumptions of the *consensus,* such conditions are likely to be insufficient or misplaced. Something more or different is necessary. Hence, the *Washington consensus* policies have contributed rather to the unfavorable development of transformation in many countries by disregarding the long-run nature of transformation and the crucial question of the complex coordination of various reforms. Instead, it overemphasized the short-run responses and overlooked the incapability and asymmetries of immature markets. In some cases those policies avoided the danger of hyper-inflation but often jeopardized the conditions needed to realize the results envisaged in the model. The missing considerations are the following:

1. Economic agents' rational behavior is bound and agents pursue opportunistically their short-run interests. This jeopardizes long-run objectives of transformation and strengthens path-dependence. Thus, long-run objectives may fail or their implementation may become more costly.
2. In one way or another, equilibrium can be reached in the market, not necessarily by competition, but possibly by monopolists or political interference.
3. Unemployment may easily become very high and production low even below the level corresponding to useless and unsalable *socialist* production.

These outcomes may invite direct intervention by the state government to overcome such an economically, politically, and socially unbearable situation. Then, private interests easily capture the state,[20] and the state intervention prevents the markets from evolving and economic actors from adapting to the markets. Thus, wrong initial policies cause undesirable policies and intervention later. What is then the desirable role of the state during transformation?

8.3   *Right* policies during transformation

The economic performance of a country is determined not only by the economic system, the environment, and policies,[21] but also by the nation's individual capabilities, particularly their knowledge, skills, and ability to undertake actions and pursue goals.[22] Research on the subject has found that fostering such capabilities requires investment with a long gestation period and risk-taking under highly uncertain circumstances including even institutional disruption.[23] It is especially important for tacit skills and complex organizational capabilities. The effectiveness of new institutions and incentives depends on the level of such capabilities in the economy. If these factors in different countries are qualitatively identical but only quantitatively different, the same type of policies may be adequate for all.

That is what the *Washington consensus* and many national policy programs presumed. First, the economic system was supposed to be broadly identical despite evident intercountry differences, i.e. the Soviet-type economic and sociopolitical system. Second, as for the environment, such factors as cultural and social heritages were regarded as irrelevant for economic performance; the geopolitical conditions were taken as being roughly the same for different countries; in addition they are endowed more or less equally with natural resources and approximately at the same level of development.[24] Finally, the crucial question of the nation's capabilities was simply disregarded, or more precisely individual capabilities were completely overlooked.

As for social capabilities, international support and some domestic reform were considered sufficient in order to set up the new organizations for policy implementation. It was assumed that fostering capabilities would be quick and not costly and would naturally follow the new policies. In addition the similarly simplistic idea prevailed that rapid devolution of old organizations could be done fast enough to prevent the old vested interests from forming coalitions and blocking the transformation. Thus, mainstream policies clearly presumed a situation different from the real conditions in the CEECs on the eve of transformation. This was so *ex-ante* before policies were implemented[25] and even more so *ex-post*. Whether such a presumption was right or not was studied by Cornia and Popov (1998).

> According to their econometric investigation differences in output performance are explained by variations in initial *structural* and *institutional* conditions and, even more so, by policy-related factors such as preservation of adequate institutional capability of the state, export promotion, establishment of competitive markets, expansion of the *new private sector* and introduction of adequate microeconomic incentives. In contrast, factors like the speed of liberalization or the level of inflation below a given threshold do not matter, and evidence on their impact is not conclusive.[26]

In other words, the initial differences in environment, the economic system, and capabilities matter as much as policies do. If a qualitatively uniform policy set is implemented in qualitatively and structurally different economies, albeit quantitatively varied, one could have expected what actually happened: highly differentiated outcomes, both qualitatively and quantitatively. As the overall context shows variety and variability, so policies should show similar features. Substantiation of this idea follows in the reform of the state in different CEECs.

8.4   The preconditions: the state before transformation

All reformers agreed that the state had to change both to prevent old coalitions from blocking transformation and to support stabilization and systemic change. There was no ready-made theory of reform, and some countries experienced severe problems of macroeconomic imbalance that required prompt solutions. International organizations and some new national governments thought that the only reasonable recipe could be obtained by learning the lessons from the Latin American experiences of the previous decade.[27] Indeed, there were some environmental similarities: a middle level of development, open economies, location relatively close to the heart of developed market economies, countries with years of dictatorship, widespread corruption, and the threat of political instability. Yet there were equally many striking differences. They were mostly in the economic system: institutions and coordination mechanisms, their capabilities, the nature of economic and social structures, and the character of the state.

The one-party state was the core pillar of the Soviet-type system, in which it was difficult to distinguish the state from the party.[28] The economic system was strongly centralized and economic activity was under the direct control of the administrative machine. The party in power controlled the latter. The core of entrepreneurial and decisionmaking functions was located in the party and the state.[29] More precisely, the state could be considered as the executive organ of the party. Top positions in the state administration were not only under the direct control of the party leadership but also monopolized by high-ranking party officials. Lower level positions were often reserved for party members. In the economy, the basic role of the state machine was to implement central planning and control its implementation. Thus, both entrepreneurial decisionmaking and control functions were concentrated in the unreformed, classical Soviet-type state.

Most countries, however, went through a process of economic reforms in the 1960s and 1980s. The latter decade also witnessed some mild political and administrative reforms. The most successful reform, despite many limitations, was undoubtedly that in Hungary.[30] Some relevant changes were also implemented in Poland. These relatively consistent and prolonged reforms visibly transformed the state machine and its economic role. The state became less political and more professional. Its role changed from being primarily political to largely being technical. Some principles and practices of checks and balances were introduced between different functions. As a result, much ordinary decisionmaking was left to enterprises.

In other countries, the situation was quite different. In Romania and Bulgaria the state remained largely unreformed and characterized by nepotism, corruption, and closed control by a limited number of party leaders. In Czechoslovakia and East Germany the state was strongly centralized and effectively politically controlled. However, professional competence and discipline were highly valued.

In the Soviet Union, the situation was originally similar to the one existing in the Balkan states, yet *perestroika* radically changed the conditions. The attempt at reforming the economic system and revitalizing economic activities by starting from politics destabilized the economic system and consequently the state. Political control of the state faded away. Yet the state lacked any proper professional structure that could have replaced political control. Consequently, the economy remained without any proper coordination, since developing market co-ordination needed time, proper institutions, enforcement, and a lack of uncertainty. The situation was not uniform, however, throughout this huge country. Indeed, the Soviet Union state was nearly destroyed by *perestroika*, but subunion states remained largely untouched and operational. Thus, the situations of individual post-Soviet countries were generally not very different compared to the Balkan countries.

To summarize, there were two types of the state among CEECs: the reformed and the unreformed. The former was organized in a relatively orderly and professional way, although it was weakly accountable to society; thus it had some capability and strength to control and run the economy. The latter was rather corrupt, weakly and undemocratically controlled by politics, and with feeble professional competence; thus it was weak at running the economy. In between, these two types there was a third, the unreformed, yet professionally run and controlled state. This was a strong type of state, possibly the strongest of the three types in running the economy and preventing macroeconomic imbalances. The real problem of this state was that it softened the incentives for economic actors that were supposed to come from the autonomy granted by the reforms. Thus quasi-market capabilities suffered under this state.

8.5   The misplaced position of the missing link

The World Bank reported (1996, 110),

> The transition from plan to market calls for a wholesale reinvention of government. The State has to move from doing many things badly to doing its fewer core tasks well. This means that government must shrink and change its nature. No longer the prime economic agent in most areas, it must instead facilitate private activity. Getting the government's own house in order—achieving tighter control on expenditure, better budget management, and tax administration, while reforming fiscal relations between levels of government—is a high priority for advanced and lagging reformers alike.[31]

There has been probably no economist or politician who, given the aim of transformation, could challenge this statement. Yet this statement is too generic for operational goals. According to the World Bank, there are some more precise aspects of restructuring and building the new state. The teachings and suggestions offered are quite reasonable, yet standard. Three different streams of change are stressed:

> First, the role of government in producing and distributing goods and services must shrink dramatically...State intervention is justified only where markets fail—in such areas as defense, primary education, rural roads, and some social insurance—and then only to the extent that it improves upon the market. Second, government must stop restricting and directly controlling private commercial activity and extricate itself from intimate involvement in the financial sector, focusing instead on promoting macroeconomic stability and providing a legal and institutional environment that supports private sector development and competition. Finally, instead of providing generous guarantees to secure adequate living standards for all, governments need to foster greater personal responsibility for income and welfare.

Although the text warns that these teachings "provide a general framework, not a rigid blueprint for changes in the role of government during transition," it continues to state that "these shifts are guided by the mix between private and public activities in a stylized market economy." One could more precisely say an Anglo-Saxon type of market economy. This is the real point. Can we really take a *stylized market economy* of any brand as the guideline for transformation? Or had we better look for different solutions, while leaving that general framework as a guideline not for transformation but for the outcome of transformation? In other words, if we are convinced that transformation should be approached not with the analytical and operational instruments of comparative statics, but with those of dynamic analysis, we should take a different approach.

More precisely: since transformation is not a *simple* problem of transition along a standard path within the same economic system, it is qualitatively different from apparently similar processes that take place within the same system like Latin America. Quantitative differences in the value of aggregates, for example, the weight of the state in the economy, are less important than qualitative differences, for example, the capabilities of the state or its role within the economic system. At the end, the report implicitly recognizes this:

> Political reforms, economic liberalization and stabilization, and new private sector opportunities all help create a demand for the many legal, financial, and social institutions discussed in this part of the Report.

They include setting new spending priorities, better expenditure control and budget management, improving tax policy and administration, and realizing fiscal decentralization. They will not arise out of thin air. Establishing these institutions and nurturing them over time may be the single greatest contribution to the long-term success of transition that governments can make.[32]

Stressing the fundamental importance of these changes is absolutely correct. Yet the report avoids the crucial question of transformation: when those different changes in the state should take place; in particular, how the coordination and possible sequencing of the different components of transformation should be undertaken. In fact, when stabilization, liberalization, and privatization are implemented, some basic reforms of the structure, the role, and policy measures of the state must have already been done. Otherwise, the outcome of the entire process of transformation would be jeopardized with the following consequences.

1. Market coordination may fail;
2. Privatization may stimulate rent-seeking activities more strongly than giving incentives to invest to compete and make profit;
3. The budget constraint of actors remains soft;
4. The foundation of new firms lags behind and those existing pursue survival strategies;[33] and
5. Competition remains weak.

The basic reason for these outcomes is that transformation is a huge, general, one-stroke, not iterative, game.[34] It fosters opportunistic behavior in most agents. Uncertainty, lack of knowledge and capabilities, and asymmetric information, etc. jeopardize collective action toward realizing an orderly and productive transformation. As a result, most actors adopt simple strategies, usually conservative, to pursue the short-run return to investment or plainly seek quasi-rents. They individually choose the best option and keep their behaviors adjusted to the old criteria unless the outcome systematically worsens the situation.[35] If actors adopting such behavior reach a critical mass, transformation policies become ineffective. Then, transformation itself becomes badly path-dependent, and the majority actors become shortsighted in plain contrast to pursuing the long-term goals.

In these circumstances, what successful transformation needs is spontaneous third-party support. It requires some minimal conditions that support decentralized coordination or some devices that make credible the threat of sanctions in the case of noncompliance. They do not naturally emerge when the new system is just a blueprint. Spontaneous third-party enforcement requires self-enforcing institutions, but blueprints alone cannot supply incentives. The first stage of transformation is necessarily almost a zero-sum game and consists largely of a one-stroke redistribution of property rights through privatization and distribution of political positions. No self-enforcing mechanism can prevent opportunistic agents from seizing distributive opportunities. Those who obtain some distributive advantages may obtain a stronger position and use it to obtain more property rights. The only *spontaneous* outcome would be that they impose enforcement that is advantageously only to themselves.

In those circumstances, spontaneous enforcement, and thus orderly productive transformation, could result only if informal institutions are powerful and of the market type, agents are altruistic, or there exists an external and coordinated set of noneconomic institutions or an external organization that could support a self-enforcing mechanism. Such a mechanism could have been supplied by a strong ideology that imposed discipline upon agents or an external organization endowed with great prestige and credibility. Such ideology did not exist nor could it have existed. The Church was the only such organization existing, but its power was inevitably weak in face of the opportunistic agents who supported transformation just so they could pursue their own material gains.

Informal institutions were not market friendly to begin with, since they succeeded a long period of Soviet-type institutions. The most traditional among them reflected even precapitalistic institutions from before the Soviet-type system. Many scholars and politicians believed, however, that there was a solution to this problem. The idea of spontaneous development in transforming economies relied on two different, though not alternative, convictions.

1. The market is the natural economic system and its institutions can develop rapidly and spontaneously at low transaction and evolution costs unless it existence is prevented by some external power like the Communist Party.
2. Market relations existed throughout the Soviet experiences in the widespread underground economy.

Neither conviction survived the test of transformation. Time proved that a developed and competitive market system does not naturally emerge, unless proper institutions organize and support its development. As to the prereform underground economy, it prospered only in a shortage economy, so that it was not of a market type and did not help to develop a market system. In fact, prereform underground firms disappeared after liberalization and the disappearance of shortages.[36] The most widely organized underground activities gave rise to organized criminality. The same holds for the now somewhat old-fashioned *robber-baron* type of development. This lies in the history of capitalist development of the United States. Comparison between the two cases proves beyond doubt that robber barons never become respectable competitive capitalists outside an economic system with the authoritative state as a crucial component.

These facts, far from showing the superfluity of the state, jointly prove that it has a fundamental and active role in transformation. The state is necessary, although it is not sufficient. A perfect transformation blueprint can do nothing without it. Yet an authoritative and effective market friendly state can compensate for the lack of a good blueprint and can react to unforeseen circumstances and negative outcomes. This perception is now well accepted by scholars, advisers, politicians, and international agencies alike and is clearly reflected in the World Bank Report.

What is not clearly understood yet is, however, that state reform is necessary before, not after, the standard stabilization and transformation measures are implemented. This conclusion is supported by economic theory and transformation experiences alike. It would not be necessary to summarize what has been discussed in previous sections about the initial and crucial stage of transformation. Since spontaneous self-enforcement did not exist in the old system nor develop rapidly in the systemic void, the only solution for an orderly transformation is the reform of the state before the other steps are implemented. Many analysts, including the authors of the World Bank Report, tacitly suppose that the state is bad, and private agents are good. Obviously this is not always true. A country where the state is bad is the one whose economic system cannot force the state or its agents to virtuous behavior. Under the same circumstances in those countries, private agents would not be better. They would often exploit the state to their own advantage.

Basic reforms of the state must take place before stabilization, liberalization, privatization, and other measures for systemic change.[37] Otherwise the reform would cost enormously and distort the new market system. The experiences of Hungary and Poland as well as Russia and other post-Soviet States offer quite convincing evidence to this conclusion as two polar examples.

8.6   The *righteous* state and its functions

Transformation involves the state as an object and as a subject. First, transformation of the state as an object is required as regards its organization, role, and activity. Second, the state as a subject is required to realize the transformation of its political and economic systems. Planning, choice of options, and implementation of policy measures go through the state. The state's own change strongly influences transformation. Therefore, the *righteous* state is the one that can minimize the risks of getting seized by conservative and rent-seeking coalitions, support entrepreneurship, and develop a competitive economy. Since individual economies differ from each other in the three dimensions mentioned above, the righteous state must be

Table 8.1   The matrix of state transformation

		Economic system			
	Level of development	A. Reformed/ middle-high + centre	B. Reformed/ middle-low + periphery	C. Unreformed/ middle-high + centre	D. Unreformed/ middle-low + periphery
Environment	Resources	E. Reformed/ rich	F. Reformed/ poor	G. Unreformed/ rich	H. Unreformed/ poor
	Size, domestic market	I. Reformed/ large	J. Reformed/ small	K. Unreformed/ large	L. Unreformed/ small

Note: The economic system can be reformed or unreformed; the level of development is middle-high or middle-low; the location of the country is central or peripheral compared to Western Europe; the resources are rich or poor; the size of the country and the domestic market are large or small.

judged differently in their own contexts. The following matrix of the state in transformation illustrates the general conditions (Table 8.1).

The matrix has two dimensions: the economic system and the environment. It includes two sets of simplifications. Along the first dimension there is a clear relation between the features of the economic system and capabilities. Therefore, capabilities and the economic system can be included in the same dimension, at the price of some generalizations. Capabilities here should be intended as those that have a (quasi-) market character i.e. those that give favorable support to the transformation in q market direction of the economic system. This is in large part the fruit of economic reforms, along with cultural and social factors. Research in this field supports this statement. Hungarian researchers found no evidence of quantitative differences throughout transforming countries concerning the pattern of entrepreneurial inclination.[38] Although quantitative differences among countries were not relevant, reforms influenced who actually became businessmen, how businessmen behaved, and their successes. The Hungarian survey supports the theory that the composition and characters of actual businessmen are determined by their occupation, the level of education, their personal values, and their connections, along with demographic factors. The influence of reform acted through the 1980s and is a major difference compared to other countries, showing that some major changes were introduced into the Hungarian economy and the society well before transition started.

Second, the environment includes different variables. The most important are the: level of development, geopolitical situation, commercial culture, natural resources, size, and domestic market. In CEECs there is a clear relation between the first three variables. The most developed countries are also those located closer to Western Europe and endowed with relatively developed commercial culture. That culture is the fruit of centuries of development and has been revived by economic reforms in some cases. For reasons of simplification, the three variables are put under a single heading: the level of development. The matrix implies that countries in different conditions require different forms of state, and hence they need different kinds of state reform. Under two different perspectives: (1) size and structure; (2) the nature and functions of the state, a review of the possible state reforms is presented.

1. The size and structure of the state. The state is called on to support systemic transformation *plus* economic development. These duties are nonstandard for the state, because the state under transformation must pursue them without its proper coordination mechanism. The size of the state can be small, if the level of economic development is high, since state support for capital accumulation is less important. As to structure, however, state offices dealing with market regulation, control and enforcement and creating opportunities for actors are more important in high level countries than in the countries with pressing problems. If, however, the low level of development causes high and persistent unemployment, relatively large state expenditures may be required for unemployment benefits and social programs. Otherwise, the social and political consequences may be damaging for economic development. Under these circumstances, the state needs to supply more services, at least until the private sector takes over, although such state services are generally less important in these countries than in more developed ones.

Resource endowment is relatively unimportant for determining the size of the state. A developing country, however, may want to use natural resources to support economic development, for example, by running their extraction and possible export directly and reinvesting the returns in the domestic economy. In this case, the size of the state will be larger. Territorially large countries with poor capital may wish to balance domestic markets throughout the country by investing in infrastructure and this would require a larger role for the state. This will make the size of the state larger than a small country taking greater advantage of international trade.

As for the economic system and capabilities, a crucial factor is the degree of reform achievement: the more consistent, deeper, and long-lasting the reform realized before transformation, the smaller the state size can be. There are two important reasons. First, after reform, the economic system becomes more market friendly, so that the coordination break that transformation produces is relatively mild and short. Thus economic actors are capable of producing more in a liberal and competitive environment and of establishing the proper market structures. Second, a reformed economy is probably less unbalanced after liberalization, because the budget constraint was hardened during reforms and prices are already close to market equilibrium. Macroeconomic stabilization is more effective, quicker, and less costly in such economies since actors have been used to reacting to quasi-market signals. Consequently, there is less need for the state to intervene.

2. Nature and functions of the state. Based on Western and other experiences, six different types of the state can be identified: (1) minimal state, (2) competitive state, (3) Keynesian state, (4) corporative state, (5) authoritarian state, and (6) developmental state. The minimal state provides a minimum level of public goods. The competitive state does all it can do more efficiently than the market.[39] The Keynesian state intervenes primarily to manage demand. The corporative state offers guarantees to social parties supporting income policies and other agreements or plays a direct role in such agreements. The authoritarian state supports the powerful government and its agents who may impose their own preferences and decisions upon private agents, perhaps in favor of one particular social group. The developmental state is an active, yet market-friendly state, that uses its power and resources to foster market agents and to give them incentives to operate in accordance with social interests, particularly in the long run.

Both the environment and the economic system are relevant to determining the nature and functions of the state. In particular, the more developed the economy is, and the more reformed the economic system was before transformation, the more the state can perform an indirect role and be structured as required for it. It can be closer to the competitive state than in any other transforming country. Some management of demand along the requirements of a Keynesian state and the use of *neo*-corporative policies do not raise the danger of interfering in institutional reform. Conversely, a less developed and unreformed economy requires a more interventionist state along the lines envisaged by the developmental state, but with some danger of getting close to an authoritarian state.

8.7   Conclusions: common wisdom and innovation in the transition state

Experiences have proved that transformation of a centrally administered economy into a market economy cannot be realized by fiat with centrally determined promarket commands, nor can be entirely an outcome of spontaneous developments. It requires a pragmatic and balanced mix of different measures and processes, whose nature is determined by the particular conditions and features of each country (Grossman 1994).

The main conclusion of the preceding analysis is that the state should be reformed before liberalization and privatization begins. This requires a period of reforms where the state machine is restructured, reorganized, transformed, and made more effective in fostering market activity. The core of this reform lies in the abandonment of central planning and plain political interference; greater autonomy for economic actors; and the development of market regulatory capabilities, structures, and instruments and of suitable control and enforcement. Since all this takes place in a hybrid economic system, i.e. the market system is only developing and central planning is disrupted, this may require transitorily greater, although increasingly indirect, control and coordination by the state. To avoid the danger of state entrenchment and interference,[40] a preannounced constitution should stipulate the conditions for further transformation of the state, linking it to observable progress in market actors, institutions, and coordination. Since these are new functions for the state, high investment in its structures, capability building, and the civil service is necessary. International support should give priority to this investment.

This is somehow the case of CEECs and East Asian countries. Above all, this is the strategy that those countries that have not yet started to transform should pursue. It is to such cases that the suggestions of the World Bank quoted above apply best. In fact these reform goals need strong commitment, but also a strong state capable of implementing such changes.

In most countries, however, transformation started with a political revolution that destroyed the core of the old system: the power monopoly of the Communist Party. This was necessary in the cases where the state and the party prevented reform. What should be done in these circumstances? Political revolution inevitably destroys the effective engine of the Communist Party and, as a consequence, dismantles the state. The entire system is left without any coordination, except for old routines and social networks, until new coordination develops itself. As a consequence, the state becomes weak and unstable, though it remains large. Under these circumstances it is difficult to reform the state, let alone the economic system.

There may be two solutions to this dilemma.[41] First, the new political elite, after it takes possession of the state, starts to reform it by using its renewed power to produce an educated and disciplined bureaucracy by imposing order and progressively developing the rule of law. This solution requires enlightened elite who pursues national interest by skimming a part of the profit generated by economic development.[42] This resembles the way that succeeded in East Asia.

The second solution is based on some kind of social contract between the polity and the society. Reforming the state is costly, time consuming, and painful. Many people risk losing their jobs and everyone else has to work hard to learn new skills. In this case, reform is only possible if the people have strong incentives, either positive or negative, to endure the sacrifices needed. In the situation of transformation countries, this may be possible only by making use primarily of moral rewards, since material resources must be concentrated on reforming structures and offices, endowing them with more modern devices, and producing better skills. In any case, resources should not be taken from the state but should be transferred to new bureaucracies, such as a privatization bureau. Even resources that are gained through reducing employment in the state machine and closing down offices such as the planning office must be reinvested in the state.

Both theoretical arguments and the experiences of different transforming countries show that the privatization of SOEs should not receive priority over state reform. Even ambiguous property rights can be beneficial for a transitory period, provided that there is effective state enforcement.[43] What really matters is that the policy of transformation and the goals to be pursued are clearly and credibly announced. This is a question that only politics can solve. Liberalization should be clearly announced and pursued consistently, but with prudence. Full liberalization of private activity should be preceded by the approval of the relevant laws, the development and regulation of capital markets, and accompanying strengthening of the state control and enforcement capability in developing market context. Liberalization of external economic relations should proceed prudently, since excessive external shocks are counterproductive for the firms that are weak in terms of market capabilities. Stimulating market expectations may be more important and may supply stronger incentives than plain liberalization. Again this depends largely on the ability of the state to implement a credible liberalization policy that is progressive through time and possibly capable of variation among different activities and branches.

Greater priority should be placed on hardening the budget constraint. This is probably the most important measure in the starting period. Experiences in Hungary and Poland show that hardening the budget constraint alone can obtain fair results in SOEs. Again, this process should proceed consistently but with some prudence in order to give firms time to adapt. Strengthening state capabilities should accompany this process to avoid decapitalization of firms or excessive degrees of bankruptcy. Here, too, a credible and preannounced policy of progressive hardening is the most promising means of disciplining firms. Some experiences in transformation countries, notably in Poland, show that under these circumstances SOEs can also improve their performance and managers can obtain incentives for restructuring.

Yet the most important and least contradictory component of transformation should consist in fostering SMEs.[44] Since apparently there is some trade-off between this and the privatization of large SOEs,[45] policies for SMEs should be given priority. SMEs are at a great disadvantage resulting from certain features of the old system: the lack of SMEs and relatively weak institutional and organizational structures, shortage of capital due to SMEs' adverse position to the financial sector, and policy support concentrated on privatization. This makes spontaneous processes unlikely to produce the needed systemic and organizational innovation and raises the question of policy remedies. By influencing the future prospects of the economy with uncertainty and risk and the overall cost and factor remuneration of SMEs relative to larger companies, general and specific policies must be devised to improve the allocation of resources to SMEs both absolutely and relatively to large companies.

The role of SMEs in general and in the CEECs in particular is crucial and specific policies are necessary, primarily because they can produce a general improvement in the economic situation at both the national and local levels by supporting employment and fostering fresh entrepreneurship in a truly market way. At the same time, they decrease the value of conservative factors, comprising transitional redistribution and path dependence.

Important implications for state reform also come from giving priority to the development of SMEs. Important measures include establishing proper state and mixed (public/private) agencies to support them, private entrepreneurial organizations of SMEs, and small local banks to finance them, in order to avoid the aversion that large banks typically have for SMEs. Since these are mostly decentralized functions, they require the decentralization of the state apparatus. Therefore, revitalizing local governments and other autonomous organizations (e.g., development agencies, competition authorities, and labor offices) is a crucial priority in the reform of the state. If this need was accepted from the beginning, its implementation would be less costly, difficult, and more effective.

Transformation is a nonstandard undertaking and unfolds over time amid continuous adaptation to external factors and internal changes in the economic system. Consequently, the role of the state and policies should go through continuous adaptation to results already achieved, until the economic system becomes a well-functioning market system. At that point, the nature and role of the state can settle to those of a *normal* state in a market economy.

One last point to be stressed is that the argument here may raise a suspicion that the state is given an excessive role. It is true, compared to the near demise of the state in many transformation countries particularly during the early years of the process. That devolution of power caused costly, heavy, and possibly irreparable consequences. However, there is no doubt that an active state raises the danger of political and bureaucratic interference and state failures. It would be easy to trade this danger off with the outcomes of the absent state in various transformation countries. A more serious point is that the state relies upon skilled and professional officials, who are rewarded with proper incentives to adapt and actively support its reform, and is made up of offices and structures that are transparent and accountable to democratically elected bodies. One important way of making democratic control of the state easier to achieve is to announce openly a countryspecific blueprint of the stages and processes of the state transformation and to report the results implemented in the transformation of the economic system. Democratic control over the implementation of this blueprint would give additional guarantees against political or bureaucratic interference and failures. After all, economic development and transformation success are not inevitable events and they depend strongly upon daily action, commitment, and engagement.

Notes

Department of Economics, University of Trento, e-mail: bdallago@risc1.gelso.unitn. it. The research on which this paper is based has been financially sponsored by the Italian Ministry for the University and Scientific-Technological Research (MURST). The author is grateful to the participants in the Second Workshop of ICSEAD and Nomura Research Institute for helpful comments on a previous version of this paper. However, any responsibility for errors remains solely with the author.

1. From the report issued by the Carnegie Endowment, Washington, DC where Chubais gave a lecture on May 17, 1999 (quoted in J. Kornai 2001).
2. Gaidar, and Pöhl (1995), p. 4.
3. For a balanced and critical account of the debate cf. Hoen (1998).
4. Kornai (2001).
5. Gaidar, and Pöhl (1995), p. 41
6. Kornai (2001).
7. According to Andreff (2005) the supporters of an evolutionary strategy in trans-forming countries in early 1990s included Andreff himself, Wlodzimierz Brus, David Ellerman, János Kornai, Kazimierz Laski, Ronald McKinnon, Lubomir Mlcoch, Peter Murrell, Gérard Roland, David Stark, and, later, Joseph Stiglitz. For an interesting account cf. Hoen (1998).
8. Cf. Dallago (1996).
9. Fisher, and Sahay (2000).
10. Fisher (2000).
11. Hanson (1999), p. 1149.
12. Kornai (2001).
13. Nishimura (2000) shows that the economic outcome in terms of long-term GDP growth was the highest in those countries that implemented softer stabilization policies. Yet these were Central European countries that reformed their econo-mies before the beginning of transformation.
14. Uvalic, and Vaughan-Whitehead (1997).
15. Cf. McIntyre, and Dallago (2003).
16. Cf. Estrin et al. (2006); Smallbone, and Welter (2005).
17. No policy blueprint can be considered righteous if it does not internalize the expectations of economic actors. It is a well known and accepted criticism of policies that the outcome of economic activity in a given period is influenced not only by policies that are implemented in that period or were implemented earlier, but also by the expectations that the very announcement of policies cre-ate. This point is linked to the *Lucas' criticism* of economic policy (Lucas 1981) and now widely accepted in policymaking in market economies. Yet policymak-ing in transforming countries needs moreover to discount the effect of other variables that cannot be taken as givens during transformation.
18. Williamson (1990).
19. Stiglitz (1998).
20. Hellman et al. (2000).
21. For this important result of comparative economics cf. in particular Koopmans, and Montias (1971).
22. I distinguish here individual capabilities from social capabilities, i.e. the institu-tions that support investment in human capital, technological competence, and the financial institutions according to Abramovitz (1986) that in my view are part of the economic system.

23. Cf. Swaan 1998.
24. For the consequences of resource endowment on the process of transformation cf. Grossman (1999).
25. Cf., for example, Dallago (1991).
26. Cornia, and Popov (1998), pp. 7–8.
27. Cf. Rodrik (1996); Stiglitz (1998).
28. Cf. Kornai (1992).
29. Cf. Grossman (1983).
30. Cf. Kornai (1986).
31. WDR (1996), p. 110.
32. WDR (1996), p. 122.
33. Scase (2003).
34. Cf. Kornai (2005).
35. Cf. Screpanti (1995).
36. Laki (1998).
37. The question of stabilization is somewhat different from the key components of transformation proper. Although it is not, strictly speaking, a component of transformation, in some cases it necessarily has priority. In fact, it is difficult to reform a macroeconomically unbalanced country.
38. Kuczi, and Lengyel (1997); Kuczi, and Makó (1998).
39. This idea was proposed by Breton (1989).
40. Wolf (1990) develops a theory of nonmarket—mostly state—failures.
41. I thank Chunlin Zhang for having brought this important point to my attention.
42. Cf. Overland, Simons, and Spagat (2001).
43. Cf. Li (1996).
44. Cf. McIntyre, and Dallago (2003). On the role of SMEs in transition cf. EBRD (1999), pp. 146–159.
45. Uvalic (2003).

References

Abramovitz, Moses. 1986. "Catching Up, Forging Ahead and Falling Behind." *Journal of Economic History* 46(2): 385–406.

Andreff, Wladimir. 2005. "Corporate Governance Structures in Post socialist Economies: Toward a Central Eastern European Model of Corporate Control?" *EACES Working Papers,* No.4 (May).

Breton, Albert. 1989. "The Growth of Competitive Governments." *Canadian Journal of Economics* (Nov.) 22(4): 717–750.

Cornia, Giovanni Andrea, and Vladimir Popov. 1998. "Transition and Long-Term Growth: Conventional versus Non-Conventional Determinants." *MOCT-MOST* 8(1): 7–32.

Dallago, Bruno. 1991. "Hungary and Poland: The Non-Socialized Sector and Privatization." *Osteuropa-Wirtschaft* (June) 36(2): 130–153.

Dallago, Bruno. 1996. "Investment, Systemic Efficiency and Distribution.", *Kyklos* 49(4): 615–641.

EBRD. 1999. *Transition Report 1999.* London: European Bank for Reconstruction and Development.

Estrin, Saul, Klaus E. Meyer, and Maria Bytchkova. 2006. "Entrepreneurship in Transition Economies." In *The Oxford Handbook of Entrepreneurship*, Mark Casson,

Bernard Yeung, Anuradha Basu, and Nigel Wadeson (eds.). Oxford: Oxford University Press: 693–725.

Fisher, Stanley. 2000. "Russian Economic Policy at the Start of the New Administration." Remarks prepared for the conference on *Investment Climate and Prospects for Economic Growth in Russia*, Moscow: Higher School of Economics, Moscow State University, Apr. 6. (http://www.imf.org/external/np/speeches/2000/040600.htm) (accessed on July 21, 2009).

Fisher, Stanley, and Ratna Sahay. 2000. "The Transition Economies after Ten Years." *IMF Working Paper*, WP/00/30 (Feb.).

Gaidar, Yegor, and Karl Otto Pöhl. 1995. *Russian Reform/International Money*. Cambridge, MA: MIT Press.

Grossman, Gregory. 1983. "The Party as Manager and Entrepreneur." In *Entrepreneurship in Imperial Russia and the Soviet Union*, Gregory Guroff and Fred V. Carstensen (eds.). Princeton: Princeton University Press: 284–305.

Grossman, Gregory. 1994. "What Was—Is, Will Be—the Command Economy?" *MOCT/MOST* 4(1): 5–22.

Grossman, Gregory. 1999. "Natural Riches and an Economic System's Fate: A Russian Century." *Economic Systems* (June) 23(2): 143–146.

Hanson, Philip. 1999. "The Russian Economic Crisis and the Future of Russian Economic Reform." *Europe-Asia Studies* 51(7): 1141–1166.

Hellman, Joel S., Geraint Jones, and Daniel Kaufmann. 2000. "How Profitable Is Buying State Officials in Transition Economies?" In *Transition*. Washington, DC: The World Bank: 8–11.

Hoen, Herman W. 1998. *The Transformation of Economic Systems in Central Europe*. Cheltenham: Edward Elgar.

Keren, Michael. 2000. "The Mafia as a Principal Actor in Transition: An Outline of an Evolutionary Game." *Economic Systems* 24(4): 360–364.

Koopmans, Tjalling C., and John Michael Montias. 1971. "On the Description and Comparison of Economic Systems." In *Comparison of Economic Systems: Theoretical and Methodological Approaches*, A. Eckstein (ed.). Berkeley, CA: University of California Press. http://cowles.econ.yale.edu/P/cp/p03b/p0357.pdf (accessed on July 21, 2009).

Kornai, János. 1986. "The Hungarian Reform Process: Visions, Hopes, and Reality." *Journal of Economic Literature* 24(4): 1687–1737.

Kornai, János. 1992. *The Socialist System. The Political Economy of Communism*. Princeton, NJ: Princeton University Press and Oxford: Oxford University Press.

Kornai, János. 2001. "Ten Years After 'The Road to a Free Economy', The Author Self-Evaluation." In Annual World Bank Conference on Development Economics 2000, Boris Pleskovic and Nicholas Stern (eds.). Washington, DC: World Bank: 49–66.

Kornai, János. 2005. *A gondolat erejével. Rendhagyó önéletrajz*. Budapest: Osiris Kiadó. [*By Force of Thought: Irregular Memoires of an Intellectual*. Princeton, NJ: Princeton University Press, 2007].

Kuczi, Tibor, and György Lengyel. 1997. "The Spread of Entrepreneurship in Eastern Europe." In *The Spread of Entrepreneurship in Eastern Europe (Survey Evidence on Entrepreneurial Inclination)*, Tibor Kuczi and György Lengyel (eds.). Budapest: Center for Public Affairs Studies, Research Reports 3: 150–170.

Kuczi, Tibor, and Csaba Makó. 1998. *A Vállalkozók társadalmi eröforrásai és a vállalkozások növekedése, életciklusai közötti össefüggések (Kutatási beszáoló)* [Relationships among the Social Sources of Entrepreneurs: Growth of Ventures and Their Life-Cycles]. Budapest: Budapest University of Economics and HAS Institute of Sociological Research.

Laki, Mihály. 1998. *Kisvállalkozás a szocializmus után* [Small Entrepreneurship After Socialism]. Budapest: Közgazdasági Szemle Alapítvány.

Li, David. 1996. "A Theory of Ambiguous Property Rights in Transition Economies: The Case of the Chinese Non-State Sector." *Journal of Comparative Economics* 23: 1–19.

Lucas, Robert E. Jr. 1981. *Studies in Business-Cycle Theory.* Cambridge, MA: MIT Press.

McIntyre, Robert J., and Bruno Dallago. 2003. (eds.) *Small and Medium Enterprises in Transformational Economies.* Basingstoke and New York: Palgrave Macmillan.

Nishimura, Yoshiaki. 2000. *Re-evaluation of Policies for Transition to Market Economy.* Kunitachi: Institute of Economic Research, Hitotsubashi University (*mimeo*).

Overland, Jody, Kenneth L. Simons, and Michael Spagat. 2001. "Political Instability and Growth in Dictatorship." Paper presented at the ASSA Annual Meeting, New Orleans, Jan. 5–7.

Rodrik, Dani. 1996. "Understanding Economic Policy Reform." *Journal of Economic Literature* (Mar.) 34: 9–41.

Scase, Richard. 2003. "Entrepreneurship and Proprietorship in Transformation: Policy Implications for the SME Sector." In *Small and Medium Enterprises in Transformational Economies*, Robert J. McIntyre and Bruno Dallago (eds.). Basingstoke and New York: Palgrave Macmillan: 64–77.

Screpanti, Ernesto. 1995. "Relative Rationality, Institutions and Precautionary Behavior." In *On Economic Institutions. Theory and Applications*, J. Groenewegen, C. Pitelis, and S-E. Sjöstrand (eds.). Cheltenham: Edward Elgar: 63–84.

Smallbone, David, and Friederike Welter. 2005. "Entrepreneurship in Transition Economies: Necessity or Opportunity Driven?" Paper presented at the VII ICCEES World Congress, Berlin, Jul. 25–30.

Stiglitz, Joseph E. 1998. "More Instruments and Broader Goals: Moving toward the Post-Washington Consensus." *WIDER Annual Lectures 2*, UNU/WIDER, Helsinki, Jan.

Swaan, Wim. 1998. "Capabilities and Institutional Change: Post-Socialist Economies and late Industrializing Economies Compared." Budapest: Institute of Economics, Hungarian Academy of Sciences (*mimeo*).

Uvalic, Milica. 2003. "Privatization Approaches: Effects on SME Creation and Performance." In *Small and Medium Enterprises in Transformational Economies*, Robert J. McIntyre and Bruno Dallago (eds.). Basingstoke and New York: Palgrave Macmillan: 171–184.

Uvalic, Milica, and Daniel Vaughan-Whitehead (eds.). 1997. *Privatization Surprises in Transition Economies—Employee Ownership in Central and Eastern Europe.* Cheltenham: Edward Elgar.

Williamson, John. 1990. "What Washington means by Policy Reform." In *Latin American Adjustment: How Much Has Happened?*, J. Williamson (ed.). Washington, DC: Institute for International Economics. http://www.petersoninstitute.org/publications/papers/paper.cfm?researchid=486 (accessed on July 21, 2009).

Wolf, Charles Jr. 1990. *Markets and Governments: Choosing between Imperfect Alternatives.* Cambridge, MA: MIT Press.

WDR. 1996. *From Plan to Market*, World Development Report. The World Bank, Oxford: Oxford University Press.

9
Can the Japan Inc. Model Be a Middle Course for Transition?: Industrial Policy and Postwar Economic Development of Japan

Yoichi Okita

9.1 Introduction

Throughout the 1990s the regular consulting meetings were held between the Japanese Economic Planning Agency and the Soviet Ministry of Economy. In particular in the middle part of the 1990s—I was a member in 1996—the Russian officials asked the Japanese officials and economists what kinds of programs would be effective to restore the Russian economy, and if we could offer a new approach different from the one recommended thus far by the IMF and American economists. They were asked if *the Japanese model* might be a promising choice for transitional economies. The Russian authorities believed that the Japanese model was an intermediate regime between a planned economy and a free market economy, and might have been trying to formulate a gradualist program in which the Japanese model could be used as a first step in the early stage of transition.

There is a mistaken view that the success of the Japanese economy in the 1950s and 1960s can be directly attributed to the Japanese model—a mixture of planned and market economies. This kind of misunderstanding originates in the observation by Abegglen (1970) describing it as *Japan, Inc.*[1] and also in the book by Charmers Johnson (1982),[2] *MITI and the Japanese Miracle*. Johnson quotes Andrea Boltho's observation:

> Three of the countries with which Japan can most profitably be compared: France, Germany, and Italy shared some or all of Japan's initial advantages—e.g. flexible labor supplies, a very favorable international environment, the possibility of using the most advanced techniques. Yet other conditions were very dissimilar. The most crucial difference was perhaps in the field of economic policies. Japanese government exercised a much greater degree of both intervention and protection than did any of its Western European counterparts; and this brings Japan closer to the experience of another set of countries—the centrally planned economies.[3]

Apparently, what *intervention and protection* meant in this context was industrial policy mostly conducted by the Ministry of International Trade and Industry (MITI). In order to judge if Boltho's statement is correct, therefore, it is necessary to pin down the basic characteristics of industrial policy in Japan and answer the question of whether it is correct to attribute Japan's higher growth rates in the 1950s and the 1960s to "the crucial difference in the field of economic policy."

Section 9.2 presents a review of the arguments in support of industrial policy. Section 9.3 is an overview of the broad categories of industrial policy employed in Japan in the 1950s and the early 1960s. Section 9.4 attempts to answer Boltho's question. The main conclusion is that Japanese industrial policy was nothing but infant industry protection and had no sophisticated designs to mitigate the undesirable effects of protection. Thus the arguments reviewed in Section 9.2 do not hold for the case of Japan. Section 9.5 presents some other explanations for Japan's rapid catch-up and the favorable initial conditions for the country. Section 9.6 summarizes the conclusions, which are somewhat different from the *Fund-Bank orthodoxy*, on the basis of the arguments above.

9.2 From F. List to *market-enhancing view* on industrial policy

The arguments by Japanese proponents of infant industry protection in the decade immediately after the World War II can be easily associated with the theory of Friedrich List. The leader of this school was Hiromi Arisawa, who maintained that trade liberalization would jeopardize *self-reliance*. He advocated that self-reliance must be achieved through industrialization with sheltered domestic producers and thought that the choice of a gradual shift toward socialism and away from capitalism was the best route to a higher living standard.[4] Kotaro Tsujimura pointed out that the kind of industrial policy adopted by the Japanese government was not at all different from the type of economic strategies taken by France, Germany, and Imperial Russia in their efforts to catch up with Britain. He said that Japan followed the standard method of latecomers in industrialization employed by these countries and perhaps pursued the method in more thoroughgoing manner than its predecessors did. In the controversy over trade liberalization in the late 1940s, those who opposed it employed the logic of *infant industry* and advocated sticking to a strategy of import substitution. James Fallows once wrote that Freidrich List, not Adam Smith, provided the theoretical backbone for policymakers in Japan.[5] Kosai (1988) concluded that the *ideology* of Japan's industrial policy in the reconstruction period was simply the *neo-mercantilist* or nineteenth century German school such as that of List or Sombart. He further said, "Industrial policy was also distinctly influenced by Marxism in that it was thought that industrial structure would inevitably advance toward the stage of monopoly. Nationalism was also an element."[6]

If industrial policy in Japan could have been interpreted as simply as above, and if it had been successful in the quarter century after World War II, then Boltho's comment would have been correct. Then we would be faced with the difficult question of why in some countries, neo-mercantilism or its successor—import substitution strategy—worked and in other countries it did not. There are two ways to answer this question. The first is to argue that some other conditions played a part in better performances in successful countries and industrial policy was not a significant factor or was even a slightly negative factor for development. This can be called as the neoclassical view, in accordance with usual terminology. This point will be taken up later. The second is to say that the industrial policies employed in East Asia were not simply import substitution strategies. They contained some special elements. Alternatively, in spite of the similar appearance of the system, its design at the implementation level was different owing to skillful management by bureaucrats.

9.2.1   Amsden's argument

Amsden (1989)[7] is one of the proponents of the second view. She admits that Germany and the United States were precursors of North East Asian countries, in the sense that they employed interventionist policies in the last half of the nineteenth century just like Japan and Korea did in the twentieth century: "[S]tate intervention intensified because the economies of Germany and the United States were required not merely to industrialize but also to catch up."[8] Economies in the process of industrialization needed government protection just because backward countries are "the least well endowed."

She distinguishes, however, industrialization in Japan and Korea from that of the nineteenth century, saying that industrialization in Britain occurred on the basis of *invention*, that in Germany and the United States occurred on the basis of *innovation* and that in backward countries on the basis of *learning*.[9] If amplified, her argument seems to suggest that a simple neo-mercantilist strategy does not work in the economies whose industrialization is based on learning. Unlike Tsujimura, she clearly denies the notion that North East Asian economies adopted exactly the same policies as those of Germany and the United States. Latecomers in the twentieth century were learners, not innovators. In Germany and the United States, protection was quite effective in promoting *innovation*, whereas in late industrializing economies, the foundation of development must be the subsidy.[10]

In the twentieth century, many countries adopted the same strategy as that employed by Germany or the United States, but failed to achieve any kind of take-off. Only Japan, Korea, and Taiwan achieved rapid economic growth in spite of their seemingly policies similar to those in the two Western economies mentioned above.[11] A natural deduction from this fact is that there is an important difference between the policy employed by these three before the take-off and that employed by other countries. Amsden claims: "In late-industrializing countries, *the state intervenes with subsidies deliberately to distort relative prices in order to stimulate economic activity*. This has been as true in Korea, Japan, and Taiwan as it has been in Brazil, India, and Turkey. In Korea, Japan, and Taiwan, however, the state has exercised discipline over subsidy recipients. *In exchange for subsidies, the state has imposed performance standards on private firms*. Subsidies have not been giveaways, but instead dispensed on the principle of reciprocity."[12]

In the minds of classical economists the world was characterized by the presence of a large number of small firms competing in the same industry or market. In this kind of *market-conforming paradigm*, competition functions as an automatic discipline. In the case of latecomers' industrialization, prices are distorted, so that a different type of discipline is necessary and must be managed by the government. Thus, subsidies are designed in most cases to rely on some performance standards. Carrots are linked to sticks or more precisely conditioned by performance. In this sense: "[t]he premise of successful late industrialization is a reciprocal relation between the state and the firm.…The more reciprocity in the state-firm relations, the higher the speed of economic growth."[13] Amsden also emphasizes that the price distortion created by the subsidy is both *conformable to the market mechanism* and *acceptable* so long as it leads to export-led growth. Table 9.1 summarizes Amsden's argument.

9.2.2 The World Bank on *contests*

The World Bank (1993): *East Asian Miracle* interprets Amsden's argument more rigorously, utilizing the theories of market failures. In backward countries, market failures are pervasive and require some corrections by the government.

A typical market failure observed more often in developing countries than in industrialized countries is lack of information, or asymmetry of information. As a result of this problem, the capital market does not function well in bringing about investment in promising businesses. The World Bank (1993) says, "Adam Smith's invisible hand paradigm argues that each individual, in pursuing his or her self-interest, also maximizes the common welfare; cooperation is therefore unnecessary. In reality, modern economies are characterized by extensive cooperation."[14] Here, "cooperation" mainly implies exchange of information. Since, "[i]nstitutional arrangements for cooperation and information exchange in developing economies are weaker than in industrial economies" and "the needs for these forms of coordination or rather, cooperation are undoubtedly greater," the creation of institutions for facilitating cooperation by governments is theoretically justified.

Table 9.1 Types of development based on Amsden's *Asia's Next Giant*

	Stage	Paradigm	Growth basis	Policy	Discipline	Target
Britain (19th century)	First Industrial Revolution	Market-conforming	Invention	Lais-sez-faire	Invisible hand (competition)	
Germany and USA (19th century)	Second Industrial Revolution	Shumpeterian	Innovation	Infant industry protection	Gales of new technology	Import substitution
Japan, Korea, and Taiwan	Late industrialization	Market augmenting	Learning	Subsidy and protection	Performance-based subsidization	Export promotion
Brazil, Turkey, India (before 1990), and Sub-Saharan Africa	Late industrialization		Learning	Subsidy and protection	None	Import substitution
India, Thailand, and Chile (recent years)	Emerging market	Market-friendly	Learning	Liberalization	Global competition	

Note: The last line is added by this author and is not based on Amsden's argument.

Another type of market failure in relation to investment in the early stage of development is the so-called *coordination failure*. The World Bank provides the most comprehensible example:

> For example, if a steel plant and a steel-using industry are needed concurrently, it does not pay to develop the plant unless there is a steel-using industry, and it does not pay to develop the steel-using industry unless there is a plant. If each awaits the other, nothing happens. Market failures due to incomplete markets, such as the absence of capital and risk markets, exacerbate this situation.[15]

Cooperation and coordination among private firms may lead to collusion or cartels. Protection and coordination by the government are prone to rent-seeking behavior in the private sector and may lead to serious inefficiency. To prevent these problems, they created *contests* by firms setting some performance criteria and rewarding better performers with some preferential treatment. The World Bank says that there are three prerequisites for the success of the contest: rewards, rules, and referee. In North East Asian economies, such rules were clear-cut and well understood, and rewards were very attractive. In most cases export performances were used as the criteria. Besides "referees, the government officials who have designed and supervised the contests, have been competent and fair."[16]

According to the World Bank, the reason why protection and subsidies effectively succeeded in bringing about a spurt in growth only in some particular countries is explicable by the presence of, and good design of, the contest including competent and clean referees. By creating some kind of *contest* using performance-based incentives, countries like Japan, Korea, and Taiwan succeeded in minimizing the harmful effects of government intervention. Other countries, which pursued the policy of protecting infant industries, failed to accelerate growth. It appears that government intervention stifled competition in their cases.

Thus revisionists, and the parts of *the East Asian Miracle*, that amplify their ideas conceive two kinds of protection for infant industries: one with *contest* and another without. The problem remains, however, whether Japanese industrial policy in general really matches the sophisticated formulation of industrial policy laid out in the *East Asian Miracle*, a point we will come back to later.

9.2.3 Coordination failure and industrial policy

At this point, it is necessary to review recent developments in the theory of coordination failure that justify the use of industrial policy. Aoki et al. (1997) say that there are two polar views concerning the government's role in the market economy. One pole is the *market-friendly view* put forth in the *World Development Report 1991* (World Bank 1991). The other is the so-called *developmental-state view* whose proponents include C. Johnson (1982),

A. Amsden (1989), and R. Wade (1990). The former states that the intervention of government in the form of industrial policies is harmful, or at best irrelevant, whereas the latter emphasizes that market failures like failure of coordination in investment decisions are so pervasive in the developmental stage that government intervention is necessary. Aoki et al. (1997) introduce a third view, the *market-enhancing view*, starting from a criticism of dichotomy between the first two views. Their logic goes as follows.

> [I]t has conventionally been thought that government control and the market mechanism are alternative mechanisms for solving resource-allocation problems. When the market fails to implement an efficient solution, government interventions may be called for as the substitute. There is no fundamental difference between neoclassical orthodoxy (the market-friendly view) and the developmental-state view. The difference may be a matter of degree in perceived market failures and in the perceived ability of the government to intervene successfully.[17]

They rigorously distinguish between coordination failures and other types of market failures. Both market-friendly and developmental-state views admit that the so-called *traditional* type of market failure like pollution and public goods must be dealt with by the government. The difference between these views lies in the recognition of whether or not the market can solve, after trial and error (*experiment and failure*, according to Aoki et al. 1997), the problem of coordination. The new, *market-enhancing view* agrees with the market-friendly view that the government should not remedy coordination failures, but disagrees with it on the following point. "[I]t is not the government's responsibility to solve the coordination problem. Rather, the government's role is to facilitate the development of private-sector institutions that can overcome these failures." But how? Because the problem lies in the lack of information exchange, the answer given by this third view is to establish a forum for the exchange of information, sponsored by the government and with the participation of mainly private entities. Mediation of information by the government itself is not desirable. Thus the only permissible government involvement is to set up deliberation councils.

An example shows this clearly. In the *East Asian Miracle*, the case of an interindustry link between a steel plant and a steel-using industry is used to explain the meaning of coordination failure. This kind of complementarity is the most typical source of the problem. Okazaki (1997) claims that in the post-war economic recovery period, because of a high degree of complementarity among steel, shipbuilding, marine transportation, and coal, if government had not done anything to coordinate the plans of these industries, ambitious, or bold investment projects needed to jump-start recovery of the economy would not have taken place. He concludes that just one deliberation council attached to the MITI served as the institution for the exchange of information among representatives from firms in the four industries mentioned above.

The market-enhancing view is theoretically quite elegant and very strict. But its conclusion supports the deliberation-council-type forum as the only justifiable government action in the face of a coordination failure.

9.3   A brief overview of Japanese industrial policy in the 1940s–1950s

In this and the next sections, we must examine if the various theories explained in the previous section really match the historical facts of Japan.

9.3.1   When were industrial policies active in Japan?

Before the *Dodge Line* of 1949 (see Section 9.5), the Japanese economy was characterized by the remains of tight and detailed control under the wartime regime. Although a large part of the economy was in the private sector, the government controlled prices of several hundred basic industrial products and set some quantitative targets for production. Some products and materials were even rationed according to a *plan* laid out by the Economic Stabilization Board. Thus, the Japanese economy was a quasi-socialist system. The General Headquarters of the Allied Forces was quite tolerant of the Japanese government's socialistic inclination, and for a short while the Socialist Party was the ruling party, so many bureaucrats and opinion formers advocated protection and control of domestic industries.

In this period, the government tried to restore the production of coal and iron to previous levels, introducing a *priority production* system. This scheme consisted of control of prices and wages (prices were set artificially low and wages were set high), preferential loans, and most notably the privileging of these industries in the rationing of materials. For example, there was a production target for coal in 1947. The central organ to implement the plan was the Economic Stabilization Board, which controlled the prices of 2,128 items in 1949 and rationed 57 items of production. These forms of interventionist policy were much more direct than industrial policies after 1950.

After the Dodge Line, almost all of the interventionist policies were abandoned. But the Japanese government kept the belief that protection of infant industry was necessary, leading to a set of so-called *industrial policies*. It must be emphasized that those industrial policies maintained some influence on the mentality of private enterprises only until the mid-1950s or a little later. Some economists describe this short period as the Golden Age of industrial policy and assert that observers from outside of Japan have been influenced by the impression given in this period. In order to understand the policies, a cursory taxonomy must be given first.

9.3.2   Brief taxonomy of Japanese industrial policy

It is difficult and perhaps not worthwhile to make a list of all kinds of policies introduced by MITI. It is, however, of some use to provide a broad idea of what categories of policies were adopted. Since MITI's course changed from time to time, we can omit periods in which their policies were not designed to accelerate the modernization of industries. According to Tsuruta (1982), MITI's policy objectives became unrealistic as early as about 1960 because the private sector of Japanese economy started to grow on its own. Evidently after the investment boom in the late 1950s, it grew by its spontaneous mechanism. Thus, it suffices to examine the industrial policy between the Dodge Line of 1949 and 1960 when the government announced the introduction of trade liberalization, which marked an important switch of government policies. There are several aspects of industrial policy to discuss in this period.

First, import protection through quantitative restrictions and high tariff rates was an important measure designed to shelter most industries. In 1960, however, the Japanese government announced *Guidelines for Trade Liberalization*. Since then, the level of protection has been steadily lowered. Besides, accession to the IMF in 1952 and to the General Agreement on Tariffs and Trade (GATT) in 1955 made many industries aware of the future threat of international competition and brought about efforts on their behalf to rationalize production processes prior to actual trade liberalization.

Second, foreign direct investment (FDI) was strictly controlled by the Deliberation Council of Foreign Capital. As a strategy for fostering promising industries, FDI is often welcomed by developing countries or regions. Lacking financial resources and advanced technology, Japanese industrial leaders and the government were, as a general principle, ready to accept foreign capital. Yet, in examining each application from abroad, the council mostly dismissed the entry of foreign firms into Japan, influenced by the interests of specific companies. Tsuruta (1982) said that while the restriction on trade had some grounds (the infant industry argument), the restriction of FDI was not justifiable at all.[18]

Third, preferential tax incentives were given to some *strategic industries* in the form of accelerated depreciation schemes. There were several types of scheme, but in all of them, the incentives were given to encourage investment in advanced machinery or technologies. Contrary to the principle of picking the winner, however, preferential treatment was also given to many declining industries so long as they tried to introduce some new machinery or equipment.

Fourth, tax credits were given to exporting industries in proportion to their performances (Export Income Deduction).

Fifth, loans at preferential interest rates from the Japan Development Bank and Japan Export Bank were allocated to several *strategic industries* at the discretion of MITI. The government also emphasized the care of the *weaker part of the economy* by providing small and medium-size enterprises and unincorporated firms with low interest rate loans. The sources of funds for these loans were mainly the postal savings system without any additional budgetary burden, but the government subsidized the administrative cost of the program heavily.

Sixth, until the late 1950s, the allocation of the foreign exchange budget was used to restrict imports and encourage exports. Those firms with supposedly good export prospects received favorable allocations of foreign currency, because their imports were expected to regenerate larger inflows of foreign currency.

It is often said that MITI intervened to the activities of the private sector by persuasion and so-called *administrative guidance*, but we can safely ignore this because such measures did not affect the behavior of the private sector unless they were combined with the policies mentioned above. Another set of seemingly important tools in industrial policy was the use of *deliberation councils*, where exchanges of information between private enterprises and government officials took place. It will be discussed later whether such exchanges were crucial in avoiding some kind of market failure and thus contributed to growth performance.

In summary, the main tools of Japan's industrial policy were protection from foreign competitors, tax incentives, and preferential loans. The first is roughly the same as an import substitution strategy. The other two might be classified as export promotion measures if they had really been targeted at promising export industries.

9.3.3 Characterization of Japanese industrial policies

Infant industry protection is the antithesis of Ricardo's theory of comparative advantage. Critics like Amsden, Wade, and MITI officials correctly pointed out its lack of dynamic perspective. It may not create desirable consequences. Even though there may be some dynamic gains from established industries some serious loss of welfare may be caused by intervention in the form of *government failure*. This danger is called the *Listian trap*.[19]

Government failure is now an established concept. It means that although government should rectify market failures in theory, in reality it tends to fail to conceive and implement correct or adequate policies. In addition, the protected industries sometimes do not grow at all, because protection provides no force or incentive for them to improve on their initial situation. Instead, they rather enjoy the rents obtainable from protection so long as they can monopolize the domestic economy.

Hayami (1997) criticized import substitution policy by saying that the victims were consumers, farmers, and unprotected industries, especially small and medium-size firms competing with foreign imports. He argues further: "Despite such sacrifice, the cases are few in which protected industries succeed in achieving internationally competitive strength in due course. Instead, protection reduces the incentives for domestic producers to keep up with productivity at an international level for the sake of survival, resulting in preservation of inefficient enterprises."[20]

These two shortcomings explain why the import substitution strategy hindered growth or equivalently, industrialization in some countries such as

India before 1990, Brazil, Kenya, and so on. Why didn't industrial policy in Japan fall into the same trap? As Amsden (1989) and the World Bank (1993) explained before, Japanese industrial policy was a careful combination of protection and other incentives and disciplines. Before examining their propositions, it is possible to provide two other answers to this question.

First, the size of domestic markets was large enough to permit competition among, if not many, at least several firms. This was the conclusion of M. Okuno and K. Suzumura derived from an extensive study reported in *Industrial policy of Japan*.[21] They pointed out that in addition to infant industry protection, another type of trade restriction was introduced to foster countervailing power in the face of a foreign monopolist or oligopoly.[22] In this case, industrial policy worked as a substitute for worldwide antimonopoly policy.

Amsden (1989) and the World Bank (1993) were concerned about the industrial structure in terms of the concentration rate, but there was ample evidence that competition among domestic firms was very keen. One such piece of evidence was the fact that MITI repeatedly issued warnings about *excessive competition* and tried unsuccessfully to persuade firms into mergers. These situations made Okuno and Suzumura assert that "the initiative and vitality of the private sector undermined the plans of the government authorities to try to utilize direct intervention in the nature of *controls*."[23]

Second, in the 1950s, Japanese firms protected by the industrial policy were anticipating trade liberalization and were aware of the necessity to prepare for competition with strong foreign firms. Although it was only in 1955 that Japan gained accession to GATT and in 1960 that the government declared the *General Principles of Trade Liberalization*. But manufacturing companies started to anticipate the coming liberalization probably as early as the time of the Dodge Line. One of the reasons why import substitution does not nurture infant industries is the lack of discipline. If firms foresee the end of featherbedding, they will certainly start preparing for the competitive situation well in advance of the opening up of the market.

9.3.4 Are subsidies in Japan really performance-based?

In the previous section, we have looked only at protective measures, because they were the main pillars of industrial policy in the late 1940s and throughout the 1950s. In the mid-1950s, another set of measures, subsidies, and subsidy-like measures was extensively introduced. These were mainly tax subsidies and loans with preferential interest rates from government-sponsored financial institutions.

The first problem with these measures was that they were extended not only to promising infant industries but also to established and internationally competitive mature industries and in some cases even to declining industries. In a slightly different context, that is, on industrial policy at large, Hayami (1997) points out that mature industries like steel mills and shipbuilding, low productivity sectors like retailing and agriculture, and declining industries like textiles were the main beneficiaries of such industrial policies and other similar protective policies and subsidies. Komiya (1988), Ito-Krueger (1992), and Hayami (1997) all enumerate industries that succeeded in growing into very competitive exporters without particularly favorable treatment by the government. Ito's list is not the longest, still covering: sewing machines, cameras, bicycles, motorcycles, pianos, and radios during the 1950s and the 1960s, color TVs, tape recorders, magnetic tapes, audio components, watches, pocket calculators, machine tools, ceramics, and robotics from the late 1960s to the present.[24]

The second problem regarding subsidy-type policies was that they were giveaways rather than performance-based rewards. Both Amsden (1989) and the World Bank (1993) claim that subsidies to promote exports and industrialization in Japan, as well as in Korea, are combined with some discipline in the form of performance criteria, as described above. The keyword is *contest*. The only two examples presented in the World Bank report are the First Temporary Measures for Machine Industry Promotion Law and First Steel Industry Rationalization Program.[25] In this table there is no explanation about the performance criteria. There are columns for *Rules*, *Rewards*, and *Referees*, but one cannot find any hint of such *criteria* by looking at all these items. This is simply because there were no such things as performance criteria. Many industries, which were not at all promising, were also given subsidies and preferential treatment, as explained above. This fact indicates that the rewards were not even based on prospective performances. In the case of the export income deduction system for the corporate income tax, the performance criterion was profit earned by export, one might say. But if one generalizes the meaning of performance criteria in that way, all the subsidies must be regarded as performance-based rewards. Then the difference between *High Performing Asian Economies* and other developing countries cannot be explained by the presence or absence of contests.

This means that the industrial policy design cannot explain the successes of Japanese export industries, nor the rapid growth of the economy in the 1950s and 1960s. One may argue that although the design of the system was not adequate, the discretion exercised by bureaucrats created the right incentives and appropriate discipline. Although foreign observers tend to say that Japanese bureaucrats were competent and trustworthy, they are overestimating the quality of Japanese bureaucrats. There are many scandals involving both bureaucrats and politicians. There is a great deal of evidence that Japanese bureaucrats are not immune from red-tape inefficiency. Besides, competence and trustworthiness do not guarantee right policies.

The lack of discipline is fatal, because reward (in our case subsidy or protection) by itself does not produce desirable outcomes. We must recall that Amsden's argument boils down to the following; catching up requires both sticks and carrots. Adam Smith argued that a stick in the form of competition and a carrot in the form of temporary monopoly followed by the competition constitute strong incentives to innovation.[26] Apparently Adam Smith theorized a different mechanism from David Ricardo's comparative advantage. Perhaps we can dismiss Ricardo's theory as being static. "But Adam Smith's argument was based on a much broader perspective. Some of the current discussions of the role of the government and the virtue of competition take this broader perspective."[27] Competition seems to be a much better form of discipline than a *performance-based subsidy* or *contest*, even though there may be some doubts about the virtue of temporary monopoly.

There is an important counterexample to the proposition that a combination of subsidy and governmental discipline is indispensable in late industrializing countries. Without the help of such an arrangement, the Japanese cotton-spinning industry succeeded in growing into an important export industry in the 1890s and thereafter. This is clearly inconsistent with Amsden's argument.[28]

In Table 9.1, the last line was added not to summarize the argument of Amsden but to show that not only alleged *market-augmenting* strategies in Japan, Korea, and Taiwan but also *market-friendly* strategies adopted by India, Thailand, Chile, and Argentina in the 1990s proved quite effective. Thus, rather than the developmental-state strategy, something else common to the latter group might have worked to bring about remarkable growth in Japan, Korea, and Taiwan.

9.3.5   Is coordination failure important?

To solve the problem of interindustrial externalities or strategic complementarity, interindustrial coordination may be needed. Okuno-Fujiwara (1997) refers to the policy to compensate for coordination failure as *guidance* of the market mechanisms. "The guiding role of the government is to help the economy move in a certain direction by providing incentives and coordinating private activities."[29] Okazaki claims that after the Dodge Line, heavy industries were troubled by their small scale, and that a coordination of investment projects was needed in order to achieve rationalization in all enterprises. If the private sector had been left alone, "complementarity among industries, economies of scale, and incomplete information" would have caused serious problems. "To resolve coordination failure, the government's coordination played an important role."[30] But information sharing and consensusmaking may not be necessary if overseas suppliers have large enough capacity or ambitious investment plans. It is simply a matter of bidding a slightly higher price than before in the world market. In the case of Okazaki's example, four industries did not have to harmonize their investment plans. Just by collecting information or statistics in the international markets for steel products and maritime transportation charges, the shipbuilding industry could decide its investment plan. Hayami (1997) says, "the interindustry coordination for effective forward and backward linkages needs not be designed within the boundary of a national economy,"[31] He uses the example of Taiwan. In contrast to the perception of Wade (1990), it was not government intervention but the linkage with foreign companies which was the crucial factor for the *remarkable* success of small and medium-size enterprises and perhaps the success of the whole Taiwanese economy.

Another difficulty with coordination failure as an important obstacle to the catch-up process is that the only legitimate government action in the field of industrial policy is to *sponsor* forums in which only private companies coordinate their investment plans and/or production plans. Matsuyama (1997) points out that even though coordination failure requires some corrective action by somebody, the private sector can reach a better solution by trial and error than through a solution imposed by government intervention. This means that the government should refrain from quick-fix mediation of information but should let the private sector go through such trials and errors unaided.[32]

The above argument leads us to the conclusion that among various types of industrial policies, the only meaningful and beneficial one was the deliberation councils sponsored by MITI. The contention that MITI's policy largely explains Japan's rapid growth really implies that such trifling operations as deliberation councils were the main factor behind the Japanese miracle. No other industrial policy was needed, or rather other industrial policies would have been harmful. If the deliberation councils had really contributed to Japan's rapid economic growth, however, they would have become well known immediately and would have been emulated by many other developing countries as a quick booster, given the simplicity and ease of reproduction.

9.4   Johnson, Amsden, and growth theories

Instead of adopting the above line of argument, it is more reasonable to say that it was not industrial policy but other, mostly economic, factors that explain rapid growth in that period. Yet, C. Johnson (1982) challenged those economists who tried to account for this growth through economic factors. His logic hinges on the following observation.

> Hugh Patrick argues, "I am of the school which interprets Japanese economic performance as due primarily to the actions and efforts of private individuals and enterprises responding to the opportunities provided in quite free markets for commodities and labor. While the government has been supportive of and indeed has done much to create the environment for growth, its role has often been exaggerated." But there is a problem, he concedes. "It is disturbing that the macro explanations of Japanese postwar economic performance—in terms of increases in aggregate labor and capital inputs and in their more productive allocation—leave

40 percent plus of output growth and half of labor productivity growth unexplained." If it can be shown that the government's industrial policy made the difference in the rate of investment in certain economically strategic industries, then perhaps we may say that its role has not been exaggerated.[33]

C. Johnson is not an economist, and because of his background he made mistakes which economists can easily detect. What Patrick is talking about as a "disturbing" thing is the so-called Solow residual. The presence of a "residual," or in more straightforward terminology, *inexplicable factors*, is surely disturbing. But this situation is not peculiar to the Japanese growth pattern. Arrow (1962) once said that "[I]t is by now uncontroversial that increases in per capita income cannot be explained simply by increase in the capital-labor ratio. Nevertheless a view of economic growth that depends so heavily on an exogenous variable, let alone one so difficult to measure as the quantity of knowledge, is hardly intellectually satisfactory."[34]

One obvious error made by Johnson is that he regarded the Solow residual as something that should be explained by noneconomic factors such as the abilities of bureaucrats. Although Arrow complained about the fact that the residual was conceived as exogenous, he did not regard the residual as a noneconomic factor. His effort to explain technological progress (which is nothing but Solow's residual) by some other economic factors bore fruit later in the form of a new school called the *endogenous growth theory*. What Johnson regarded as an inexplicable portion of Japan's remarkable economic achievement was explicable by economic but exogenous factors according to conventional economics. The new growth theories even try to explain it as a part of an economic model.

Another of Johnson's errors is that he tried to explain the residual through the government's industrial policy and resulting differences in *the rate of investment in certain economically strategic industries*. Since we are concerned with some factors other than the contribution of the increases in inputs including capital and labor, it is apparent that he is mixing up what is *in* (contribution of inputs) and what is *out* (technology or efficiency or total factor productivity).

In any case, if we can explain the technological progress endogenously, then there is no room for Johnson's argument. Recent studies in the field of growth theory advance the view that the contribution of capital (including human capital) to the growth of output is greater than conventional measurements based on growth accounting. In other words, "the elasticity of final output with respect to physical capital will be larger than the share of capital income in value added."[35] The logic behind this observation is that capital investment is accompanied by large positive externalities. Thus the contribution of capital increase to output growth is so large that there is no residual left. This is tantamount to saying that capital increase is accompanied by parallel improvements in efficiency or technology, and that capital and output increase proportionately.[36]

Amsden, using a much older idea, develops an intuitive version of endogenous growth theory applicable only to late-industrializing countries. She claims that there is a reverse causality running from growth to productivity, utilizing the work of Kaldor. This is contrary to the causality generally found in traditional economic theories which runs from technological progress and productivity to growth. In catching-up economies, both normal and reverse causalities are working, and hence "there is circular and cumulative causality."[37] There are three mechanisms through which the above *reverse causality* is brought about.

First, foreign technology embodied in plant and equipment raises productivity, and investments in plant and equipment depend on growth. Second, "it will be easier to realize scale economies embodied in imported foreign technology when output is growing." Third, the faster output is rising, the faster the process of learning-by-doing proceeds. In all of these three items, investment plays a key role. By adding to these three mechanisms the causality from a high growth to high saving ratio, then to a high investment ratio, and finally to the substantial contribution of embodied technological progress, the circular process is completed.

According to this proposition, industrialized economies cannot enjoy the cumulative process, because technology borrowing in a latecomer economy is a crucial factor to the process. Thus, in spite of Kaldor's initiative to get the reverse causality started, the British economy did not achieve vigorous growth in the 1960s. This is consistent with one of the conclusions of the Solow growth model; rich economies cannot grow as fast as some latecomers. Kaldor's theory can also be applied to the Japanese economy in the rapid growth era when Japan was utilizing the pool of technologies invented by Westerners.

There is another mechanism that contributes to the growth-to-productivity relationship (the reverse relationship). High growth rates and resulting high investment ratios created many new high productivity sectors to which inputs shifted from low productivity sectors. Using Japanese data, Denison estimates that "improved resource allocation" pushed up the annual growth rate in 1953–71 by 0.95 percentage points, out of which 0.64 can be explained by "contraction of agricultural inputs," and 0.30 by "contraction of non-agricultural self-employed."[38] According to the author's rough calculation, the contribution of contraction of agricultural labor input alone contributed to annual growth by almost 1 percentage point during the period 1955–70. Although this is a rather intuitive estimation, it is clear that these contractions of low productivity sectors were induced by job opportunities resulting from rapid capacity expansion elsewhere. Thus, a significant part of growth in the rapid growth era can be explained by such induced, that is, endogenous improvement of efficiency.

Whichever argument one may use, it is possible to explain the high contribution of the Solow residual mentioned by Patrick using economic terms. Actually, Romer's *proportionality model* and Amsden's *circular model* (or virtuous circle model) are essentially the same argument. They are both consistent with the development of the Japanese economy. During the period between 1955 and 1970, the capital-output ratio did not show a significant rise. Thus, one can observe a rough proportionality between capital and output. According to Kosai and Ogino (1980), the capital-output ratio for the whole Japanese economy was 2.5 in 1955–60, 2.9 in 1960–65, and 2.9 again in 1965–70.[39] These figures are quite low. Many economists had expected that the ratio would rise to a level comparable to those of Western industrialized countries as a result of the diminishing marginal productivity of capital.

When Johnson published his book, *MITI*, it might have been difficult to provide a clear-cut counterargument to his claim that a large part of the rapid growth in the postwar Japanese economy could be explained by non-economic factors. These days, however, we are equipped with the above arguments. There can be differing views about the role of the government in prewar economic development, but as far as the postwar period is concerned, it was neither the government nor industrial policy that brought about rapid economic growth.

After examining some recent arguments, we come back to the conclusion of Okuno and Suzumura (1988) quoted in Section 9.3 that the competitive market was the main cause of the rapid development of Japan. Then we need to find out how this competitive situation was established. There seems to be two policies that radically changed the situation immediately after the World War II. The first was the dissolution of family-owned *Zaibatsu* conglomerates combined with the introduction of the Anti-Monopoly Law and Excessive Concentration Elimination Law in 1946. The second was the Dodge Line in 1949. Nakamura (1994) called the combination of these two *revolutionary*.

9.5   The Dodge Line—a starting point

It is worth making some comments on the Dodge Line at this stage. In the wake of the World War II, the Japanese economy was devastated partly as a result of bomb damage and partly because the industrial structure was heavily biased toward the munitions industry. The level of industrial production in 1946 was as low as almost one-fifth of the wartime peak. There were serious bottlenecks of supplies, especially in materials and energy. The government was running a large deficit financed by the printing of money. The deficit was further swollen by the effort of government to subsidize the energy industry and some strategic industries such as iron and steel. Prices soared due to the bottlenecks and increased money supply, which was aggravated by an increase of loans to strategic industries as well. Inflation was running at the annual rate of 216 percent in 1947 and 173 percent in 1948. Black market prices were rising faster than those quoted. Everybody was becoming aware of the necessity to stop this. The Japanese government under the occupation was trying to formulate a gradualist approach to tightening the nation's belt. Then, in late 1948, Washington decided to encourage the recovery of the Japanese economy with the aim of building a bulwark in the Asian front against communism. Indeed, stabilization was one of the main ingredients of the newly formulated policy. But because of resistance from both the General Headquarters of the Army of Occupation and the Japanese government, a compromise, *the Nine Principles for Economic Stabilization* was reached between Washington and Tokyo. A few months later, Special Ambassador Joseph Dodge arrived in Tokyo, and introduced a much more radical set of policies that could be called *shock therapy*. It must be remembered that he was a hardline Republican and had participated in the formulation of the German stabilization policy immediately after World War II.

The first measure in the program was to balance of the real overall budget.[40] This means that the entire central government budget including special budgets (off-budget special accounts) had to be balanced. The second measure was the abolition of all subsidies. The third was the suspension of both bond issues and new loans from the Reconstruction Finance Bank. This served as a quite stringent tightening of monetary policy. Fourth, price controls on commodities were abolished leaving only some 20 items under government regulation. Fifth, the dual exchange rate system was terminated and a single rate of 360 yen per dollar was set.

Okazaki said that the Dodge Line was a transition to a market economy.[41] Furthermore, it was a *shock therapy* transition. The deficit was eliminated from the national budget for fiscal year 1949. Owing to this measure and the suspension of the activities of the Reconstruction Finance Bank, the expansion of the money supply was kept in check. This therapy worked quite well in bringing the economy into a market economy. Prices were stabilized. Thus, the aims of the *market-friendly approach* can be summarized in two key words: liberalization and stabilization. What the Dodge Line brought about was a combination of the two. The liberalization of international trade was delayed somewhat, but keen domestic competition was sufficient to pave the way to smooth functioning of competition and thus the market mechanism.

Although it is not possible to compare the impact of the Dodge Line and industrial policy in the 1950s and 1960s quantitatively, it is quite clear that the former was decisively more significant. This is a minority view, because the Dodge Line was very unpopular among most Japanese economists active in the 1950s and the 1960s, who were mostly directly or indirectly involved in the formulation of the gradualist approach killed by Special Ambassador

Dodge.[42] Many younger economists who support the view that private sector initiative was the mainstay of the growth in the 1950s and the 1960s, did not pay enough attention to the role of the Dodge Line because of the recession that followed its introduction. It is indeed difficult to answer the question: what would have happened if the Dodge Line had not been introduced? It is not too difficult to imagine, however, relying on the various results of convergence or growth regression, that prolonged inflation and a featherbedding policy would have stifled the private initiative to introduce innovative technologies and ideas. We should give higher credit to the legacy of the shock therapy prescribed by Dodge than the average Japanese view would give.

9.6   Conclusion

If we interpret Japan's experience in the above manner, what kind of policy does it suggest in the context of a strategy for development and/or transition from a planned economy to a market economy?

Recently, the IMF's recommendations to some Asian countries that underwent a financial crisis in 1997 were unfavorably received, because the IMF's menu of reform programs included some unnecessary and excessive belt-tightening policies such as severe tightening of fiscal policy in the countries with fairly sound financial positions or budget balances. In some transition economies the shock therapies of the IMF produced a prolonged decline in the level of production and living standard, although in some cases the decline was followed by remarkable recovery and sustained growth. These events created a considerable distrust among policymakers and economists toward the IMF's credo of neoclassical economics and shock therapy approach.

Some Japanese economists including K. Ohno (1998) recently initiated an effort to reconsider the *Fund-Bank orthodoxy* and neoclassical doctrine of emphasizing macroeconomic stability and the free market, saying that there are three problems in such a view:

1. it is not always true that the market mechanism is an ideal type;
2. dynamism of noneconomic factors is neglected; and
3. it separates of economic efficiency from all other value systems such as religion, education, ethnicity, morality, culture, etc.

They say that Japanese experience presents some guide to nonorthodox approaches for development and/or transition. Their disagreement with the orthodoxy is mainly based on their experience in designing Japanese aid programs for developing countries. In this regard, it is true that laissez-faire ideology or the market-friendly approach is not a panacea. Gerschenkron (1962) stressed the role of government in a very early stage of development, mentioning the examples of Russia in the 1880s and Hungary around the turn of the century. He also emphasized the role of institutions in industrialization or the catch-up process depending on the stage of development. Investment banks in France and Germany, for example, played crucial roles in realizing ambitious investment projects including railroad construction.

As Ohno and Gerschenkron say, institutions play a key role at certain stages. In one stage, the role of government, not only as a referee but also as a player, may be extremely important. In some other situations, institutions, such as nineteenth century *private* investment banks in continental Europe, may be necessary. In the economic history of Meiji era Japan, one can find some examples of government initiatives to establish some industries including railroads, which eventually helped the development of private industries. Yet in other periods, such as postwar Japanese, the stabilization and market economy made possible by the Dodge Line were the main factors that paved the way to rapid growth.

It must be remembered that recent empirical studies in the field of *growth regression,* which is based on the Solow-Swan growth model, noneconomic factors and financial institutions were given quite a significant position. It is clear, however, that noneconomic factors such as political stability are important just because they are a fundamental basis for drastic change in the policy toward economic stabilization and liberalization. Other findings of growth regression suggest that price stability and openness of the economy are important, as are the starting level of the economy, savings ratio, and education. This seems to be consistent with the following conclusion. Japan's industrial policies in the postwar period do not provide a lesson for either transition strategy or industrialization strategy. The Japanese economy at the end of World War II was institutionally sufficiently mature, so to speak, and waiting for a kind of shock therapy very much akin to the one recently prescribed by the IMF.

Depending on the stage of development, culture, and political background, the prescription needs to deviate from the neoclassical orthodoxy. But we can conjecture that in the present world economy, there are many economies that reached the stage where a market-friendly approach can provide better results than others such as a market-augmenting approach, a market-enhancing approach, or a developmental-state approach, etc.

Notes

As a postscript, the author wishes to add that the conclusion is not only affected by the recent development of international trade theory with increasing-return-to-scale assumption but also supported by new empirical studies on Japan's industrial policy.

1. Abegglen (1970, 71). Abegglen says as follows. "The Japanese government corresponds to corporate headquarters, responsible for planning and coordination,

formation of long-term policies and major investment decisions. The large corporations of Japan are akin to corporate divisions, with a good deal of operating autonomy within the overall policy framework laid down by corporate headquarters..."

2. Johnson (1982).
3. Boltho (1975), pp. 188–189.
4. Tsuruta (1982).
5. Fallows (1994), p. 179.
6. Kosai (1988).
7. Amsden (1989).
8. *Ibid.*, p. 12.
9. *Ibid.*, p. 3.
10. "The First Industrial Revolution was built on laissez-faire, the Second on infant industry protection. In late industrialization, the foundation is the subsidy-which both protection and financial incentives" (*ibid.*, p. 143).
11. Amsden says as follows. "Learners do not innovate (by definition) and must compete initially on the combined basis of low wages, State subsidies (broadly construed to include a wide variety of government supports), and incremental productivity and quality improvements related to existing products" (*ibid.*, p. 5).
12. *Ibid.*, p. 8.
13. *Ibid.*, p. 146.
14. World Bank (1993), pp. 90–91.
15. *Ibid.*, p. 92.
16. *Ibid.*, p. 94 (Box 2.2).
17. Aoki et al. (1997), p. 8.
18. Tsuruta (1982).
19. See Hayami (1997), p. 209.
20. *Ibid.*, p. 211.
21. Komiya, Okuno, and Suzumura (1988), p. 554.
22. *Ibid.*, p. 553.
23. *Ibid.*, p. 552.
24. Ito (1992), p. 201.
25. World Bank (1993), Table 2.2, "Examples of Contest," p. 95.
26. This argument is based on the summary by Joseph E. Stiglitz (1988), p. 71.
27. *Ibid.*
28. See Hayami (1997), pp. 216–217.
29. *Ibid.*, p. 394.
30. Okazaki (1997), p. 94.
31. Hayami (1997), p. 228.
32. Matsuyama (1997), pp. 134–160.
33. Johnson (1982), p. 9. Quotations by Johnson are from Hugh Patrick, "The Future of the Japanese Economy: Output and Labor Productivity," *The Journal of Japanese Studies*, 3 (Summer 1977), p. 239 and p. 225.
34. Arrow (1962).
35. Aghion, and Howitt (1998), p. 33.
36. See Romer (1987) and "Comment" by Martin N. Baily in the same volume.
37. Amsden, pp. 109–112.
38. Denison, and Chung (1976), p. 98, Table 2–13.
39. Yutaka Kosai, and Yoshitaro Ogino (1980).
40. Takafusa Nakamura (1994), p. 160.
41. *Ibid.*, p. 94.

42. Hisao Kanamori, a leading economist who wrote some books on the postwar economic history, and who used to be an economist in the Economic Stabilization Board, once said that he disliked the Dodge Line, although he changed his view later.

References

Abegglen, J. C. (ed.). 1970. *Business Strategies for Japan*. Tokyo: Sophia University/TBS Britannica.

Aghion, P., and P. Howitt. 1998. *Endogenous Growth Theory*. Cambridge, MA: MIT Press.

Amsden, A. H. 1989. *Asia's Next Giant: South Korea and Late Industrialization*. Oxford: Oxford University Press.

Aoki, M., H. K. Kim, and M. Okuno-Fujiwara (eds.). 1997. *The Role of Government in East Asian Economic Development: Comparative Institutional Analysis*. Oxford: Clarendon Press.

Arrow, K. J. 1962. "The Economic Implication of Learning by Doing." *The Review of Economic Studies* (June) 29(3): 155–173.

Boltho, A. 1975. *Japan: An Economic Survey, 1953–73*. London: Oxford University Press.

Denison, E. F., and W. K. Chung. 1976. "Economic Growth and Its Sources." In *Asia's New Giant: How the Japanese Economy Works*, H. Patrick and H. Rosovsky (eds.). Washington, DC: The Brookings Institution.

Fallows, J. 1994. *Looking at the Sun: The Rise of the New East Asian Economic and Political System*. New York: Pantheon.

Gerschenkron, A. 1962. *Economic Backwardness in Historical Perspective*. Cambridge, MA: Harvard University Press.

Hayami, Y. 1997. *Development Economics: From the Poverty to the Wealth of Nations*. Oxford: Oxford University Press.

Ito, T. and A. O. Krueger. 1992. *Japanese Economy*. Cambridge, MA: The MIT Press.

Johnson, C. 1982. *MITI and the Japanese Miracle*. Palo Alto, CA: Stanford University Press.

Komiya, R. 1988. "Introduction." In *Industrial Policy of Japan*, R. Komiya, M. Okuno, and K. Suzumura (eds.). Tokyo: Academic Press Japan, Inc.: 1–22.

Komiya, R., M. Okuno, and K. Suzumura. (eds.). 1988. *Industrial Policy of Japan*. Tokyo: Academic Press Japan, Inc. [A translation of *Nihon no Sangyo Seisaku*, 1984, Tokyo Daigaku Shuppankai].

Kosai, Y. 1988. "The Reconstruction Period. (Chapter 2)" In *Industrial Policy of Japan*, R. Komiya, M. Okuno, and K. Suzumura (eds.). Tokyo: Academic Press Japan, Inc.: 25–48.

Kosai, Y., and Y. Ogino. 1980. *Nihon Keizai Tembou* [A Perspective on the Japanese Economy]. Tokyo: Nihon-Hyouron-Sha.

Matsuyama, K. 1997. "Economic Development as Coordination Problem." In *The Role of Government in East Asian Economic Development: Comparative Institutional Analysis*, M. Aoki, H. K. Kim, and M. Okuno-Fujiwara (eds.). Oxford: Clarendon Press: 134–160.

Nakamura, T. 1994. *Lectures on Modern Japanese Economic History 1926–1994*. Tokyo: LTCB International Library Foundation.

Ohno, K. 1998. "Overview: Creating the Market Economy." In *Japanese Views on Economic Development: Diverse Path to the Market*, K. Ohno and I. Ohno (eds.). London and New York: Routledge.

Okazaki, T. 1997. "The Government-Firm Relationship in Postwar Japanese Economic Recovery: Resolving Coordination Failure by Coordination in Industrial Rationalization." In *The Role of Government in East Asian Economic Development: Comparative Institutional Analysis*, M. Aoki, H. K. Kim, and M. Okuno-Fujiwara (eds.). Oxford: Clarendon Press: 74–100.

Okuno-Fujiwara, M. 1997. "Toward a Comparative Institutional Analysis of the Government-Business Relationship." In *The Role of Government in East Asian Economic Development: Comparative Institutional Analysis*, M. Aoki, H. K. Kim, and M. Okuno-Fujiwara (eds.). Oxford: Clarendon Press: 373–406.

Okuno, M. and K. Suzumura. 1988. "Conclusion." In *Industrial Policy of Japan*, R. Komiya, M. Okuno, and K. Suzumura (eds.). Tokyo: Academic Press Japan, Inc.: 551–558.

Romer, P. M. 1987. "Crazy Explanations for the Productivity Slowdown." *NBER Macroeconomic Annual 1987*, Vol. 2. Cambridge, MA: National Bureau of Economic Research: 163–210.

Stiglitz, J. E. 1988. *Economics of the Public Sector.* 2nd Edn., New York: W. W. Norton.

Tsuruta, T. 1982. *Sengo Nihon no Sangyou Seisaku* [Industry Policy in Post-war Japan]. Tokyo: Nihon Keizai Shibun-Sha.

Wade, R. 1990. *Governing the Market: Economic Theory and the Role of the Government in East Asian Industrialization.* Princeton, NJ: Princeton University Press.

World Bank. 1991. *World Development Report: Challenge of Development.* New York: Oxford University Press.

World Bank. 1993. *East Asian Miracle: Economic Growth and Public Policy.* Washington, DC: World Bank.

10
Market and Political Justice in Postsocialist Poland
Witold Morawski

10.1 Objectives of analysis

This chapter is focused on distributive justice, which is a neglected aspect of the postsocialist transformation in Poland. The transformed system has established many new institutions like the free market, but all to often they neither function effectively nor much care about social justice. An important problem is how the Poles assess the performance of such institutions as the free market and the democratic state. Unless they appreciate them as being better than the old regime, their legitimacy can not be established. This chapter examines first how the new system answers the questions of what and how political and economic goods are distributed, by whom, for whom, and when. Then, it tries to evaluate the new system from the viewpoint of social justice in distribution.

Social justice is concerned with the various inequalities in the society. One must admit that some of the economic, social, and other inequalities may be not easily removable and defended (Barry 1989, 3). Some others, however, should be removed or mitigated in order to reduce the negative effects of certain systemic changes or deliberate policies and to match the values and interests of the people, that is, their perception of social justice. Social organs such as the state, local governments, voluntary associations, the parish, etc. are responsible for this.

Since the events of 1989–91, central planning has been rejected, and the market has become the only available hardware for economic coordination. The proper software is also needed; namely, adequate laws, reliable élites, a sensitive welfare state, active citizens, changed mentalities, etc. If the new capitalist system accompanies these conditions, it may be accepted as legitimate (Dahrendorf 1999). A number of opinion surveys show the Poles' perception of realized social justice.

Two surveys from 1991 and 1997 show how the market and the state were perceived in the 1990s (Cichomski and Morawski 1991, Cichomski, Morawski, and Morawski 1997) and show that the Polish people's dissatisfaction with the functioning of the market and the state institutions was very high, although few people questioned the advisability of strengthening either the market economy or the democratic state. This confirmed that people accepted the systemic change undertaken in the name of *the return to normalcy* that had existed in the form of mature democracies for a long time. It might be, however, that to some extent their low opinions of the new social order reflected their lack of concern over social justice. In this regard a fundamental proposition articulated by John Rawls, a theorist of liberal social justice should be remembered (1971, 3). "Justice is the first virtue of social institutions, as truth is of systems of thought. A theory, however elegant and economical it may be, must be rejected or revised if it is untrue. Likewise, laws and institutions, no matter how efficient and well-arranged, must be reformed or abolished if they are unjust."

As an aside, comparisons with Western thought would be useful, since the social market economy is *its* culture as one article in Poland's Constitution of 1997 says. Although the relationship between market and polity in Poland will be greatly influenced by the EU, some remarks on American society by Robert E. Lane (1986, 383) on the two different types of social justice of the market and the state have great relevance to our arguments. They are concerned with the Anglo-Saxon concepts worth taking into consideration. The market generates justice based on individual *inputs* and the rewards proportional to them (microjustice), whereas the democratic state (the polity) generates political justice based on political reactions to collective pressures in the democratic process (macrojustice). He maintains the superiority of the former form of justice. "The defence of capitalism in America is rooted in a preference for the market's justice of earned deserts over the justices of equality and needs associated with the polity."

Americans consider the market a more honest distributor than the state. They believe that people appreciate the goods ensured by the market, for example, wages more highly than the goods ensured by the political system, for example, freedom and equal rights. This means that Americans rank the consequences of the market procedural rules higher than the substantial decisions of the political process. American thinking is a characteristic of their liberal and individualistic culture, whereas collectivist elements are stronger in the Polish culture. Such a mentality has been shaped by the system of state socialism, traditions of national struggles, religion, etc.

10.2   Who distributes better?

It was impossible to find in the opinions expressed by the Polish citizens to get an explicit answer to the question: which distributes better: the market or the democratic state. It was only found that both institutions were highly appreciated. The Poles were convinced that the market economy was of fundamental importance to the country's economic development, and the degree of this conviction was very high (in 1991, 72.9 percent and in 1997, 74.5 percent). They were also convinced that privatization was advantageous for the development of the economy (in 1997, 62.9 percent). As regards the political sphere, people believed that they had the possibility of real choice (in 1991, 60.8 percent and in 1997, 67.3 percent).

An overall assessment of Polish views, however, revealed a rather negative outlook, reflecting a low degree of satisfaction with realized conditions of the democratic state and the market economy. They seemed to think as follows: "We do have a democracy but a bad one. We do have a market-private economy but a bad one." The percentage of people dissatisfied with the operation of both institutions were considerably larger than those of the satisfied. Furthermore, the assessment of the democratic state worsened between 1991 and 1997. For example, the proportion of people who suspected that public officials were not concerned with their duties as much as the respondent would expect, rose significantly from 76.6 percent in 1991 to 84.5 percent in 1997. Only one person in five in 1991 and one in ten in 1997 was convinced of the honesty of court trials. Only one person in five believed that the government exercised power for the benefit of all the people.

The actual functioning of the market-private economy is not judged any better. Privatization of state-owned enterprises (SOEs) is generally seen as a process that threatens the interests of the majority (in 1997, 63.5 percent). Only 34.1 percent of Polish people agreed with the opinion that privatization paves the way to improving the living standards of most people. Half of the respondents believed that privatization causes the plundering of public property. All in all, people considered privatization to be advantageous for economic development but that the benefits derived from it are uneven, so it does not strengthen social justice.

People were undecided which of the market or the state should be given more power (PGSS 1997). They were of the opinion that both institutions should have only as much power as they had at the time (economic institutions, 54.3 percent and the government, 57.0 percent). These were the highest percentages among all the postsocialist countries (the Czech Republic, Hungary, Bulgaria, Russia, and the former German Democratic Republic) and Western countries (the USA, the former Federal Republic of Germany) analyzed. It seemed that Poles had not yet managed to formulate their own opinion regarding which of these institutions would be a better distributor of goods.

In comparing Poland with mature democracies, its percentage of respondents who felt that both institutions had too much power was only half of those in the countries like the United States and West Germany. In the West, a citizen of the state and a customer in the market can sometimes feel that their autonomy is threatened, because these institutions are strong enough to impose strict rules of the game upon the people. People need not necessarily feel powerless in face of these institutions, but they may simply respect them. People in Poland, however, assess that the market and the state have too much power less often than in the West and significantly more frequently feel that these institutions have too little power. This view is two to three times more prevalent in Poland than in the West. Poles are correct in claiming that these are weak institutions. They have good reason for not knowing which of them should be favored and is more trust-worthy, although recent political discourse in Poland could give the impression that the market is beginning to gain an advantage over the polity. Opinion about political institutions in Poland is low. For example, people have a negative conviction about the quality of the political class. Thus, we must conclude that the absence of any firm opinion on whether more or less power to the state or market is a sign not of volatility of views but rather a symptom of the weakness of the market, the state, and of society: both institutions are more or less equally accepted, rejected, and tolerated.

Can this irresolution be treated as a symptom of *escape from freedom*: the freedom which has been enlarged considerably by the market economy and the democratic state? (Tischner 1993). Such an interpretation would be premature, as the declared willingness of "escape into state protection" cannot be perceived solely as a symptom of the statist mentality if one remembers that basic needs are not satisfied on mass scale in Poland yet. This is a result of cultural backwardness as well as transformation itself. More people are inclined to consider themselves to be *losers* rather than *winners* in transformation.

10.3   What should be distributed: material goods vs. postmaterial goods?

The ideas I am going to discuss now come from Ronald Inglehart's books on the culture shift in advanced industrial societies (Inglehart 1990; Inglehart 1997). If we accept his view that materialistic values are: *"fight rising prices" and "maintain order in the country,"* and that postmaterialistic values are: "give people more say in the decisions of the government" and "protect freedom of speech," we find that materialistic values predominated in Poland. In the United States their predominance was estimated at 3 to 1, in Poland at 4 to 1. This level was persistent throughout the 1990s. The goal of *maintaining order in the country* was considered the most important by half of the respondents in 1997 and was more strongly supported than in 1991, whereas the material goal: *fight rising prices* had weakened a little. Although the positions of three or four particular goals changed significantly between 1991 and 1997, no big difference was observed with regard to freedom of speech, and the overall picture largely remained the same.

It is interesting to compare data from the 1990s with those from the first half of the 1980s when "maintaining order in the country" was ranked significantly lower. It expressed a "concern" of the authorities. "Fight rising prices" was more or less at the same level as in the 1990s. It may be surprising to notice that postmaterialistic values were more frequently treated as priority values in the 1980s than in the 1990s. In 1980 and 1984 the goal "to maintain order in the country" was ranked highest by only 17 and 21 percent of the respondents respectively, "to fight rising prices" by 37 and 38 percent, "to give people more say in the decisions of the government" by 22 and 18 percent, and "to protect freedom of speech" by 17 and 13 percent (Siemieńska 1988, 199). Did the weakening of the priority of postmaterialistic values in the 1990s imply that they had already been realized? The answer could be positive as some of those values had been realized. People's answers indicate that they were of the opinion that they achieved free political choice after 1989, which seems to explain that our society was more politically passive in the 1990s than in the 1980s.

Then, a new question may be asked: does it mean that market mechanism and liberal democracy discourage people from using instruments of freedom? The disturbing fact was that influencing the democratic state became the secondary value for most people in the 1990s. This is disturbing because people were still dissatisfied with their basic material needs. This contradiction often ignited a criticism of the political class in Poland, which claimed that it knew societal needs well. Then, it really did not know how to practice democracy that was already a live value in the world (Held 1996; Naisbitt 1997). Polish politicians seemed not to know the way to organize the interactions between the political élite and the ordinary citizens, which is a prerequisite of the stable social order in Poland now.

10.4 For whom—who and what?

Questions concerning for whom goods should be provided are inseparable from the answers of who provides these goods. If, for instance, people are not ready to cover the cost of education by themselves, the state must cover the expense. This requires citizens to pay taxes to the state. Only then can the state allocate budgetary resources for education. Thus, the idea that the government should ensure social transfers, even though the idea may lead to constant state intervention in economic decisions, is highly likely to get social support. Such expectations are characteristic of all postsocialist countries (Mason 1995). The surveys indicated almost universal support among Poles for the idea that the government should attempt to ensure work for everybody who wants to work. This idea was voiced by 87.7 percent of respondents in 1991 and again in 1997. Systemic transformation had brought only a slight drop in this expectation, because in 1988 this postulate was advanced by 90.2 percent (Morawski 1994, 292).

Equally interesting is the percentage of respondents supporting the view that the government should fix an upper ceiling on individual incomes. This proposition was put forward by 47.2 and 50.5 percent of respondents in 1991 and 1997 respectively. Surprisingly, this was more frequently advocated in the 1990s after transformation than in 1988 before transformation, when 39.2 percent only accepted income limits for persons with the highest incomes (Morawski 1994, 291). The picture is crystal clear. Although people are aware that the goal of economic reform is the market economy, intervention in economic decisions is often advocated to the government. The figures below show their support for various forms of such intervention (PGSS 1997):

- administrative control of wages: 60.4 percent (in 1988, 73.2 percent: Morawski 1994, 292);
- administrative control of prices: 74.1 percent (in 1988, 87.8 percent: Morawski 1994, 292);
- financing by the government of projects creating new jobs: 90.5 percent;
- subsidies for industry for developing new technologies and products: 84.2 percent;
- support for sunset industries to protect jobs: 66.1 percent; and
- shortening working time to create new jobs: 40.6 percent.

No doubt the realization of such wishes would have created conflicts, because of the limits of the state budget. The nature of conflicts over public choices during systemic transformation is usually revealed by parliamentary debates on the budget. In order to shed more light on the dilemmas faced by citizens and their political representatives, references are made to public opinion surveys. First, data are shown about which is more important for the government, to maintain low inflation or low unemployment. (PGSS 1997). Respondents were asked also to choose between keeping spending on social services unchanged and reducing them to decrease the budget deficit. The answers to these questions reveal a big split in public opinion. The result is quite interesting: although 87.7 percent of respondents expected the government to ensure a job for everyone wanting one, when asked to choose between fighting unemployment and decreasing inflation, only 51.4 percent of respondents were in favor of maintaining low unemployment, and 48.6 percent opted for low inflation. We may interpret these data that 36 percent (87 percent *minus* 51 percent) hoped that achieving low inflation would be more favorable for the economy or lead more effectively to the elimination of unemployment. However, another result showed that 67.6 percent of Poles were in favor of preserving social benefits at the existing level even though it would mean that the budget deficit would remain the same. It could be interpreted from the above facts that public opinion in Poland was closest at the time to the position of Social Democrats, who regarded the budget deficit as a necessary evil.

This interpretation is strengthened by public opinion concerning the lack of readiness among those benefiting from social services to pay for services out of their own pockets. More precisely, they were ready to incur only a minority of the costs or no cost at all, for example, outlays on costs for surgery, higher education, etc. Only about 12 percent of respondents were ready to cover the half or more of the costs of hospitalization. A clear change of thinking occurred only in the area of the costs for employee vacations and kindergartens, with the majority of respondents being ready to cover these costs themselves.

A closer look at the structural and subjective determinants of the above opinion shows that among those who were willing to pay for medical expenses, there are statistically significant variations. Specialists and top executives are more often ready than others, although less than three times so, to pay a larger part of or even full costs for such visits, but as much as 70 percent of people describing themselves as upper class are in favor of fully or partially free social services. As for the remaining social services, opinion differs significantly about who should pay.

The result seems strange, because substantial amounts of household income are often spent, especially for higher education, at the booming private schools. It is difficult to interpret these results, but it seems to suggest the necessity of seeking compromises between the sense of social justice and requirements of economic effectiveness. A strong interest in having a college diploma proves that meritocracy criteria are often respected in the operation of various institutions in Poland, and people are looking for every possible source—from the state budget to their own pocket—to get the means to achieve a higher education. The following data will help to shed light on the empirical facts mentioned above.

10.5   How to distribute: criteria and procedures

Opinion about realized and postulated principles of social justice seem to be the most useful measures to assess the market and the state. The most important result of the entire survey concerns answers to questions regarding *equal opportunities to get ahead*, followed by principles of *rewards* for *inputs*. Robert E. Lane wrote about the requirements of recognizing institutions as just in the United States: "For the market to be considered fair, two related procedural requirements must be met: there must be perceived openness, if not equality, of opportunity, and the market must be considered responsive to effort—to hard work. For the polity to be considered procedurally fair, there must be *adherence to a general norm of political equality*, at least among groups if not among individuals (Verba and Orren 1985, 214), and one must believe that the government is responsive to one's influence. By and large, the market passes the test but the polity does not" (Lane 1986, 386).

The market is considered just in the United States even if it *pays out* unequally, provided that it ensures implementation of the liberal principle of *equal opportunities* and that *rewards* proportionally correspond to *inputs*. Meanwhile, the state is expected to observe a criterion of equality to all citizens. In practice, citizens' needs are recognized as justified demands on the state or the whole political system. Thus, the liberal principle of equal opportunities is both a value and a means. It is equality at the start, or the lack of barriers. It should be stated simultaneously that the final result—life success—depends on how people transform their *inputs* (such as effort, hard work, skills, intelligence, etc.) into *rewards* (such as earnings, career, professional satisfaction, etc.). If merits or equity between *inputs* and *rewards* are achieved, or in other words if *rewards* are proportionally dependent upon *inputs*, then *rewards* will be unequal but just. The principle of equal opportunities realizes social justice as a process, but equal opportunities are created for individuals at the starting point by relevant legislation, activity of the state, assistance provided by nongovernmental associations, local governments, etc. But the principle does not assume that an automatic mechanism will be operating later on, because the only goal is removing barriers at the starting point. In short, apart from ensuring openness of the economic and political systems, everything else depends on individuals themselves.

Ensuring equality of opportunities is not a simple matter, but it is a sort of value which is imposed upon the society to protect the dignity of individuals. Consequently, the principle is interpreted as equality of access to definite means or also as equality of existence or nonexistence of specific barriers or constraints (Sen 1992). Although we assume that understanding of this principle is similar in Poland, we did not investigate ways in which this principle was defined by respondents. We can add, however, that such a definition spontaneously came to people's minds, because at the same time we were asking them about other social justice principles.

The empirical result is quite explicit. Only one Pole in four or five thought in the 1990s that people were actually assured equal opportunities to get ahead. Equally interesting is the fact that this conviction was slightly weaker in 1997 than in 1991 (down from 24.8 percent in 1991 to 21.3 percent in 1997). The most disturbing finding of the survey occurred when the comparative context was taken into account: in the United States, three times as many people (65.9 percent) and in former West Germany (FRG), twice as many people (54.6 percent) claimed that the principle of equal opportunities was implemented. (Alwin et al. 1995, 121). Thus, it is not surprising that the United States and the FRG ranked first and second among 13 countries in the ranking of economic system legitimization undertaken by the International Social Justice Project. (Alwin et al. 1995, 121) Western countries are characterized by considerable socio-economic inequalities. The difference between these countries and Poland lies not so much in the degree of inequalities which can be similar or close, but in the fact that Western inequalities are considered *just* inequalities or legitimized inequalities. In Western countries equal opportunity provides people more chances to get ahead, while Poles who are deprived of equal opportunity have qualitatively smaller chances to get ahead. Other sources of the system's legitimization exist in Western countries that are analyzed here in the form of meritocratic principles.

Let us look more closely at these. Respondents were asked in two ways about these issues: firstly, about the implementation of the principle *"effort* or *hard work* is rewarded," and secondly, about the implementation of the principle "intelligence/skills are rewarded." These principles are not identical, because Polish findings depart from those characterizing Western countries. In Poland, answers to the question about the implementation of the principle "effort is rewarded" range between 16.2 and 21.4 percent (1991 and 1997, respectively). Corresponding shares in the United States and FRG reach as high as 71.4 percent; in Japan, 48.3 percent; in Britain, 48.1 percent ; and in the Netherlands, 49.1 percent. (Alwin et al. 1995, 121) With regard to rewards for intelligence and skills, the contrast between Poland and Western countries is even greater: 17.0–25.2 percent in Poland to about 75 percent in the United States and FRG (Alwin et al. 1995, 121).

Despite major differences in comparison with the West, Polish data contain an optimistic element, since the percentage of persons who are convinced of the implementation of these principles tended to rise in the 1990s. It rose by about 6–9 percent between 1991 and 1997. This would imply that the emerging system would become increasingly meritorious. Speaking metaphorically, if the pace of approaching the West were similar in the future to that recorded in our survey—about 1 percent annually—it would take Poland about 40 years to catch up to leading Western countries, more or less as much time as the Biblical Israelites needed to cover the distance from Egypt to the Holy Land.

Figure 10.1 shows the opinions of respondents about the realization of justice principles in Poland against the background of selected Western countries. It should be added that certain variations in opinion appeared according to structural and social consciousness variables.

- People who define themselves being as the left, agree with the opinion that the principle of equal opportunities is implemented less often than those who define themselves as in the centre or to the right. Let us note that the right began to withdraw from this opinion in 1997, which can be attributed to the fact that the leftist coalition was in power at that time.
- As regards the principle "effort or hard work is rewarded," all respondents, apart from farmers, are of the opinion that this principle is more and more frequently implemented. This positive trend is visible in the opinion expressed not only by specialists and top executives but also by unskilled workers. The opinion of skilled workers was even more positive.
- Distributions of opinion about the implementation of the principle "intelligence, skills, or abilities are rewarded" were more complex. In 1991, social groups holding lower positions or groups defining themselves as being lower or the middle class were much more often convinced that

Equal opportunities to get ahead	Effort is rewarded	People get what they need	Skill is rewarded
			*75.4 FRG
		*73.8 Japan	*75.2 USA
	*71.4 USA		
	*71.4 FRG		
*65.9 USA			
		*63.5 Netherlands	
			*62.6 Japan
*54.6 FRG		*54.0 FRG	
*45.8 Netherlands	*49.1 Netherlands		
*24.8 Poland 91			*25.2 Poland 97
*21.3 Poland 97	*21.4 Poland 97		
	*16.2 Poland 91		*17.0 Poland 91
		*7.9 Poland 91	
		*5.1 Poland 97	
Equal opportunities to get ahead	Effort is rewarded	People get what they need	Skill is rewarded

Figure 10.1 Beliefs about the realization of principles of justice

Notes: *Those employed in the private sector as a whole express the opinion that equal opportunities are on the increase in Poland. Farmers, however, also belonging to the private sector claim that equal opportunities are lower.

The questions asked were: "Please tell me how much you agree or disagree with the following Statements: In (the country) people have equal opportunities to get ahead;" "In (the country) people get what they need;" "In (the country) people get rewarded for their effort;" "In (the country) people get rewarded for their intelligence and skill" (Alwin et al. 1995, 121–125).

Reference to effort or hard work refers to the individual's measurable achievements, while intelligence or abilities refers instead to the individual's character, that is, to their personality: "*What counts here is not what one does but what one is*" (Fowler and Orenstein 1993, 70).

Source: (Poland 1991 and 1997, Western Countries 1991; percentage of "strongly agree" and "somewhat agree").

this principle was implemented. The situation looked different when assessments were made according to political self-identification; namely, persons locating themselves as being in the centre and to the right confirmed the implementation of this principle more frequently than those on the left.

To summarize, if only one Pole in four or five Pole believes that he/she has equal opportunities to get ahead, it means that he/she seldom comes across barriers. The other life trajectory is not much better either, because the level of implementing meritocratic principles is quite low. Although fortunately it displays an improving trend, the two survey findings taken together substantially reduce the possibility of rapid legitimization of the market economy and the democratic state in Poland. While Western societies are characterized by openness, as two-thirds to three-fourths of responses admit, Polish society is only partially open, as admitted by 16–25 percent of respondents. In Western countries the percentage of positive opinions on meritocracy are two to three times as high as these results from Poland indicate. There are some other important reasons for that feeling of social injustice in Poland. They are related to the sources of poverty and wealth as well as the power of trade unions.

10.6 On the sources of poverty and wealth

Among seven possible choices concerning the source of wealth in Poland, respondents ranked informal contacts and connections first. This opinion was expressed by more than 70 percent of the respondents and increased from 73.1 percent in 1991 to 78.5 percent in 1997. They also pointed to dishonesty as a source of wealth: the share of respondents expressing such an opinion rose from 63.0 percent in 1991 to 72.7 percent in 1997. The two factors were closely related in the opinion of respondents, with a generally-held a strong conviction of the existence of patron-client relations and corruption. The above findings warrant a consideration of the hypothesis that *networks* are an analytical alternative to hierarchical coordination or control developed in the structure of the state on the one hand, and to horizontal and dispersed coordination developed in market mechanisms on the other (Stark and Bruszt 1998, 116–136; Bruszt and Stark 2000, 115–120). It appears that the category of *networks* can be useful not only in the analysis of old and new nomenclatures (élite formation) but also in the analysis at the grass-roots level. Unfortunately our survey was not aimed at verifying hypotheses of this kind. Nevertheless, additional survey opinions are presented below, as they seem interesting and revealing:

- The first finding concerns a growing consensus that the economic system allows the rich to "reap unjustified benefits." This opinion was held by 52 percent of respondents in 1991 and 62.7 percent in 1997. The judgment regarding the emerging system is as follows: it is increasingly effective, but it arouses moral doubts because it is not governed by rule of law or meritocratic principles, but primarily by various informal connections.

- The second concerns a declining conviction that the ineffective economic system is the cause of poverty. Such an opinion was shared by 66.0 percent of respondents in 1991 and 56.3 percent in 1997. The result is somewhat optimistic, given this accusation directed to the economic system was common even prior to 1989.

- The third one concerns the place held by lack of *equal opportunities* as a cause of poverty and a source of wealth. The lack of equal opportunities to get ahead was listed by 46.7 percent of respondents in 1991 and 52.4 percent in 1997 as the cause of poverty. Meanwhile, *better opportunities to get ahead* are treated as a source of wealth by a clearly growing percentage of the population: 56.6 percent in 1991 and 66.3 percent in 1997.

10.7 The power of trade unions as a test of justified advancing of demands

Opinions about the new democratic state in the results demonstrate a high degree of dissatisfaction. In this context, it would be interesting to look closely at one of the most legitimized institutions of public life in Poland; namely, trade unions. Assessments of the trade union *Solidarity* as a pressure group within the state would be a particularly adequate test for advancing justified demands. *Solidarity* was a major social force that played a decisive role in the downfall of the socialist state during the 1980s. It can be said generally that trade unions produce collective goods on which people can count, through collective strategies when strategies of individuals fail. It remained to be seen if the trade unions were able to fulfil their conventional tasks, among which the most important are: decent pay and employment security (Cichomski, Kulpińska, and Morawski 1998; Morawski 2000).

Before discussing trade unions, it must be pointed out that before the end of the 1990s no cohesive system of labor relations had emerged in Poland. It was partly neocorporatist in character, as approximately one quarter of MPs elected in 1997 were representatives of trade unions in both political groupings: Solidarity's government and the opposition. Although trade unions are politically important, their membership tends to steadily decrease, and membership at the end of the 1990s was much lower than it was at the time of the first *Solidarity* (1980–81). In total, only one-third of employees in Poland at that time were trade union members, which was on a par with the UK, a little more than in Germany, and far less than in Scandinavian countries.

As for the power of trade unions, the survey results show: (1) there is strong conviction that trade unions in Poland had as much power as they should; but (2) about one-third of respondents agreed that trade unions had too much power. Compared with other postsocialist countries, the percentage in Poland was much higher, and the percentage of respondents believing that trade unions had too little power was much lower (PGSS 1997). This demonstrates the specific situation in Poland connected with the traditions of the powerful social movement *Solidarity* (1980–89), the first independent trade union in the history of state socialism.

Our survey was done in 1997, when Poles chose the Solidarity political alliance as an alternative to the leftist coalition which had not been able tosatisfy their needs before, despite very high economic growth during the postcommunist coalition government. People were hoping that the Solidarity government formed after the parliamentary election in 1997 would be more effective in satisfying their material needs. In 2001, the material situation of the people had not changed much, but unemployment had gone up again to more than 16 percent. Forces on the right of the political spectrum interpreted the swing as being caused not so much by economic reasons but as the second rejection (after the first in 1989) of a postcommunist alternative.

10.8   Tentative interpretations

Looking for analytical-theoretical categories which would correspond to the empirical findings presented above, it seems appropriate to start with considering the usefulness of two traditional perspectives: conflict and cooperation. Were social moods in Poland at the beginning of the twenty-first century closer to the conflict perspective, in which economic and political relations are perceived by people as becoming similar to a zero-sum game, or were they closer to the cooperation perspective, in which all players can profit in a positive sum game?

The collected data can be interpreted according to both schemes. The potential for dissatisfaction with the real functioning of the market and the state in postsocialist Poland has been so great that it would seem to justify interpretation within the conflict perspective. A number of arguments can also support the cooperation thesis, however, such as the high acceptance of the values of the free market and the democratic state as well as the high readiness to accept principles of meritocracy. Nevertheless, it seems that both theses are inadequate.

A more promising interpretation of the presented empirical data can be made with game-theoretic categories and relevant analytical tools. The theory of games "examines the interaction of individual decisions given certain assumptions concerning decisions under risk, the general environment, and the cooperative or non-cooperative behavior of other individuals" (Pearce 1989, 166). Neither conflict nor cooperation disappears in it, but the game paradigm positively synthesizes both conflict and cooperation approaches and seems to suit better the new circumstances in economic relations and labor relations from 1989. First of all, it assumes a high level of calculation on the part of all game participants, because their activities are conditioned by the market, which becomes increasingly global, as well as by democracy, which becomes increasingly determined by various external factors like human rights, the UN, the EU, etc. Under such conditions, the content of calculations of social actors boils down to various trade-offs.

For example, employees all over the world face dual commitments: with their trade unions and their management. (Le Grand and Ishikawa 2000) Such double identification was very rare 30–40 years ago. Nowadays, employees are acutely aware that they are in the same boat as their managers. If a firm goes bankrupt, they lose their jobs. Such reasoning is forced by conditions of a global economy, which as far as employment goes, almost mimics constant depression (Krugman 1999). Various forces within the firm must cope autonomously with a stormy environment. It does not mean that people resign from conventional aspirations such as pay and employment, but it means that they are ready to abandon aggressive strategies to reach more ambitious goals.

There is an incessant game between everybody. It is not a class struggle aimed at mutual annihilation, nor is it a fully peaceful cooperation. Our data about trade unions and others can be interpreted better from the perspective of games. Let us recall that people postulated that they should have the same amount of power as they had at the time. This speaks volumes, taking into account that "people get what they need" at the level of only 7.9 percent and 5.1 percent in 1991 and 1997 respectively. Theoretically speaking, this fact could lead people to adversarial moods; that is, to give more power to trade unions. What we observed, however, was quite the opposite mood: every third respondent was of the opinion that trade unions had too much power, as if he/she did not want to benefit from their help.

Opinion stressing the large role played by informal networks in becoming rich or staying poor also directs our attention to networks with intensive games in the workplace and outside. In these games old and new nomenclatures gain advantages. This is the way that so-called political capitalism emerged (economic rent from power for those who have political connections). In this situation, respondents advanced postulates about respecting the principle "to everybody according to needs" on the one hand, but on the other very frequently according to the principle of "to everybody according to effort made or hard work." This proves that they prefer to develop individual strategies rather than collective ones pursued by trade unions. Of course, people are not against trade unions, but people realize that their power has to be limited nowadays; hence they regard the trade unions as actors that have to cope with other actors in wider social, economic, political, and global frameworks.

Our respondents voiced opinions as rational individuals who want to make free choices on the basis of input in the form of *effort, hard work,* or *skill*. Despite such desires, he/she cannot make such choices, because he/she has to benefit from networks, which in many instances are of dubious character. Such opinions can be treated as indicators of the fact that the new institutions of an open society in Poland, the market and political democracy, have not yet consolidated the new rules of the game. First of all, the rule of law, and more generally, transparency in social, economic, and political relationships is below a satisfactory level for the people. In this situation, our respondents would like to improve their positions, not only through collective institutions like trade unions, political parties, or the state apparatuses, but also by individual strategies. It cannot be claimed, however, that experiences show the victory of *homo economicus* in Poland. He is after all a theoretical abstract. Instead, it may be claimed that our respondents would like to realize their values more individually than before, and that they are perfectly aware of numerous constraints that do not permit them to fulfil their wishes without overcoming larger obstacles.

Our data support the hypothesis that Poland at the end of the twentieth century was a *half-open* society, where various mechanisms created barriers making "an equal start" somewhat impossible and hampered implementation of nonegalitarian principles (meritocracy). Contrary to appearances, Poles do not accept fully the principles of political justice, although they formulate many expectations towards the state which come from a low level of satisfaction of basic needs. Poles are ready to accept market justice principles. But many conditions must be fulfilled in order for these principles to be fully realized. At that point in time, they were not, which cast a long shadow on the transformation, because it had not lived up to the dreams of the 1980s. The transformation divided people, however, into those accomplishing their dreams ("winners") and those impatient to accomplish them ("losers"). The transformation processes strengthened doubts as to whether the nature of the emerging social order corresponded to those dreams. Admittedly, many dreams were pure illusions but not all. What is perhaps more important is that the spirit of dreams and hopes may evaporate somewhere and some time.

References

Alwin Duane F., Gornev Galin, and Khakhulina Ludmila, with the collaboration of Antoncic, Vojko, Arts, Will, Cichomski, Bogdan, and Herkmens, Piet. 1995. "Comparative Referential Structures, System Legitimacy, and Justice Sentiments: An International Comparison." In *Social Justice and Political Change. Public Opinion in Capitalist and Post-Communist States*, James E. Kluegel, David S.Mason, and Bernd Wegener (eds.). Hawthorne, NY: Aldine de Gruyter.

Barry, Brian. 1989. *Theories of Justice*. Berkeley, CA: University of California Press.

Bruszt, László, and David Stark. 2000. "Post-Communist Networking: Secret Agents, Mafiosi and Sociologists." *East European Constitutional Review* 9(1–2). Zima-Wiosna: 115–120.

Cichomski, Bogdan, Jolanta Kulpińska, and Witold Morawski. 1998. "Employment, Commitment and Trade Unions: Continuity or Change in Poland 1985–1995." In *Workers, Firms and Unions. Industrial Relations in Transition*. Roderick Martin, Akihiro Ishikawa, Csaba Mako, and Francesco Consoli (eds.). Frankfurt: Peter Lang.

Dahrendorf, Ralf. 1999. "The Third Way and Liberty. An Authoritarian Streak in Europe's New Center." *Foreign Affairs* (Sept.–Oct.) 78(5): 13–17.

Fowler, Robert Booth, and Jeffrey R Orenstein. 1993. *An Introduction to Political Theory. Toward the Next Century*. New York: HarperCollins College Publishers.

Held, David. 1996. (reprinted) *Democracy and the Global Order. From the Modern State to Cosmopolitan Governance*. Cambridge: Polity Press.

Inglehart, Ronald. 1990. *Culture Shift in Advanced Industrial Societies*. Princeton: Princeton University Press.

Inglehart, Ronald. 1997. *Modernization and Postmodernization: Cultural, Economic and Political Change in 43 Societies*. Princeton: Princeton University Press.

Krugman, Paul. 1999. *The Return of Depression Economics*. Harmondsworth, England: Allen Lane/The Penguin Press.

Lane, Robert E. 1986. "Market Justice, Political Justice." *American Political Science Review* 80(2): 383, 386.

Le Grand, Carl, and Akihiro Ishikawa. 2000. "Workers Identity with Management and/or the Trade Union." In *Workers, Firms and Unions 2: The Development of Dual Commitment*, A. Ishikawa, R. Martin, W. Moravski, and V. Rus (eds.). Frankfurt: Peter Lang.

Mason, David S. 1995. "Justice, Socialism, and Participation in Postcommunist States." In *Social Justice and Political Change. Public Opinion in Capitalist and Post-Communist States*, James R. Kluegel, David S. Mason, and Bernd Wegener (eds.). New York: Aldine de Gruyter.

Morawski, Witold. 1994. "Modele reformy a zmiana systemowa w Polsce" [Reform Models and Systemic Change in Poland]. *W: Zmierzch Socjalizmu Państwowego. Szkice z Socjologii Ekonomicznej*. [Twilight of State Socialism. Sketches from Economic Sociology]. Warsaw: Wyd. Naukowe PWN.

Morawski, Witold. 2000. "Changing Images of Trade Unions." In *Workers, Firms and Unions 2: The Development of Dual Commitment*, Akihiro Ishikawa, Roderick Martin, Witold Morawski, and Veljko Rus (eds.). Frankfurt: Peter Lang.

Naisbitt, John. 1997. *Megatrendy* [Megatrends]. Warsaw: Wyd. Zysk i S-ka.

Pearce, D. (ed.). 1986. *MIT Dictionary of Modern Economics*. Cambridge, MA: MIT Press.

PGSS. 1997. *Polski Generalny Sondaż Społeczny: Poglądy Polaków 1997. Rola Rządu* [Polish General Social Survey: Views of Poles 1997. Role of the Government]. Warsaw: Institute of Social Studies, University of Warsaw in the Framework of the International Social Survey Program.

Polska 1991: Cichomski Bogdan, and Witold Morawski. 1991. *Sprawiedliwość społeczna w Polsce. Badanie międzynarodowe* [Social Justice in Poland. International Survey]. Warsaw: Institute of Social Studies, University of Warsaw.

Polska 1997 (Poland 2000): Cichomski Bogdan, Witold Morawski, and Paweł Morawski. 1997. *Sprawiedliwość społeczna w Polsce w latach dziewięćdziesiątych. Badania porównawcze* [Social Justice in Poland in the 1990s. Comparative Study. (2000)]. Warsaw: Institute of Social Studies, University of Warsaw.

Rawls, John. 1971. *A Theory of Justice*. Cambridge, MA: The Belknap Press of Harvard University Press.

Sen, Amartya. 1992. *Inequality Reexamined*. Cambridge, MA: Harvard University Press.

Siemieńska, Renata. 1988. "Political Materialist-Postmaterialist Values and Their Determinants in Poland in Cross-National Perspective." *International Review of Sociology* 3: 199.

Stark, David, and László Bruszt. 1998. *Postsocialist Pathways. Transforming Politics and Property in East Central Europe.* Cambridge: Cambridge University Press.

Tischner, Józef. 1993. *Nieszczęsny dar wolności* [Unfortunate Gift of Freedom]. Kraków: Znak.

Verba, Sidney, and Gary Orren. 1985. *Equality in America: The View from the Top.* Cambridge: Harvard University Press.

Part IV

Lessons Beyond the First Decade of Transformation

By now western massmedia give credit
to Perestroika and talk about a *second revolution*,
about the irreversible nature of restructuring,
or about a *fresh leap* on the basis of
newly-established economic and legal reforms.
We are criticized by the *left* for the pace
of restructuring being *too slow*, and
by the *right* for taking leaps being *too great*.
But all agree that Soviet leadership
is implementing reforms in earnest.
                    —M. Gorbachev, *Perestroika*, 1987

11
Facts and Lessons of Ten Years of Transformation in Central Europe

Tsuneo Morita

11.1 From what to where

11.1.1 Transformation vs. transition

The two words depict two different ways of observing movement or change. Transition suggests a movement from one state to another, whereas transformation implies a shift from one system to another. Since the contemporary events in the former socialist countries in Central Europe have been such a fundamental change in the social system, I use *transformation* rather than *transition*.

11.1.2 Socialism to capitalism

To refer to the transformation in the present day context as a switch from a socialist to a capitalist economy is an oversimplification. There has been neither a "pure" capitalist economy nor a "pure" socialist economy in the world. What exist in Europe now are mixed economies with various means for income redistribution. Welfare states like the UK and Scandinavian countries possess more socialist features than some former socialist countries.

Particular characteristics in institutions and beliefs must be specified, toward which the transformation is directed. Is a voucher-privatized economy in Russia a market economy? Often the term *capitalist* is used in a symbolic or superficial sense to describe the emergence of capitalistic behavior or ways of thinking in a society undergoing transformation.

11.1.3 Socialist economy to market economy

The two concepts are not mutually exclusive. The contrast between the two concepts may reflect ideological distortions in the socialist economies. The contrast implies the transformation from a politically distorted to a nonpolitically organized economy.

11.1.4   Planning to market

The two contrasting concepts are often properly used in the publications of international organizations, but no effectively functioning planning systems existed in ex-Socialist economies. Therefore, this contrast is not sufficient to describe the essence of the transformation. Besides, this contrast is related more to the institutional working of coordination in the economy and less to any fundamental differences in conducting economic activities.

11.1.5   Allocation to exchange

The contemporary transformation in socioeconomic activity is understood to be a fundamental change in world history. Morita (1994) proposed the two key concepts: *allocation* and *exchange* as contrasting socioeconomic coordinating principles. While *from planning to market* also refers to coordinating institutions, the historic change in the economic activities of human society is better represented by the contrast of allocation and exchange.

11.2   The conceptualization of transformation

11.2.1   Asymmetry of transformation

Early in the 1990s many economists expected that a *market revolution* could be achieved as quickly as the earlier *socialist revolutions*. This was a widespread misunderstanding of our age. The two transformations were entirely asymmetrical in time span and complexity. The historical socialist revolutions were first and foremost political movements and resulted in political regulation and control of the national economy. Control by planning was just a simplification of economic functioning. Every socialist revolution did this by means of the direct *allocation* of economic goods. In that case transformation was from complexity to simplicity, which required only a relatively short time.

Transformation from direct control to markets, however, requires all the participants to learn and adapt themselves to the working of market mechanisms. This cannot be accomplished in a short period. Natural law decrees that evolution from a simple state to a complex state is a long process and is not to be taken for granted. Degeneration can come about rapidly through destruction. It is easy politically to destroy an economy's adaptive capacity for development but extremely difficult to build the capacity back up. This asymmetry is essential to understanding contemporary transformation. No miraculous way exists of shortening the long process of transformation. Reducing the transformation time by inviting a large amount of foreign capital is another question.[1] That is the main reason why this paper rejects the contrast between shock therapy and gradualism.

11.2.2 Socioeconomic factors of exchange and allocation

Complexity or simplicity in economic and social behavior depends on the socioeconomic factors associated with allocation or exchange. Allocation activity in socialist economies caused a continuous degeneration of human behavior and ultimately destroyed the whole society, whereas exchange activities lent vitality to human behavior, even when state redistribution was substantial. The reason why vitality was lost entirely in socialist society is the continuous degeneration brought about by state allocation (Table 11.1).

The table shows the inevitable functioning of both allocation activity and exchange activity in every sphere of the socioeconomic dimension.

First, since exchange is a bilateral activity and allocation is almost a unilateral activity, the communication involved in exchange is informational and anonymous. It is also transmitted as a universal message equally to all participants, whereas the communication involved in allocation is transmitted through personal channels to a specified organ or person in a specified physical unit.

Second, exchange autonomously organizes the market mechanism, whereas allocation needs bureaucratic organizations. The market mechanism can change itself and adapt to new surroundings for further development, whereas bureaucratic organizations cannot adjust flexibly to new environments.

Table 11.1 Comparison of the socioeconomic factors of allocation and exchange

Socioeconomic factor[a]	Basic economic activity[b]	
	Exchange	Allocation
1. Communication	Informational and bilateral	Physical and unilateral
2. Institutionalization	Self-organizing market system	Bureaucratization
3. Personal relationship	Depersonalized civilization	Personalized decivilization
4. Organization	Open and transparent	Closed and secret
5. Social behavior	Independent and self responsibility	Dependent on authority
6. Complexity	Continuously increasing	Degeneration into simplicity
7. Self-development	Autonomic and continuous	Destructive and deteriorating

Notes: [a] A socioeconomic factor is a driver for autonomous development.
[b] Every national economy consists of the two main economic activities: exchange and allocation. The question is the mixture of the two in a given economy.

Third, exchange liberates personal interdependence as a result of the universality of information and the anonymous nature of activity, whereas allocation presupposes some kind of subjective personal obedience to organizations. Depersonalization under exchange results in promoting modern civilization, but personalization in allocation maintains feudalistic human relationships and thus results in decivilization.

Fourth, a market institution can be changed and further developed as new types of transactions are introduced. The rules of exchange are transparent and open to all the participants, otherwise it would never work. Bureaucracy, however, is closed to the outside world and aims at maintaining its organization at any cost, so information is not fully made available to all the participants.

Fifth, exchange promotes independent personal activities with their own range of responsibilities, whereas allocation enforces obedience and dependence on the authority, leading to the loss of self-responsibility.

Sixth, exchange is ready to meet the needs of complex activities with many positive devices, whereas allocation tends to move away from complex human activities by simplifying the rules.

Seventh, exchange promotes the autonomous adaptation of organizations and individuals, whereas allocation limits the flexibility of organizations and individuals degrades them to self-destructive ends.

11.2.3   Why did the allocation-dominated system collapse?

1. *The initial factor: political decisions suppressed rationality.* In the allocation-dominated system economic decisions are subordinate to political judgments. It is well known that the communist parties in the former socialist countries possessed stronger decisionmaking power within companies than the managers. Not only in the microeconomy but also the macroeconomy, the superiority of politics over economic rationality prevailed there. The structure of economic activity was distorted, and such distortions cumulated throughout the whole history of socialist society and led to the collapse of the system itself.

2. *The second factor: subordination to the authorities suppressed individual initiatives.* Allocation strengthened the vertical relationship of companies to the authorities who severely limited voluntary exchange in order to keep their power intact. Voluntary and individual initiatives for promoting horizontal relationships among companies were banned and punished, so exchange activities atrophied. This suppression continuously lowered the level of economic activity and produced lasting stagnation.

3. *The inevitable effect: simplicity defeated complexity, leading to degeneration.* Planning demands intensive calculations that cannot be accomplished even with an advanced computer system. The Soviet Union attempted to plan activity in the national economy de facto by using manual calculations,

which soon ended up as merely setting routine rules for rationing materials and products. Thus, planning of the national economy never actually existed in the strictest sense of the word in any socialist planned economy. What really existed was only the implementation of routine rules and political decisions. This *impossibility of planning* made it inevitable that the planning procedures would be simplified. Simplicity defeated complexity with the result of the people and society falling into continuous degeneration.

4. *The final consequence: degeneration led to deviation from civilization and finally the collapse of society.* Degeneration of society prevailed in every form of social and economic activity from the legal framework to social norms. People gave up their initiative and handed over decisionmaking power to the authorities and simply obeyed as a "guided mass." In some ways it may have become an easygoing way to be provided with a guaranteed daily life. This has the knock-on effect of making people increasingly lazy and ignorant: in other words the degeneration of society and the subsequent diversion of society from civilization.

11.2.4   The transformation task: reconfirmation

Transformation is by no means an easy or straightforward process. Table 11.2 shows the data on the percentages of redistribution of GDP in former socialist Central European countries and confirms these countries have already become exchange-based economies at least in a macroeconomic sense.

The redistribution rate in 1998 was already well below the average of the EU 15, and appears to be likely to decrease further as is the case of the less

Table 11.2   Comparison of tax structure and size of redistribution (% of GDP, 1998)

	A. Direct tax	B. Indirect tax	C. Contribution to social security	A + B + C Redistribution rate
Hungary	10.1	14.9	14.1	39.1
Poland	13.1	14.0	12.9	40.0
Czech Republic	9.5	12.0	16.9	38.4
CE average	10.9	13.6	14.6	39.2
Germany	10.2	12.6	19.6	42.4
Sweden	24.1	16.6	15.1	55.8
Britain	16.6	14.9	7.8	39.3
Portugal	10.3	14.8	12.1	37.2
Greece	8.3	15.0	12.8	36.1
Ireland	13.6	14.1	4.0	31.7
EU 15 average	13.7	14.4	15.2	43.3
USA	14.8	6.8	9.1	30.7
Japan	9.1	8.3	11.0	28.4

Source: Based on OECD data.

developed members of the EU. Since transforming countries need to create a deeply cultivated domestic market, it is necessary to lower tax burdens. In spite of the macroeconomic facts, the actual deepening of the market economy is still far from accomplished. The microeconomic process, like the income redistribution of inhabitants, seems to show an entirely different picture. The personal income tax rate is very low in Central European countries (Table 11.2), which seems accurately to describe the decreasing tendency of the income redistribution rate.

If the highest rate of income tax is only 40 percent as Table 11.3 shows, it is in fact very low when compared to developed countries. If this is the case, then the Central European countries are already at the level of developed market economy with respect to income redistribution.

If, however, the highest tax rate is applied to almost all incomes, then the tax burden in fact becomes very heavy. In Hungary, for example, 20 percent income tax must be paid by those earning the minimum wage. Almost everyone, except for unskilled workers, quickly reaches the highest taxation bracket, which cuts in at US$ 4,000 annually. On top of this, inhabitants have to pay 25 percent value added tax (VAT) and local government tax out of the remaining income. Thus, roughly calculating, the total tax burden for inhabitants in Central European countries exceeds 50 percent of their personal income.

The paradox between the heavy tax burden of inhabitants and the low redistribution rate measured by percentages in GDP can be attributed to the inefficient collection of corporate income tax, which distorts the income and tax structure. The paradox can be observed universally in the transforming countries even after a decade or more. At the same time, it explains the slow expansion of the domestic market. Figure 11.1 illustrates a rough comparison in the structure of production and income distribution among the main types of economic systems.

The heavy tax burden on inhabitants in transforming countries is explained by the fact that many state and public institutions still operate free of any radical reform even today after almost two decades of transformation. A huge amount of money and human resources is wasted in maintaining inefficient public services. This leads not only to the irrational tax burden on inhabitants but also the sluggish expansion of the market economy.

Table 11.3   Tax rates in Central Europe in 1999 (%)

	Hungary	Poland	Czech Republic
Standard rate of VAT	25	22	22
Corporate tax	18	34	35
The highest rate of personal income tax	42	40	40

Source: Based on OECD data.

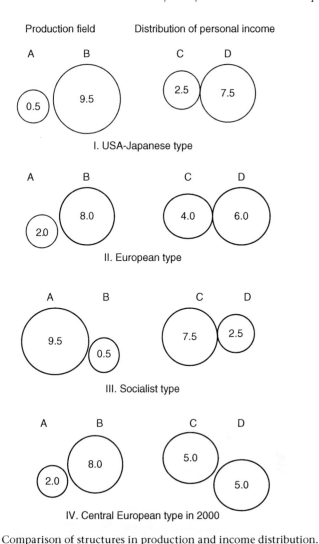

Production field   Distribution of personal income

I. USA-Japanese type

II. European type

III. Socialist type

IV. Central European type in 2000

Figure 11.1   Comparison of structures in production and income distribution.

Note: A and B represent the weight of state-public enterprise and private enterprise respectively. C and D show the distribution of personal income between the portion paid to the public budget and the remaining portion available to inhabitants.

If the analysis above is correct, then the task for the second stage of transformation (the convergence period) in the next decade will be mainly to reform the state and public services. They will require a change in the structure of tax and income of inhabitants. Thus, transformation to exchange-dominated economies has been only half achieved from the viewpoint of economic development.

Moreover, we should not forget that the transformation is not confined to merely an economic sense. As described above, the transformation task encompasses everything from the economic system to the social norms. The new social norm calls for the creation of civilized rules of behavior in society, which were neglected and disappeared under the old regime. It takes at least one generation to establish a civilized social norm: social discipline, social justice, and morals.

11.3   False criterion: shock therapy vs. gradualism

In the first half of the 1990s, soon after the separation of Czechoslovakia, IMF economists praised the voucher privatization scheme in the Czech Republic as a form of shock therapy. At the same time, they criticized Hungarian privatization for its slow gradualism. Thereafter, the comparison between shock therapy and gradualism has been a popular criterion by which to judge the advancement of market economic reform.

As is widely known, Polish shock therapy was introduced to bring down quickly the hyperinflation caused by the collapse of the old system. The Polish case was relevant only to a country which encountered the same type of crisis in the early stage of transformation. However, the Polish case is not relevant to Hungary or the Czech Republic, where the initial shock of transformation was mild. Advocates of radical policy misunderstand the nature of transformation, that is, the asymmetry of transformation. Laws required institutionally for the working of a market economy can be regulated without a workable market economy. Mere legislation does not produce a market economy.

The transformation from allocation to exchange in the principle of socioeconomic activity is not just an evolutionary movement from one platform to another. Transformation in our age is not a mere change in the legal framework of society, but a fundamental change in socioeconomic discipline in individuals and organizations in society. It will take at least a generation to complete the process. There is no easy way to create a shortcut to the transformation. Lately, discussion about shock therapy and gradualism has been subsiding, because the vaunted Czech approach of voucher privatization has been showing signs of failure. This clearly supports the arguments presented above.

11.4   Voucher was virtual: no shortcut to privatization

After appraisal and recommendation by international organizations, almost all transforming countries attempted to follow the Czech and Slovak miracle of voucher privatization (Table 11.4). There was a reason and necessity for these countries to follow voucher privatization, but there has been no miracle anywhere at all. There are two ways to find the capital resources required for privatization: from domestic capital and foreign capital. Except

Table 11.4 Mass privatization programs in Central and Eastern Europe and the CIS countries

Country	Year voucher distribution began	All shares issued in waves or continuously?	Are vouchers bearer, tradable, or nontradable?	Is investment in funds allowed, encouraged or compulsory?
Albania	1995	Continuously	Bearer	Encouraged[a]
Armenia	1994	Continuously	Bearer	Allowed[b]
Bulgaria	1995	Waves	Nontradable	Encouraged
Czech Republic	1992	Waves	Nontradable	Encouraged
Estonia	1993	Continuously	Tradable[d]	Allowed[e]
Georgia	1995	Continuously	Tradable	Allowed[b]
Kazakhstan	1994	Waves	Nontradable	Compulsory
Kyrgyzstan	1994	Continuously	Bearer	Allowed[f]
Latvia	1994	Continuously	Tradable	Allowed[e]
Lithuania	1993	Continuously	Nontradable	Allowed[e]
Moldova	1994	Waves[g]	Nontradable	Encouraged
Poland	1995	Waves	Tradable	Compulsory
Romania[h]	1992	Continuously	Bearer	Compulsory[i]
Romania	1995	Waves	Nontradable[j]	Allowed
Russia	1992	Continuously	Bearer	Encouraged
Slovakia	1992	Waves	Nontradable	Encouraged
Slovenia	1994	Continuously	Nontradable	Allowed
Ukraine	1995	Continuously	Nontradable	Allowed

Notes: [a] By July 1996 only one or two funds had applied to receive vouchers.

[b] Although a legal entitlement exists to invest vouchers in funds, in practice this option was limited.

[c] The results of the first voucher auction were cancelled in March 1995, and fund licenses were suspended from then until August 1996.

[d] Vouchers were nontradable at the outset of the program, but cash trading was legalized in the spring of 1994.

[e] Citizens could also exchange vouchers for other things such as apartments or land.

[f] Citizens could invest their vouchers in housing as well as shares. They can sell their vouchers to funds, but no formal mechanism exists for them to subscribe to funds.

[g] Although the design of the Moldavian program was based on the offer of companies in waves, the waves were small in the early stages, and thus had many of the characteristics of a continuous issue.

[h] In 1991 Romania introduced a scheme based on the distribution of certificates of ownership in five private ownership funds. In 1995 a supplementary mass privatization program was introduced involving the distribution of coupons that could be exchanged for company shares or fund shares, after which the funds were to be transformed into financial investment companies.

[i] Under certain circumstances certificates of ownership in funds could be exchanged for company shares.

[j] Certificates of ownership were bearers, coupons were registered and nontradable.

Source: Saul Estrin," Some Reflections on Privatisation in Belarus," Economic Trends Quarterly Issue *Belarus*, July–September 1999.

in the case of the Czech Republic, domestic capital was not sufficiently available for privatization in any transforming country in the early 1990s, when no sufficient foreign capital inflow was expected. There was no choice, therefore, regarding privatization methods but to distribute national assets among the inhabitants and wait for new domestic entrepreneurs to emerge. This explains the widespread use of voucher privatization.

Here we should determine what privatization actually is. The IMF urged that any kind of privatization was preferable to state ownership, and was an active supporter of voucher privatization. Voucher methods possess no magic at all. An elaborate framework does not substitute for reality and substance. Privatization is expected to bring about some essential changes to the roles of capital, management, and technology. A change of management may push a first step toward the reform of enterprise. If the new managers are sufficiently capable, then they can manage to accumulate capital and introduce new technologies to the enterprise. This is an ideal view of privatization. The question is whether one can find such competent managers from the old regime or not. This is the *aporia* (unsolvable contradiction) of privatization. Unless one can break through the *aporia*, there is no miracle in voucher privatization whatsoever.

Even the Czech Republic, where the conditions were favorable for privatization, is suffering from an awfully distorted market system resulting from voucher privatization. That is why Czechs began to reprivatize the enterprises that were once privatized through voucher methods. Then, what was voucher privatization? The answer should be that it was virtual privatization. The Czech miracle has faded away. The Czech example demonstrates that there is no "easy road" or a shortcut to system transformation, because it is really a historic process that no one can instantly go through.

11.5   Klaus's failure

11.5.1   Overvaluation of domestic technology and undervaluation of FDI

There were very ambiguous attitudes towards FDI in Poland and the Czech Republic in the early 1990s. Only Hungary has been active throughout the whole period under study in receiving capital from abroad. Poland was very cautious towards foreign capital because of its default of external debts. The Czechs were so proud of their competence in the manufacturing industries that they did not need foreign capital and technology. Then, Poland changed its mind as it realized that there would be no economic progress without sufficient capital and advanced technology. In the contrast, the Czech government abolished preferential conditions for FDI after its separation from Slovakia in 1993.

It was just after the currency crisis in 1997 that the Czech government seriously began to reconsider the importance of FDI, simply because it recognized that Czech industry had been lagging behind the rest of the industrialized world by more than one generation in terms of technology.

11.5.2   Misunderstanding the policy of foreign exchange

At the end of 1995, when Nomura Research Institute Europe forecast the devaluation of the overappreciated Czech koruna by as much as 20 percent after the general election in 1996. Prime Minister Klaus was furious. "Nomura's forecasts have always been wrong, and it is mere commonsense that the Czech koruna can only appreciate in the future and will never be devalued because the Czech koruna is greatly undervalued," he retorted in a press interview.

He considered that an undervalued currency, such as the Czech koruna with strong industrial backing, would appreciate continuously in the long run. The point was that he confused the nominal exchange rate with the real exchange rate and short-term exchange rate policy with long-term policy. An underdeveloped market economy generally tends to force its currency to be undervalued, but its currency's appreciation can be realized with the development of the market economy in the long run. In the short run, a more flexible exchange rate policy is needed that fits the conditions of the national economy. In particular, under inflationary circumstances, exchange rate policy is not nearly as straightforward as Klaus thought. If the nominal exchange rate appreciates annually by 10 percent through monetary policy under 10 percent inflationary conditions, then roughly speaking the real exchange rate will appreciate by 20 percent. It would be impossible even for a relatively healthy economy like the Czech Republic to appreciate its currency annually by 20 percent through its transformation period. The undervaluation of a currency simply cannot be solved over a short period of time. However, Klaus mistakenly assumed that appreciation could be achieved in a straightforward manner in relatively short time.

More sophisticated currency policy is necessary for a transforming economy under inflationary circumstances. The nominal exchange rate should be devalued if the inflation rate is high, but the real exchange rate should be allowed to appreciate to some extent. This can be done by keeping the devaluation rate lower than the inflation rate. It seems to be highly contradictory, but only such a deliberate exchange rate policy can effectively support transforming economies. This is the reason why "the crawling peg" policy was effective in Poland and Hungary in 1990s. What is the proper rate of real appreciation? This is not a political question, but is rather a question of monetary policy that is judged by measuring growth potential in both the short run and the long run.

11.5.3   Manipulation of data

Economists representing international organizations were easily deceived by "tricks" that manipulated macroeconomic indicators in the Czech Republic. One is the rate of unemployment and the other is the state budget deficit. Almost all kinds of macroeconomic data in the Czech Republic were incomparable with those in other transforming countries during the early years of transformation: there was no inflation, no unemployment, no state budget deficit, no large deficit in the balance of payments, etc. This really appeared to be a miracle.

Nowadays, it is widely known that the low rate of unemployment can be explained by lagged restructuring of quasi-privatized companies, and indeed recently the rate has been increasing as restructuring has proceeded. It was about 9.5 percent at the end of 1998, which was already more than that of Hungary.

The World Bank compiled accurate data on the deficit of the state budget (See Tables 11.5A and 11.5B) with the cooperation of the Ministry of Finance. The difference between the official data and the corrected data is the hidden deficits that have been put off of the official budget. They consist mainly of nonperforming loans from commercial banks that have been concentrated and accumulated as assets in the Bank of Consolidation (KoB: Konsolidacni Banka). So long as the Bank of Consolidation exists, the accumulated bad loans are not treated as losses that add to the state deficit in a legal sense, but the losses cannot be transferred to a third organization forever.

Recently, a similar type of data manipulation can be observed with FDI data in Poland. Two organizations publish FDI data in Poland: the National Bank of Poland and Polish Information and Foreign Investment Agency (PAIZ; PAIiIZ now), a state organization for investment promotion. In the two years from 1998 to 2000 the discrepancy of data between the two organizations

Table 11.5A   Government implicit fiscal deficit, 1993–98 (% of GDP)

	1993	1994	1995	1996	1997	1998
Reported state budget fiscal deficit	−0.5	−1.3	0.3	0.5	1.1	1.4
"Hidden" fiscal deficit in transformation institutions (KoB, CI, CF and NPF)[a]	3.2	1.9	1.0	0.5	1.0	2.0
"Hidden" fiscal deficit in guarantees net hidden subsidy (risk-adjusted)	0.0	0.0	0.1	1.0	3.1	1.5
Implicit fiscal deficit (including transformation institutions and guarantee net hidden subsidy)	2.7	0.6	1.4	2.0	5.2	4.9

Note: [a]See Table 11.5B.

Table 11.5B   Sources of "Hidden" fiscal deficit, 1993–98 (CZK billion)

	1993	1994	1995	1996	1997	1998
Konsolidacni Banka (KoB)[a] Net public expenditure	7.7	7.3	4.5	0.9	10.6	28.8
Ceska Inkasni (CI) net public expenditures	20.1	6.6	4.9	4.8	3.1	2.7
Ceska Financi (CF) net public expenditures	–	–	–	–	0.6[b]	1.8[b]
National Property Fund (NPF) net public expenditures (excluding KoB, CI)	4.2	8.2	4.3	1.9	2.0	2.6
State guarantees net hidden subsidy (risk-adjusted)	0.1	−0.4	1.3	14.9	51.5	26.7

Notes: [a] Activities of KoB include providing credit to finance the Stabilization Program of CF. Therefore, the table includes only interest payments by CF (which are then reported as interest income of KoB).
[b] These figures are interest payments to KoB on credit taken by CF from KoB to finance the Stabilization Program. In addition, CF paid interest of CZK 0.8 billion and CZK 2.8 billion in 1997 and 1998, respectively, to the Czech National Bank on its credit from Czech National Bank to finance the Consolidation Program.
Source: World Bank, *Czech Republic,* September 1999.

roughly amounts to $10 billion, which paints a confusing picture for economists. Since PAIZ is a promotional organ for inviting foreign investment and not a statistical unit for Poland, we should not treat its data as official. FDI data from the National Bank of Poland is based on the balance of payments and may be used in comparison with other countries' data.

11.6   Market functionalism vs. industrial policy

Various measures are used to compare the advancement of reforms. They are mainly the criteria related to market functioning such as the privatization and liberalization of prices, the banking system, and trade and capital transactions. These are the conditions and infrastructure for market functioning and are important for creating the market economy. Forming a legal and institutional framework is a necessary condition in creating a market economy but not sufficient in itself. The contents of the market are the activities of people themselves, which depend on the internal and external deepening of the market across the entire economy as well as the level of personal income. Economic activity must be increased by the industrial policy of the government.

International advisers tend to make proposals within given frameworks, because their task is universal for any country irrespective of its level of economic development. This is the fallacy of market functionalism. It is much more difficult to find the industrial policy appropriate for the long-term development of the economy concerned. A thorough knowledge of industrial situations and resources available in the economy and a long-term strategic perspective are called for on the part of policymakers. This task is usually neglected by international advisers with the excuse that industrial policy is an old-fashioned form of government intervention. A warning case is the Russian crisis of 1998 that showed just how vulnerable an economy can be if the support by market functionalism is not supplemented by proper industrial policy. Market functionalism is also compatible with financial liberalism, which can superficially develop the capital market without a strong real economy. The failure of international advisers in the case of the Russian economy can be explained by this fallacy of sheer market functionalism. Thus far, arbitrary privatization has brought about neither the restructuring of enterprises nor effective capital accumulation without the government's industrial policy. It has merely resulted in the sharing of state wealth amongst newly born entrepreneurs who are actually former high-ranking bureaucrats, élite employees of state companies, and ex-leaders of the Communist Party and communist youth league.

11.7 Who governs the quasi-privatized enterprises: "The New Holy Trinity"?

11.7.1 Quasi-privatization

A voucher-privatized company is called a quasi-privatized company and cannot be seriously regarded as a private company. Nevertheless, international organizations have recognized them as private companies if the state stake in them is below 50 percent. This is a somewhat mechanical judgment, taking only the legal form into account. This explains why the share of the private sector was high in those countries where voucher privatization was applied. The rate itself is extremely high as Table 11.6 shows. However, by what means is it possible to shift the national economy from state ownership

Table 11.6 Private sector share of GDP in % (rough EBRD estimate)

	1995	1996	1997	1998	1999
Czech Republic	70	75	75	75	80
Hungary	60	70	70	80	80
Poland	60	60	65	65	65
Slovakia	60	70	75	75	75
Russian Federation	55	60	70	70	70

Note: Rough estimate of European Bank for Reconstruction and Development (EBRD) at the middle of 1999.

Source: EBRD, *Transition Report*, 1995, 1996, 1997, 1998, 1999.

Table 11.7 Ownership structure of voucher-privatized commercial banks in the Czech Republic (1994)

	Ownership structure (%)			
	Voucher	Foreign capital	National Property Fund	Others
Ceska sportelna	37	0	40	23
Investicni banka	52	0	45	3
Komercni banka	53	0	44	3

Note: Already all three banks are privatized (2000).

Source: Taken and reformatted by the author from date of the Vienna Institute for Comparative Economic Studies.

to private ownership in such a short period? Is what Table 11.6 shows a real picture or just an inflated picture courtesy of voucher "magic"?

As Table 11.7 shows, the large Czech banks were considered to be private when they underwent voucher privatization in 1994, since state ownership was decreased to less than 50 percent. Thus, almost all voucher-privatized companies with minority state ownership were judged to be private and the weight of the private sector zoomed up. As has been already described, the voucher-privatized Czech banks were reprivatized by West European banks. This example clearly reveals that a voucher-privatized company is still not private but just quasi-private, and surely requires reprivatization in the future.[2]

11.7.2 Sharing of national assets by the *New Holy Trinity*

To date, voucher privatization in itself has brought about a reallocation of existing national assets among national players. This is only the first round of privatization and should be followed by successive rounds of privatization in a more correct way. As long as a company remains quasi-private, it is only a "state monopoly" capitalist-type company, over which competent bureaucrats of the old regime, reform-oriented managers, and influential politicians have de facto control. Thus, a new type of *Holy Trinity* among bureaucrats, managers, and politicians has been established in many quasi-privatized companies.

This new *Holy Trinity* forms and expands its own power group by including other companies and establishing its own banks and media channels as can be typically observed in Russia. How can we characterize this type of industrial group?

11.7.3 Patterns of original accumulation

1. *Russian case: enclosure of national assets.* The acquisition of national assets by the new *Holy Trinity* in Russia seems to be nothing but an example of the original accumulation of capital, as Marx described in *Das Kapital*, that is

typically observed in the early stage of capitalistic development. This type of capital accumulation is generally observed in former Soviet Union (FSU) countries, where natural resources are rich, old political power is still relatively strong, and development of the market economy is weak. It is obvious that during the course of acquisition that key companies established various types of subsidiaries around them and made their money flows extremely complex and nontransparent. Thus, even if the key companies were quasi-privatized, their managers could easily confiscate personal wealth by leaking money through subsidiaries to their own nominally existing companies. Otherwise, it is inconceivable how company hierarchy can afford their luxurious lifestyles from their official salaries.

The subsidiary tactic is widely utilized in Central European countries as well. It is said that a large portion of the Ft 120 billion loss of Postabank in Hungary was distributed to politicians, managers, and others through various ostensible payments of the bank's subsidiaries, which in turn had their own subsidiaries with cross-ownership structures.

2. *Czech case: insider transaction.* In a more civilized society where the market was far more developed than in Russia, different methods of original capital accumulation took place. The Czech Republic, the pioneer of voucher privatization, showed another way of accumulating capital by the use of insider transactions. Rapid privatization had transformed almost all of the state-owned enterprises (SOEs) into joint-stock companies, and their shares were freely traded among investment funds. Because of the lack of strict transaction rules and disclosure requirements, however, frequent insider transactions were observed. Consequently, many unidentifiable investor groups could acquire enough stakes in large companies or even in big banks, and suddenly mysterious owners appeared in the Czech business world.

In the Czech Republic, politicians tried to establish good relationships with quasi-privatized commercial banks and large companies in order to maintain their economic and political influences. Donations from large banks and companies were the main sources of election campaign funds for the ruling Party, ODS (civic democrats). The president of the largest Czech commercial bank, Komercni Bank, was until recently a famous senator of the ODS and a colleague of Klaus. The fourth largest bank, IPB banks, was also a major contributor in the 1995 election campaign.

The delay in the real privatization of big banks in the Czech Republic caused several serious problems in the banking sector. The Klaus government did not take effective measures to consolidate accumulated bad loans but instead continued the easy option of bailing out companies. Consequently, large banks kept past business routines with strong holdings of nonfinancial business companies, regardless of their profitability. This further worsened the situation of the banking sector and left semiprivatized nonfinancial companies unrestructured.

All of these factors were mutually beneficial to the Czech ruling party, ODS, and the managers of large banks and companies, because they could maintain their positions and politicoeconomic benefits in cooperation. The direct cause of the resignation of Klaus in December 1997 was, however, the unexpected disclosure of a secret party bank account in Switzerland. Foreign companies' lobbying fees were transferred to this account in connection with privatization deals as well as secret donations in the Czech Republic.

Thus, hasty privatization in the Czech Republic deeply upset market disciplines and rules, although Klaus himself praised it as real liberal capitalism. All of these brought about chaotic business situations especially in the banking sector and the capital market. The recession of the Czech economy in the second half of 1990s could be attributed to the rapid voucher privatization, which was carried out in accordance with the wishes of international organizations in 1993 and 1994. Anyway, through voucher privatization and insider transactions, the Czech style reorganization and redistribution of national assets was established, and this characterizes the Czech method of original capital accumulation.

3. *The Hungarian case: dependence on foreign capital.* In Hungary neither natural resources nor domestic capital were sufficient, so the only way to accumulate capital was by importing it through foreign strategic investors. They could pave the way for new capital accumulation. However, not every country can rely on imported capital, because where to invest is not a given country's decision but an investor's decision. Fortunately Hungary succeeded in attracting foreign capital and has so far accumulated sufficient capital partly by selling state companies to strategic investors and mainly by inviting greenfield investment.

Privatization by foreign capital only takes one round and does not require reprivatization as voucher methods do. However, the problem of how to encourage and "bring up" domestic entrepreneurs remains unsolved.

4. *Polish case: mixed type of latecomer.* Compared to the three countries mentioned above, the Polish case cannot be decisively characterized by typical methods of capital accumulation. Trade unions hold strong powers and represent an independent social power that largely contributes to political democracy, although they put limitations on the privatization process.

Thus, the Polish privatization process has been delayed, in spite of several attempts to quicken it, because of a lack of social consensus. Finally, as the latest user of voucher methods, Poland tried to introduce a uniquely revised form of voucher privatization, that is, through NIF: the National Investment Fund. By inviting foreign investment banks and consulting companies to manage voucher-privatized companies, the Polish government sought to avoid the typical weakness of the voucher methods experienced in the Czech Republic.

The revised methods, however, seem to be neither revolutionary nor miraculous. The results so far may be a little better than voucher methods and function without the assistance of experienced foreign management companies. But they does not show any remarkable merit, which confirms that there is no easy shortcut to privatization.

The recent rush of foreign capital into Poland seems to show that the direct sales of individual companies are proceeding successfully mainly thanks to the large domestic market, not the success of NIF. In this sense, too, the Polish way to privatization is of the mixed type.

11.8   Opportunism and corruption: the legacy of the old system

During almost two decades of transformation, an enormous amount of public money and national wealth has been slipping into the hands of individuals and private companies through legal and illegal channels alike. There are some typical ways of making personal wealth in the transformation period.

The first channel is privatization itself. Politicians of a governing party can obtain some insider information about privatization plans. They can participate in intermediating not only in large privatization matters, but also relatively minor matters and thereby collect small benefits. Of course, the participation of politicians themselves is not permitted in almost all cases, but that of their family members and cooperators is not illegal. If the matter in question is an international tender, then the size of the success fee for lobbying could be enormous.

The second is that not only bureaucrats but also politicians have also been appointed as supervisory board members of quasi-privatized and fully privatized companies. Each honorarium may not be large, but enough money can be acquired to buy cars and flats from many nominal supervisory jobs offered by company managers who are looking for political and governmental connections.

The third channel lies in, the ruling party's decisionmaking power in distributing the state budget. Here again, politicians can get insider information on where money flows. By proposing ways of expanding budgets or suggesting where money should be spent, they can get earnings through intriguing channels.

Interestingly enough no concept exists of abuse of status, insider transactions, and bribery in most transforming countries. There does not seem to be any social norm that regulates the people's ethics of social behavior and justice. Almost no legal accusations have been made by prosecutors of bribery and corruption.

In the transforming countries the prosecution system is under construction, whereas in the old regime there was no prosecution system independent of the ruling party. The spread of corruption without legal punishment is the legacy of the old regime under which people are still living.

11.9   The loss of ideals, but since when?

In the general election of 1998 the so-called center right FIDESZ (young democrats) coalition won in Hungary, and the so-called left wing Social Democrats won in the Czech Republic. Do these results show opposing political trends in the two countries? No, not at all. Both political outcomes reflect exactly the same choice in the sense that voters welcomed the social policies neglected by previous governments. It may seem strange that the center right party in Hungary adopted such social policies, almost all of which were features of the socialist era.

It is worth noting that a stereotypical classification of political parties is no longer relevant to the political analysis of the former socialist Central European countries today, where the old left is strongly pursuing a market economy approach and the old right is oriented toward social policies. Thus, earlier positioning of political parties should be inverted by exactly 180 degrees; left became right and right became left. Table 11.8 shows that an old-fashioned and obsolete analysis of political maps by a pair concept of right and left in former socialist countries is already inappropriate for analyzing the political situation in this region. It is also worth listening to the leader of the Hungarian Socialist Party, László Kovács, elected after the loss of general election in 1998. He said that the party strongly opposed the taxation plan on real estate and interest on bank deposits. Nobody could believe his words.

When did the Hungarian Socialist Party become a capitalist party? Something must have eaten away the ideals and conscience of the Hungarian

Table 11.8   A superficial political map

	First postcommunist government	Next	1998
Bulgaria	Right	Left	Right
Czech Republic	Right	Right	Centre-left
Estonia	Right	Mixed	Right
Hungary	Right	Left	Right
Latvia	Right	Mixed	Mixed
Lithuania	Right	Left	Right
Poland	Right	Left	Right
Romania	Left	Left	Right
Slovakia	Right	Left	Left
Slovenia	Left	Left	Mixed

Source: *The Economist*, May 30–June 5, 1998.

socialists who had enjoyed political power and economic benefits too much in the ruling period.

A Japanese proverb says: sufficient food and clothing make good manners. What we seem to observe in Hungary, however, is that sufficient food and clothing make men throw away the ideals and become snobbish or vulgar. It is difficult to believe that this is the case with the behavior of Hungarian socialists. It does not seem that such a degeneration of socialists happened in such a short period during transformation. It has a long history, because as Table 11.2 showed, the allocation system does not have any chance of developing civilized relationships in society. In the sense of economic rationality and social morality, the old regime lost its legitimacy a long time ago. The reign of the Communist Party merely maintained the formal legitimacy. Even that formal legitimacy was lost when the old regime collapsed. Since then, socialists, including reformers, have lost their ideals both as a political party and individuals, because they could not tell themselves what a socialist or a socialist party should represent in the transformation era.

11.10   How is it possible to restore social justice?

It is essential to restore social justice in a transforming society by imposing taxes on accumulated wealth in the form of real estate and financial assets. This is because the sources of valuable real estate and other liquid assets are nothing but various types of incomes that have evaded taxation. It is surprising to discover that no effective taxation on real estate exists in Hungary or other Central European countries. The state budget depends on a very high level of taxation of personal income and on VAT. The prevailing system of taxation in Central European countries is heavily dependent on current incomes and expenditures which disproportionately burden the poor and favor the rich. As is observed in developed countries, low income earners do not have any way of evading taxation, whereas high income earners have certain ways of evading taxation. The evaded incomes are exempt from taxation and transformed into real estate and financial assets. Contemporary Central Europe seems to be a paradise for the rich. The reason why Hungarian socialists are so strongly against a real estate tax is that many of their MPs built houses during their ruling term. Certainly this is not the way for socialists to restore social justice in Hungary.

Almost every general election in Central European countries in the years after the beginning of transformation led to a change in government. Thanks to the changes, most major parties have already enjoyed the ruling periods and have learnt which channels of money flow are connected with privatization and state budget distribution. Interestingly enough, this change of government has realized a de facto mutual surveillance system which checks extraordinary abuse of status among politicians. In this sense public votes have so far played an important role by judging the ruling of government parties on behalf of unreliable and politically dependent prosecutors.

In connection with general elections, one comment ought to be made. Although the Hungarian Socialist Party did not take any responsibility for the notorious Tocsik scandal that emerged in 1996, it obtained the largest support in the following election. However, it did not succeed in keeping power. In the same way, Prime Minister Klaus in the Czech Republic was forced to resign over the matter of the secret bank account. But surprisingly voters still supported the ODS and the parties split from the ODS. These are very interesting phenomena of social and political norms in the former socialist Central European countries. People are incredibly tolerant of political scandals so that the scandals do not cause terminal damage to the parties concerned.

Although foreign investors do not like frequent changes of governments, the changes in political power so far have at least brought about the cleaning-up of the quasi-bribery activities of politicians, bureaucrats, and managers. Thus societies have barely maintained minimum social justice in a society where an independent prosecution system does not function at all.

The disclosure system of individual assets of MPs was introduced in the 1990s in Hungary, but no one trusts their self-declarations, most of which are so laughable that no form of media has anything to do with them. This might be so, partly because the media itself does not work as a social checking and critical power in Hungary, and partly because people are very tolerant of bribery and government corruption. This can be explained by the long period of silence from the people about any type of government and party corruption under the old regime, where people's protests against the ruling power were severely punished.

As described above, people in the former socialist Central European countries, except in Poland, are tolerant, obedient, and silent regarding social injustice and corruption concerning the government and parties. These societies are actually in some sense similar to Western European societies where the acceptance of the *status quo* is rather strong among people. People conform to the current structure of social class and strata, the distribution of wealth between the rich and the poor, and the relationship between authority and governed.

Social mobility is far higher in Asian countries than in Europe; that is, the opportunities exist for people to move up from one social class or status to another by their own efforts. This possibility has produced tremendous energy among people who are struggling for social advancement. At the same time it has opened up every type of corruption to ruling government and parties. Thus, Asian society can be characterized as one of high mobility, strong social conflict and political antagonism, large-scale corruption, high demand for social disciplines and ethics because of the lack of either, a strong and independent prosecution system for maintaining minimum social order, and high ideals for social justice as integrating objectives.

On the other hand, Western European society can be characterized as one of low social mobility, moderate social conflict, peaceful political dialog, small-scale corruption, established social disciplines and ethics, a prosecution system highly dependent on government, and a quiet voice of social justice, partly because a social welfare system is already established.

In these respects Central European society is different from Western European society. Central Europe is in a somewhat mixed position in every aspect of the social comparisons described above. That is, the level of social mobility is low, political struggle is less antagonistic, corruption is widespread, social discipline and ethics are low, and demand for social justice is also weak. Central European countries and societies seem to require more energy and power to advance to a higher level of social and economic progress. At the same time social disciplines and ethics should be restored in order to lessen de facto bribery and corruption that pervades spreading government and semiprivatized institutions.

Thus, Central European governments should motivate people to play a more active role in business and social life not only by encouraging economic measures but also by establishing justified social norms in public life. In order to show the social disciplines needed for a developed and civilized society, the public must learn new social norms and fight strongly against social injustice and corruption in social and business organizations. The will to fight itself shows the activity level of a society, and the converse is also true that the activity level of society remains low as long as people are afraid of fighting corruption and social injustice.

Notes

1. The Central European countries that received a relatively large amount of direct investment succeeded in relatively swift transformation. Direct investment is the only way of shortening the transformation time, which I emphasized in my book as an "almighty method" behind the successful change of a national economy. However, even if a superficial, swift transformation can be realized in a relatively short amount of time by foreign capital, it will have brought about a dual structure for the national economy, i.e. one in which a highly developed economic sphere comprising foreign companies with foreign management and imported high technology coexists with a comparatively small-scale pure domestic economic sphere that relies on low technology.

2. By 2002 almost all of the large Czech banks had been sold to West European banks which finally finished privatization of Czech banks in rather an ironic manner. This example clearly shows the failure of voucher privatization and that the privatization could only be completed by the introduction of foreign capital, and not in a favorable way that kept Czech pride intact. This example also shows us that swift transformation cannot be accomplished without foreign capital and management along with the introduction of cutting-edge technology. The full

implementation of the foreign model might not be the final stage in transforming an economy. The assimilation process of dominant foreign companies to become essentially domestic companies will be the next stage for the transforming economies.

References

EBRD. 1994–99. *Transition Report*. London.

"Is Central Europe, along with Hungary, Turning Right?", *The Economist*. 1998, May 30, pp. 49–50.

Estrin, Saul. 1999. "Some Reflections on Privatization in Belarus." *Economic Trends*, Quarterly Issue: Belarus (July–Sep.).

Morita, Tsuneo. 1994. *Taiseitenkan no keizaigaku* [*Economics of System Transformation*]. Tokyo: Shinseisha Publisher. [In Japanese.]

WIIW. 2000. *Countries in Transition 2000*. Vienna: Vienna Institute for International Economic Studies..

World Bank. 1999. *Czech Republic*. Washington, DC: World Bank.

12
Czech Republic 1990–2000: Lessons from the Economic and Political Transformation

František Turnovec

12.1 Milestones of economic transformation in the Czech Republic

Until the 1989 *velvet revolution* Czechoslovakia was one of the most conservative socialist countries. Even compared to other former socialist countries in Central Europe its economy was exceptional as regards privatization with only 4 percent of GDP produced by the private sector and 10 percent produced by the cooperative sector in 1989. No experiments with liberalization of economic and political systems had been attempted in the 1970s and 1980s. The rigid party form had to live with the legacy of post-1968 normalization and ran the country. At that time, more liberal segments of the communist party and the Czechoslovak political and intellectual establishments were eliminated or expelled from the country. They were isolated or persecuted for as long as two decades.

The radical political change in the last months of 1989 was supported by the majority of the population but was possible only under the influence of international changes initiated by the Soviet *perestroika*. The people asked for democracy and at the very beginning almost nobody proposed an economic program going beyond the *democratic market socialism* rhetoric.

In the absence of even partial market reforms, relatively competent management of the fully state-controlled and centrally planned economy paradoxically left the country at the end of the 1980s with initial conditions better than those in more liberal and market-oriented socialist countries like Hungary and Poland. The country had no significant external debt, low inflation, a positive trade balance, and a balanced government budget. The uncompetitive structure of the economy forced it to be completely subordinated to the strategic objectives of the Soviet Union and Warsaw Pact and oriented to undemanding Communist Economic Community (COMECON) markets and underdeveloped countries' markets.

In 1990, however, the strategies of transition became the priority agenda. Important topics were, for instance, price and trade liberalization, privatization, and reorientation of foreign trade to Western markets, together with the creation of a corresponding social safety net in order to make the transformation process socially feasible and a significant reconstruction of institutional and legal frameworks to facilitate transition from a centrally planned to a liberal market economy. Surprisingly no concept of economic transition was on the table at the end of 1989. Neither dissidents in former socialist countries nor the experts in the many Western institutes of Soviet or Eastern studies anticipated seriously the collapse of the communist regime and its practical implications.

The concept of radical economic reform won support, at least theoretically, in the new political establishment, and ideas of *democratic market socialism* lost their attraction for the majority of the Czech society. Optimistic but not very rational expectations prevailed, and people were ready to suffer for a while in the expectation of prosperity afterward. The political pendulum moved to the *right*. In this relatively favorable social atmosphere in 1991 the economic transition started.

To illustrate and justify periodization of the first ten years of economic transition a timetable of selected macroeconomic data is provided in Table 12.1.

Together with macroeconomic fundamentals (the real growth rate of GDP, the rate of inflation measured by the Consumers' Price Index (CPI), the rate of unemployment, and the current account balance as a percentage of GDP), a synthetic measure (SR)—given by the sum of the GDP growth rate (GR) and the current account balance as a percentage of GDP (CA) minus the sum of the rate of inflation (IR) and the rate of unemployment (UR)—sometimes called the index of economic misery is introduced. Clearly the higher the value of SR observed, the better the performance of the economy. To illustrate also absolute performance, the level of GDP as a percentage of 1989's level and the cumulative level of consumer prices are provided.

The curve SR provides a relatively good reflection of the following periodization of the first ten years of the transformation process of the Czech economy:

1. 1990, a pretransformation period, when a minimal legislative framework had to be prepared to start the reform. Two-tiered banking system established. Trade and Co-operation agreement with the EU. Relatively mild decline from 1989.

2. 1991, a liberalization shock, caused by trade liberalization and liberalization of prices, and deepened by the collapse of COMECON as an external shock. First steps to currency convertibility, depreciation of Czech koruna (CZK), fixed exchange rate based on currency basket of US dollar and German mark with a daily fluctuation band of 0.5 percent. Small-scale privatization started. Restitution law and competition law. Association agreement with the EU. Significant adverse jump in price levels, inflation, and GDP.

Table 12.1 Czech Republic 1990–2000, basic macroeconomic indicators

	Real Growth of GDP (GR)	Rate of Inflation (IR)	Rate of Unemployment (UR)	Balance of Current Account in % of GDP(CA)	Synthetic Rate of macroeconomic performance (SR=GR+CA−IR−UR)	GDP level in % of 1989	Consumer price level in % of 1989
1990	−1.2	9.7	1.0	−1.1	−13.0	98.80	109.70
1991	−11.5	56.6	4.1	4.5	−67.7	87.44	171.79
1992	−3.3	11.1	2.6	−1.0	−18.0	84.55	190.86
1993	0.1	20.8	3.5	1.3	−22.9	85.06	230.56
1994	2.2	10.0	3.2	−2.0	−13.4	87.78	253.61
1995	5.9	9.1	2.9	−4.4	−10.3	93.40	276.69
1996	4.8	8.8	3.5	−7.0	−14.5	97.04	301.04
1997	−1.0	8.5	5.2	−6.2	−20.9	98.01	326.63
1998	−2.2	10.7	7.5	−1.9	−22.3	95.57	361.58
1999	−0.8	2.1	8.7	−2.7	−14.3	95.37	374.60
2000	3.1	3.9	8.8	−2.2	−11.8	97.96	388.83

Sources: "Zpráva vlády o stavu české společnosti" [The Government Report], Hospodářské noviny, March 5, 1999; Countries in Transition 1999, WIIW Handbook of Statistics, Vienna 2000; Statistical Yearbook of the Czech Republic 1999, CSU Prague 1999; "Report of the Czech Statistical Office on the 2000 GDP," Lidové noviny, March 22, 2001.

3. 1992–93, economic recovery, slowed down by a second external shock—division of the country (former Czechoslovakia) in 1993. First wave of voucher privatization. Central European Free Trade Agreement (CEFTA) membership (1993). Value Added Tax (VAT) introduced (1993), stock exchange began trading. Bankruptcy law enacted. Association agreement with the EU renegotiated (1993).

4. 1994–96, disequilibrium of growth, generated by increased domestic demand caused by privatization revenues of households and indirect (hidden) government subsidies through bad bank credits of state-controlled banks. Second wave of voucher privatization. WTO and OECD membership (1995). Full current account convertibility introduced. Forced administration of largest private bank (Agrobanka). Application for the EU membership.

5. 1997–99, a postprivatization recession resulting from unfinished restructuring, over-restrictive response of the central bank to external disequilibrium, and problems of state-controlled banking sector. Currency crisis (1997), floating exchange rate system introduced. Restrictive measures in government budget, austerity packages. Political crisis and series of minority governments. NATO membership (1999).

6. 2000–, first signals of economic recovery, privatization of residual state property and state-controlled banks, restructuring and reprivatization of the country's largest industrial conglomerates, unsuccessfully privatized during mass privatization.

12.2   The privatization game: a success or a failure?

The Czech privatization was considered a success story for several years. The issue of privatization became a top-priority item on the agenda immediately after the fall of the communist regime. By 1998 private sector contribution to GDP was officially estimated to have increased from 4 percent in 1989 to 90 percent.[1] Several forms of privatization were used (Kotrba and Svejnar 1994): restitution, both small-scale and large-scale privatization, direct transfers to municipalities, and the transformation of cooperative property. The relative weights of the different forms are in Table 12.2.

The first step was a restitution program: returning property to former owners (during 1990–92). It allowed the natural restitution of property expropriated after the communist takeover of 1948. Since a major part of the Czech (and Czechoslovak) economy was nationalized before 1948, natural restitution accounted for a relatively small fraction of the total property (in accounting value about 130 billion CZK out of a total of about 1,700 billion.).

Property transferred by law directly (free of charge) from the state to municipalities accounts for about 350 billion CZK. So-called small-scale privatization was officially ended in December 1993. The law permitted the sale or leasing of real and movable property possessed by state-owned

Table 12.2   Summary of weights of different forms of privatization (in 1998)

	Accounting value in billions of CZK	Share (%)
1. Restitutions	130	7.71
2. Transfer to municipalities	350	20.75
3. Small-scale privatization	23	1.36
4. Large-scale privatization	934	55.36
Including		
Voucher privatization	333	19.74
Other methods	391	23.18
State-owned (not then privatized)	210	12.45
5. Transformation of cooperatives	250	14.82
Total	1,687	100

Source: "Estimates of Ministry of Finance, National Property Fund, Czech Statistical Office." Hospodářské noviny. March 5, 1999.

enterprises (SOEs) and federal, republican, and local governments. Property in accounting value of about 23 billion CZK was sold at auction.[2]

The most important form, considering the importance and size of privatized property, was so-called large-scale privatization. Large-scale privatization was carried out through the following basic methods:

1. transformation of an SOE into a joint-stock company and a transfer of shares,[3]
2. direct sale to a predetermined buyer,
3. public auction or public tender.

The voucher privatization program, which offered citizens the chance to purchase shares in large companies for a small registration fee met with popular enthusiasm (see Table 12.3). Within two years (1993–94) nearly every Czech had become a shareholder; indeed, the Czechs were the largest per capita shareholders of any country, including the United States (Schwartz 1997).

Voucher privatization was a game (Kotrba 1995).[4] For a registration fee of 1,000 CZK (about US$ 35 at that time) every Czech citizen over the age of 18 residing permanently in former Czechoslovakia obtained a voucher book formally worth 1,000 points. Individual investors could allocate the investment points of their voucher book to one or more of the companies listed on the supply side. Bidding for shares was organized in several rounds. Before each round the authorities announced the share price (in investment points) of each company, the number of available shares and the extent of excess demand registered in previous rounds. In the first round the price was set identically for all companies and was adjusted individually for each enterprise thereafter. At the end of each round, the Center for Voucher

Table 12.3   Number of individual shareholder accounts (in millions)[5]

	September 1994	September 1995	December 1996	December 1997	January 1999	December 2000
Total number of accounts	7.26	7.4	7.3	5.9	3.95	3.7
Empty accounts	0.95	2	2.5	1.8	1.03	1.0
Individual shareholders	6.31	5.4	4.8	4.1	2.92	2.7

Note: Data are cumulative (stock): number of accounts at the date indicated (end of the month).

Source: "Středisko cenných papírů." *Lidové noviny*. January 9, 2001.

Privatization and Ministry of Finance processed the bids: if the demand for shares of a given company was equal to or less than the supply of shares, all orders were met at the price set for this round. The authorities then reduced the share price for excess supply companies. If demand exceeded supply, the demand was satisfied only partly or no transaction took place; the investment points were returned to their owners, and the authorities raised the share price for the following round. The prices were set according to a complex algorithm that was never revealed.

Originally the privatization game was designed for individual investors as players. But lacking access to relevant information they were not prepared for the game. To assist individual investors' choices Investment Privatization Funds (IPF) were established. They became the major players in the game and also the major winners (Bohatá 1998). IPFs were supposed to act as collective investors to diversify their portfolios in order to minimize the risk. Before the bidding, individual investors could allocate the entirety or parts of their voucher books to one of several IPFs and then become their shareholders. Successful advertisement campaigns for IPFs encouraged a majority of individual investors to commit their voucher points (or voucher books) to IPFs (72 percent of investment points in the first wave and 63 percent in the second wave). Voucher privatization became a game dominated by the IPFs and the role of individuals in voucher privatization was marginalized.

Czech banks (mostly controlled by the state) played a crucial role within the process of voucher privatization. They established investment companies, those investment companies established dozens of IPFs, and these funds became the major players in the both waves of voucher privatization. While the major Czech banks themselves were subjects of voucher privatization, at the same time the Fund of National Property retained more than 40 percent of the shares in major Czech banks.[6]

To classify large-scale privatization outcomes we can consider the following sectors: the state (public) sector (state-controlled companies); companies privatized by the voucher method, companies privatized by standard methods (public auctions, public tenders, or direct sales) to Czech owners, and companies privatized by standard methods to foreign owners. Table 12.2 above provided data about the weights of different forms of large-scale privatization (at the end of 1998): the voucher method accounted for 19.74 percent of national property, standard methods (both to Czech and foreign owners) for 23.18 percent and state-owned for 12.45 percent (considering accounting value).

After the liberalization shock and decline in 1991–93, deepened by the external shocks of COMECON's collapse and the division of the country, GDP started to grow in 1994 (Table 12.1). Privatization seemed to be successful. In 1996 the Czech government publicly announced that the transition was over and that the posttransitionary period was underway.

12.3   Postprivatization recession

Such illusions began to vanish in 1997 when the Czech public first learned that several managers of the investment funds designed to invest the public's vouchers were instead systematically stealing from their own investors. The Czech Ministry of Finance has since enumerated 15 techniques for stealing.[7]

While the *synthetic rate* of economic performance (see Figure 12.1) shows that negative trends started in 1996 (current account), the first signals of real GDP decline appeared in first quarter 1998. Then nine consecutive

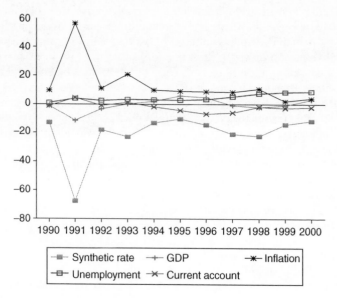

Figure 12.1   Czech Republic: macroeconomic indicators 1990–2000

Table 12.4 Comparison of performance of sectors by method of privatization in manufacturing industry (value added per employee in thousands of CZK)

	1997	1998	% sales 1998
Public/state sector[a]	360.9	465.6	16.5
Firms privatized by voucher method	277.2	321.5	23.4
Firms privatized by standard methods[b]	306.5	343.9	8.1
Sector under foreign control	680.3	743.2	16.3
Other[c]	318.1	373.2	35.7
Total	326.4	389.2	100.0

Notes: [a]State enterprises, state-controlled joint-stock companies, and municipal enterprises.
[b]Public auctions, public tenders, and direct sales (into "Czech hands").
[c]Mixed or nonidentifiable forms of privatization.
Source: "Zpráva vlády o stavu české společnosti." *Hospodářské noviny.* March 5, 1999.

quarters exhibit deepening decline (with growth rates with respect to the same quarter of the previous year of –0.9% percent in 1997/II, –2.1 in 1997/III, –1.4 percent in 1997/IV, –1.1 in 1998/I, –1.8 percent in 1998/II, –2.5 in 1998/III, –3.3 in 1998/IV, –3.7 in 1999/I, and –0.8 in 1999/II).[8] While the GDP level as a percentage of 1989's GDP was 98.01 percent in 1997, it declined to 95.37 percent in 1998.

It appeared that the voucher privatization and standard privatization into *Czech hands* almost exclusively in credit, did not restructure or improve the performance of privatized firms but rather led to the crisis in the banking sector.[9] The biggest improvements in performance may be observed in the foreign-controlled sector (Table 12.4). This sector represented about 16 percent of the total industrial sales and grew by more than 3 percent in the first half of 1998, leading industrial growth. Foreign investors have been continuously enhancing productivity which is currently 41 percent above the average in the remaining sectors. The worst results exhibit firms privatized by the voucher method and standard methods into Czech hands. They are behind the state sector firms.

The methods of privatization adopted generated a highly nontransparent ownership structure (Turnovec 1999, 2000), led to *fuzzy* design of corporate governance (Bohatá 1998) and, in the absence of prudent regulation of capital markets and the banking sector (Matoušek 1998), contributed to the slowdown of economic performance of the Czech economy after 1996. It was not the only factor in the postprivatization recession, but certainly the most significant one.[10]

12.4 Political implications

While expectations, raised by the privatization strategy, associated with the Civic Democratic Party of Václav Klaus, had paved the way to an impressive victory for the center-right coalition in the 1992 election (Turnovec 1995), postprivatization recession went hand in hand with growing political instability.

From 1992 the government coalition consisted of three center-right parties: the Civic Democratic Party (ODS), the Christian-Democratic Union (KDU-ČSL), and the Civic Democratic Alliance (ODA). After the 1996 parliamentary election these three parties formed a minority coalition government, controlling 99 of the 200 seats in the Lower House and 53 of the 81 seats in the Upper House. This was tolerated by the Social Democratic Party, who abstained in a vote of no confidence in July 1996. Out of 16 government offices, eight were held by the ODS, four by the KDU-ČSL, and four by the ODA.

Voters' preferences for political parties changed significantly during 1997. This was an expression of the growing criticism of political and social development and the economic problems that had been neglected for a long time by the ruling coalition. Restrictive economic policies introduced in the spring of 1997 were accompanied by only cosmetic personnel changes in the government. The false expectations raised by overly optimistic government propaganda were dashed by economic recession, which led to a decrease in real incomes, the exchange rate crisis, and the crisis in the banking sector.

In November 1997 the culmination of these problems led to the dissolution of the government coalition. During the prime minister's absence from the country, two smaller parties, the ODA and KDU-ČSL, withdrew from the coalition and, after President Havel's intervention, the government resigned on November 30. While the immediate reason for the government crisis was related to the unclear financing of the Civic Democratic Party, indicating possible corruption during privatization, the November collapse of the government reflected the general instability of the Czech political environment. The causes were the dissatisfaction of a substantial portion of the population with recent economic development, disapproval of the leading coalition party's political style, friction among coalition parties, and power struggles among different segments of the Czech political establishment.

Observing growing animosity among politicians and the inability of political parties to agree on the composition of a viable government, President Havel appointed Josef Tošovský, the generally respected Governor of the Czech National Bank with no party affiliation, as the new prime minister on December 17, 1997. The new government, based not on the parliamentary power of political parties but supported by two small former coalition partners of the Civic Democratic Party (The Christian Democratic Union and Civic Democratic Alliance), was appointed by the president on December 30, 1997. After complicated negotiations and an explicit commitment by the government to hold new parliamentary elections in the spring of 1998, the government received the support of the Lower House of the Parliament on January 28, 1998, despite the opposition of the Civic Democratic Party, but with the unanimous approval of the Social Democratic Party. In January 1998 the Civic Democratic Party split. The members who opposed Chairman Klaus's interpretation of the political crisis left the party as a move against both the party and him personally, and established a new party called the Union of Freedom.

The economic recession continued in 1998. With a limited mandate the *provisional government* of Josef Tošovský, while praised by the public, did not have enough authority to initiate significant changes in economic policies. The June 1998 early election of the Lower House failed to provide any clear answers.

The Czech Social Democratic Party (ČSSD) achieved a historic success with the strongest popular support with almost one-third of the voters casting their votes for the ČSSD. The Civic Democratic Party demonstrated its skill in political tactics and ranked second, losing only 2 percent of its electoral support compared to the 1996 election. Shortly after the election, President Havel authorized the chairman of the Social Democratic Party, Miloš Zeman, to negotiate the composition of the new government. He failed to compose a center-left majority coalition with the Christian and Democratic Union and the Union of Freedom. On the other hand, personal animosity among the leaders of the former coalition partners, the Civic Democratic Party, the Christian and Democratic Union, and the Union of Freedom, prevented the establishment of a center-right majority coalition. A grand coalition of the ČSSD and ODS was explicitly excluded by the electoral programs of both parties. A resolution to the deadlock was found in the so-called *opposition treaty* between the ČSSD and ODS. The ODS committed itself to tolerating a minority one-party government of the ČSSD in exchange for a dominant role in the Lower and Upper Houses and participation in preliminary consultations on important issues between the ČSSD and ODS. Having between them a qualified majority in both houses, the ČSSD and ODS declared their intention to work together to stabilize the Czech political environment and to change the constitution and electoral law to strengthen majority elements in a proportional voting system. The abstention of the ODS in the vote of no confidence allowed the one-party minority government of ČSSD to get the support of the Lower House in August 1998.

12.5   The end of the 1990s: a slow economic recovery

After the end of voucher privatization in 1994, no significant progress was made in the transfer of state property into private hands before 1998.[11] However, several interesting issues did arise (Turnovec et al. 1998b).

First, so-called *spontaneous privatization* emerged during 1998. Financially strong groups realized that after voucher privatization, state-owned companies existed with diverse ownership and in which the state's stake was below 50 below. These groups started massive yet silent buyouts from investment funds and small, private shareholders. As a result, they were able to gain a higher stake in ownership than that controlled by government agencies and therefore to override the state's influence in these firms. Such takeovers were successful in the case of several firms operating in the coal mining industry, and there were attempts to take over others. A similar situation first occurred in 1997 when the "Nomura Group" acquired a larger stake than the government in the Investment and Postal Bank (IPB). Nomura controlled more than 34 percent and obtained veto power in the bank. Therefore, the government was left with Nomura as the only potential buyer.

Second, government officials took offensive action in response to the first few hostile takeovers. The National Property Fund authorized cooperating brokerage houses to buy the shares of the remaining endangered companies, namely of utility distributors, to increase the state's stake to above 50 percent in order to maintain control. This might be viewed as a step backward or as a corrective action to undo the wrongs of the previous privatization method. There was also a shift in the government's privatization strategy towards favoring public tenders and direct sales to strategic investors, usually to strong multinational groups.

As a reaction to the recession, the new Czech government of Social Democrats publicly announced its intention to *revitalize* large industrial holding companies. The cabinet approved a final version of the industrial revitalization plan in April 1999. Nine collapsing firms of national importance were selected for the program.[12] It was estimated that about US$ 200 million would be needed to help these companies to survive. The restructuring was supposed to be controlled by the Revitalization Agency, established as a corporate vehicle, using a combination of several instruments like debt for equity swaps (using nonperforming loans), interest rate subsidies for selected firms, export guarantees, buyouts of certain debts and writeoffs, and other standard and non-standard methods of industrial policy. The Revitalization Agency was mandated to purchase nonperforming loans of Czech commercial banks at a fair market value. Selected assets of the state-owned banking institution, Consolidation Bank, which had itself in the past bought a number of bad loans of commercial banks, were to be transferred to the Revitalization Agency under the same terms. Furthermore, the Revitalization Agency was supposed to manage, restructure, and/or convert nonperforming loans into equity of selected large industrial corporations experiencing financial distress. The idea was to increase state influence on the companies, exercise corporate governance and promote restructuring, and to find new strategic partners for selected companies or for their viable parts. The only company on the list in which the Revitalization Agency's role was brought to an end was ZPS Zlín, which was sold in 2000 to Italian investor Tajmac, but by time a few other companies, however, had also started negotiations with potential investors (Hanousek and Munich 2000).

Third, it was generally recognized, that the key issue was privatization of the state-controlled banks. The first, not very successful, step was made in March 1998, when state's share in IPB was sold (for a nominal price) to Nomura Group.[13] A second step followed in June 1999, when the most successful Czech Bank, CSOB (Czechoslovak Trade Bank) almost fully owned by the state, was sold for 1 billion US$ to the Belgian KBC bank. The third step was privatization of the Czech Saving Bank (CS) into the hands of the Austrian Erste Spaarkasse Bank in 2000. Privatization of state shares in the last (and most problematic) of the major Czech banks, KB (Commercial Bank), was finalized in October 2001 by selling it to French banking group Société Générale. The total cost of bank restructuring was estimated to reach 350–400 billions CZK.

An important part of the government's industrial policy after 1998 was to stimulate FDI through such investment incentives as tax vacations, subsidies on new working places, and tax-free importation of new technologies.[14] They were introduced by the provisional government of Josef Tošovský in 1998, significantly extended by the Social Democrat minority government, and contributed to the steep increase of FDI during 1999 and 2000. Moreover, the privatization of banks and manufacturing and distribution firms was implemented and conducted primarily with the aim of find strategic foreign partners. Large numbers of the best known multinational companies soon set up operations in the Czech Republic. In total, there were more than 2,200 foreign-owned or partly foreign-owned companies at the end of 1999 (Hanousek and Munich 2000).

Table 12.5 provides flow and stock data about FDI during 1990–2000. FDI inflow expressed as a percentage of Czech GDP was 9.6 percent in 1999.[15]

Table 12.5 Foreign direct investments in the Czech Republic (in millions of USD)

	Inflow	Stock
1993	654	3,423
1994	869	4,292
1995	2,562	6,854
1996	1,428	8,282
1997	1,300	9,582
1998	3,718	13,300
1999	6,324	19,624
2000	4,986	24,610

Source: Countries in Transition 2000, WIIW Handbook of Statistics, Vienna 2000; Report of Ministry of Industry and Trade, *Právo*, March 10, 2001.

The first signals of recovery, indicating progress in restructuring, the successful privatization and FDI strategy, and growth in the EU countries, appeared in the second half of 1999. After nine quarters of decline, GDP increased slightly in third quarter 1999 compared to the same period of 1998. In September 1999 the trade balance was positive for the first time in 49 months. Growth of industrial production was reported in August 1999. Growth of GDP was reported in six consecutive quarters: in 1999/IV by 1 percent, in 2000/I by 4.3 percent, in 2000/II by 2.1 percent, in 2000/III by 2.2 percent and in 2000/IV by 3.9 percent. After three years of decline the annual GDP growth rate in 2000 was 3.1 percent.

12.6　Concluding remarks

What lessons can be drawn from the ten years of Czech transition experience? (See also Mlčoch, Machonin, and Sojka 2000; Tošovský 2001.)

First, the Czech experience shows that formally privatizing x percent of former state property might still keep the state responsible for considerably more than (100-x) percent (Turnovec 1999). Resignation of the state from exercising property rights and absence of a reasonable doctrine of temporary state capitalism contributed to the problems in the Czech economy and Czech society (Schwartz 1997). Fast Czech privatization at state expense, resulting in "Potemkin's villages,"[16] could not solve the problems of transition to the market economy (Mlcoch 2000).

Second, institutional reform is perhaps at least equally important as formal privatization. No invisible hand itself can automatically guarantee the smooth functioning of the market economy.

Third, the economic transition in the Czech Republic was not over at this stage: completing privatization of the state-controlled banks and restructuring of big industrial conglomerates were crucial issues for starting stable economic growth to close the gap between the Czech Republic and the EU average.

Fourth, the optimal sequencing and intensity of transition steps are not only a question of understanding the economics of the process and social feasibility, but also the question of political courage: to make the correct and perhaps painful steps at the right time and not compromising with the political cycle.

One final remark: the Czech transition economy was never in the good shape that it appeared from overoptimistic external evaluations at the beginning of the 1990s (strongly supported by official government propaganda), but neither was it in such a bad situation as some external auditors implied at the end of the decade. The recovery that began then held out no promise of a *Czech economic miracle*, as had been presented in the early 1990s, but a steady step by step improvement of economic performance of the country on its way to accession to the EU.[17]

Notes

This research was undertaken with support from the Grant Agency of the Czech Republic, project No. 402/00/0263. The author is grateful to Eva Ehrlich from the Hungarian Academy of Sciences for her helpful comments. Prepared for the ICSEAD workshop "Transitional Economies in Central-Eastern Europe and East Asia," Hungarian Academy of Sciences, Budapest, November 24–25, 2000.

1. Report of Ministry of Finance of the Czech Republic on the Law on Capital Market Regulation, 1997. For comparison: Hungary 25% in 1990 and 75% in 1996, Poland 31% in 1990 and 78% in 1996 (Turnovec et al. 1998a).
2. The revenues of the Fund of National Property (FNP) from auctions in small-scale privatization exceeded 30 billion CZK, more than the accounting value.
3. After transformation of SOEs into joint-stock companies the shares were distributed through voucher privatization to citizens, sold directly to a domestic or foreign owner, sold through intermediaries (the stock exchange and other capital market instruments), sold to employees, issued to former owners as compensation, or transferred free of charge to public institutions or municipal ownership. A significant part of the shares were transferred to the Fund of National Property representing the state as an owner.
4. There were two waves of voucher privatization: the first wave in former Czechoslovakia (1991–92) and the second wave in the Czech Republic only (1993–94). Each wave was organized in several rounds.
5. The shares are stored and updated electronically at individual investor's accounts in the Center of Securities.
6. A closed loop appeared: the state controls the bank; the bank owns the investment company; the investment company establishes several IPFs which control (on behalf of individual investors) hundreds of "privatized" companies. The question arises: to what extent are formally privatized companies really private?
7. One of the common techniques: The investment fund managers sell company shares in the portfolio to dummy companies at absurdly cheap prices. The dummy companies sell the shares on the market. The dummy companies deposit the ensuing profits into overseas bank accounts. The fund investors are left with nothing.
8. CESTAT, Statistical Bulletin 1999/1, CSU, Prague, August 1999, *Lidove noviny*, March 23. 2001.
9. The share of classified loans remained at around 30 percent of all loans in 1999, equivalent to 20 percent of GDP.
10. The central bank (Czech National Bank, CNB) was heavily criticized for over-restrictive monetary policies contributing to the credit crunch (high interest rates, minimal reserve requirements) focused on exchange rate stability and inflation targeting (V. Klaus 1999) and for imperfections in regulation of the banking sector during the first years of transition. Neither can it retreat from its part of the responsibility for the problems in the economic development of the country. But the dispute about the responsibility of the CNB frequently has too strong a political flavor and reflects a more general issue: how independent should the central bank be?
11. Despite the massive scale of the voucher privatization in 1998 there still remained a substantial number of companies where the state was involved. In 1998 it had involvement in 369 companies with an overall book value more than 440 billion CZK. The book value of the state share in these companies was almost 177 billion

CZK. A great number of these companies were partially privatized through the voucher scheme but the state had not privatized them entirely (E. Kočenda 1999, 2000).

12. Aliachem. a.s. (chemical industry), CKD Praha Holding, a.s. (machinery manufacturing and equipment), Hutni montaze Ostrava, a.s. (construction), Spolana a.s. Neratovice (chemicals), Skoda a.s. Plzen (machine making), Tatra a.s. Koprivnice (machine making), Vitkovice a.s. (steel), Zetor a.s. Brno (machine making), ZPS a.s. Zlin (machine making).

13. Facing the threat of a collapse of IPB under Nomura supervision, which could lead to collapse of the whole banking sector, the Czech government together with the Czech National Bank took over IPB in June 2000 and immediately sold the bank to the CSOB.

14. The national "investment incentive package" offers incentives to manufacturing investors, which invest at least US$ 10 million and fulfill the eligibility criteria.

15. In Poland 4.2 percent, Hungary 4 percent, and Slovakia 1.7 percent (*Právo*, March 10, 2001).

16. "Potemkin's village" is a generally known concept from the history: in the Russian empire, Duke Potemkin before the visit of Tsar Jekaterina to the countryside created artificial nice looking decoration, creating impression that everything is beautiful and hiding dirty and poor Russian villages.

17. Next eight years of development (2001–08) had confirmed this expectation. Accelerating GDP growth exceeded 6% in 2006, the cumulative stock of GDP achieved 42,500 millions of US$ at the end of 2004. Left center government dominated by social democrats, reelected in 2002, brought country to the European Union (the Czech Republic, together with nine other countries, became a member of the EU in May 2004). Eight years of economic expansion were interrupted only in the second half of 2008, when the first signals of recession appeared as an echo of global financial and economic crisis.

References

Bohatá, M. 1998. "Some Implications of Voucher Privatization for Corporate Governance." *Prague Economic Papers* 7(1): 44–58.

CSU. 1999. Statistical Yearbook of the Czech Republic 1999. Prague.

"Estimates of Ministry of Finance, National Property Fund, Czech Statistical Office." *Hospodářské noviny.* Mar. 5, 1999, Sep.

Hanousek, J., and D. Munich. (eds.). 2000. *Czech Republic 2000, Quo Vadis?* Prague: CERGE of Charles University and EI of Academy of Sciences of the Czech Republic.

Klaus, V. 1999. *Země, kde se již dva roky nevládne.* Prague: CEP.

Kočenda, E. 1999. "Residual State Property in the Czech Republic." *CERGE-EI Discussion Paper Series,* Discussion Paper No. 1999-14, Prague, Sep.

Kočenda, E. 2000. "Zbytkový státní majetek a vlastnická práva." *Politická ekonomie* 48: 393–400.

Kotrba, J. 1995. "Privatization Process in the Czech Republic." In *The Czech Republic and Economic Transition in Eastern Europe,* J. Svejnar (ed.). San Diego, CA: Academic Press: 159–198.

Kotrba J., and J. Svejnar. 1994. "Rapid and Multifaced Privatization, Experience of the Czech and Slovak Republics." *MOST* 4: 147–185.

Matoušek, R. 1998. "Banking Regulation and Supervision: Lessons from the Czech Republic." *Prague Economic Papers* 7(1): 44–58.

Mlcoch, L. 2000. "Ten Lessons from the Ten Years of the Czech Way." Lecture at the Conference of the Czech National Bank "Lessons and Challenges in Transition", Prague, Sept. 22.

Mlcoch, L., P. Machonin, and M. Sojka. 2000. *Economic and Social Changes in Czech Society after 1989 (an Alternative View)*. Prague: Charles University in Prague, The Karolinum Press.

"Report of the Czech Statistical Office on the 2000 GDP." *Lidové noviny* Mar. 22, 2001.

"Report of Ministry of Industry and Trade." *Právo* Mar. 10, 2001.

Schwartz, A. 1997. "Market Failure and Corruption in the Czech Republic." *Transition.* 8(6): 4–5.

"Středisko cenných papírů" [Center of Securities]. *Lidové noviny.* Jan. 9, 2001.

Tošovský, J. 2001. "Ten Years On (Some Lessons from the Transition)." *Prague Economic Papers* 10(1): 3–12.

Turnovec, F. 1995. "The Political System and Economic Transition." In *The Czech Republic and Economic Transition in Eastern Europe*, J. Svejnar (ed.). San Diego, CA: Academic Press: 47–101.

Turnovec, F., et al. 1998a. *Czech Republic 1997, The Year of Crises.* Prague: CERGE of Charles University and EI of Academy of Sciences of the Czech Republic.

Turnovec, F., et al. 1998b. *Czech Republic 1998, Facing Reality.* Prague: CERGE of Charles University and EI of Academy of Sciences of the Czech Republic.

Turnovec, F. 1999. "Privatization, Ownership Structure, and Transparency: How to Measure the True Involvement of the State." *European Journal of Political Economy* 15: 605–618.

Turnovec, F. 2000. "Privatization and Transparency: Evidence from the Czech Republic." In *Financial Turbulence and Capital Markets in Transition Countries*, J. Holscher (ed.). London-New York: Macmillan Press and St. Martin's Press: 83–101.

The Vienna Institute for International Economic Studies. 1999. *Countries in Transition 1999.* WIIW Handbook of Statistics. Vienna.

The Vienna Institute for International Economic Studies. 2000. *Countries in Transition 2000.* WIIW Handbook of Statistics. Vienna.

"Zpráva vlády o stavu české společnosti" [Government Report about State of Affairs in the Czech Society]. *Hospodářské noviny* [Economic News], Mar. 5, 1999.

Name Index

Subject Index